THE LIFE AND TIMES OF HENRY PLUMMER

978-1-64367-029-4

The Life and Times of Henry Plummer is an entertaining historical novel that plays out against the panorama of the Old West.

Linda Buxbaum's action-packed historical novel *The Life and Times of Henry Plummer* follows west-of-the-Mississippi lawlessness during the Civil War era.

The end is clear from the prologue, wherein real-life historical figure Henry Plummer is dragged from his cabin and lynched as a thief and murderer. Whether the act is a last resort to rid the town of a corrupt lawman or a gross miscarriage of justice is left hanging.

The novel follows Plummer's life leading up to his hanging. Though certain characters have been added to the historical record in order to flesh out the cast, the book's basic elements are true: Plummer served as a marshal for two different towns, did time in San Quentin for murder, and lived a life of constant flux. He sometimes gambled, drank, and escaped one scrape only to get into another. At other times, he settled as a homeowner and rancher. At his last stop in Montana, he was believed to belong to a gang of marauders who preyed on the rich lodes of gold and silver bound for the east, using Plummer's position as cover.

The book sets off at a fast pace and maintains a high-speed gallop to the end. Episodes that send Plummer careening from one situation to the next are credibly imagined, and his itinerant wanderings bring the vast openness and prevalent lawlessness of the west to life. Features of the story that might otherwise seem farfetched gain credibility when viewed through the context of the times—how a drifter with a checkered past could be elected town marshal, for example. The writing is unsophisticated but lands on firmer ground as the plot unfolds, though the sex scenes laced throughout are an awkward blend of flowery romanticism and graphic detail.

Plummer is sympathetically portrayed. He wants to do the right thing, has compassion for those who need it, and realizes that his fondness for gambling and drinking are flaws to be overcome. He makes frequent attempts to walk a straighter path and is less a varmint than a man with a deep capacity for self-justification.

Occasionally, the text's situations are stretched too far in order to preserve Plummer's innocence, making him seem naïve. Best drawn are the women who befriend and love Plummer. They are a lively cast, including saloon girls with hearts of gold, a freed slave pregnant with her master's baby, a neglected housewife looking for a brief moment of passion, and the preacher's daughter he eventually marries.

This book does not render a final judgement regarding Plummer; that door is left provocatively ajar. *The Life and Times of Henry Plummer* is an entertaining historical novel that plays out against the panorama of the Old West.

Reviewed by Clarion/Foreword Reviews
October 10, 2018

The Life and Times of
HENRY PLUMMER

LINDA BUXBAUM

Copyright © 2023 Linda Buxbaum.

All rights reserved. No part of this book may be reproduced, stored, or transmitted by any means—whether auditory, graphic, mechanical, or electronic—without written permission of both publisher and author, except in the case of brief excerpts used in critical articles and reviews. Unauthorized reproduction of any part of this work is illegal and is punishable by law.

ISBN: 979-8-88640-791-4 (sc)
ISBN: 979-8-88640-792-1 (hc)
ISBN: 979-8-88640-793-8 (e)

Because of the dynamic nature of the Internet, any web addresses or links contained in this book may have changed since publication and may no longer be valid. The views expressed in this work are solely those of the author and do not necessarily reflect the views of the publisher, and the publisher hereby disclaims any responsibility for them.

One Galleria Blvd., Suite 1900, Metairie, LA 70001
1-888-421-2397

CONTENTS

The End	1864	vii
Chapter 1	1851	1
Chapter 2	1852-1854	10
Chapter 3	1855	28
Chapter 4	1857	40
Chapter 5	1858	48
Chapter 6	1859	60
Chapter 7	1859-1860	75
Chapter 8	February 1861—April 1861	90
Chapter 9	June 1861—August 1861	126
Chapter 10	November 1861—May 1862	153
Chapter 11	May 1862—November 1862	176
Chapter 12	November 1862—April 1863	195
Chapter 13	June 1863—January 1864	207

THE END

1864

Henry could smell the stench of death. It, along with the ice-cold air, stung his nose. He could taste it, like he had so many times before, acrid, iron tang of adrenaline that humans give off before killing or being killed. It was all around him trapped in the circle of seventy-some men and their horses, ambushed in the 30-below-zero air, like him. They had come and taken him out of his sickbed where he had been attempting to sleep off the latest assault on his weak lungs by this God-forsaken land and its unforgiving arctic weather. The small mining camp of Bannack in the newly declared Montana Territory had been an ice box for the last four days, and Henry coughed a body-wrenching hack, spitting out blood, again. He almost hoped his own body would rob him of life before they could.

They had bound his hands behind his back and he walked the circle of vigilantes using his last and only available weapon, his gift of persuasion. He had talked himself out of so many other dire situations in the past. He stopped before each old friend he saw and tried to reason with him. They only shook their heads, regretful. "No, Henry," they spoke out, "not this time. You're on the list. Red fingered you, said you were in with them."

Henry shook his head in denial, claiming as loud as his poor lungs would allow him, "No! You listened to him? You know what kind of a man he is!"

"Was!" corrected a man as he spit out his juiced-up tobacco. "Was, Henry. He's gone now. He confessed and named every man in the gang before we hanged him."

Henry shook his head and searched the enclosure of men for a sane, reasonable person. "There's no gang! Where's Thompson? He knows I'm innocent. Sanders? Where's Sanders?"

The man laughed, choking on the brown spittle left in his mouth. "Hey, boy. Don't yuh know, Sanders and Lott, they's the ones that swore us all in. You's sunk, you sissified, dressed-up sheriff. We's all vigilantes now."

Sanders stepped out from the ring of men who were horseless. "It's useless, Henry, you're to be hanged. Don't beg for your life. It's been decided. Can't be helped. I feel as bad about it as you but I wouldn't save you if I could."

Henry stood silent for a moment. He hoped this was just another one of his wretched dreams. Must be. He was innocent, and certainly not a common thief, horse, gold dust, or otherwise. He attempted to defend himself once more. "I'm not a thief, never have been. The only men I have killed were about to kill me, and the rest, I was just keeping the law as sheriff or marshal."

The men all around him just shook their heads, and Henry could smell it again, the smell of death. The men and their horses were restless, anxious to return to their homes, to their warm beds and stables. The horses tossed their heads in the freezing cold, snorting out snot and what seemed to Henry, contempt. Their long eyelashes icicled as did the men's moustaches and beards. Many of the men had wrapped scarves around their necks and mouths making them difficult to recognize. Henry mostly identified them by their muffled voices.

Henry, still not believing this was happening to him, asked to spend the last few minutes of his life writing a note to his wife and then one to his family back in Maine still not believing this was happening to him. He was grateful that his dear mother had died years ago so she would not have to bear the heartbreak of his untimely, horrible end.

CHAPTER 1

1851

By the time Henry's father died at sea in 1850, the heat of the California gold rush had spread throughout the nation, even as far as remote Maine. Henry had spent three miserable, sick-in-the-lungs winters and decided he needed to find a more suitable climate or die young. He felt restless and had read as much as he wanted in his study of the law and knew he could take his knowledge with him anywhere he chose to go. Jeffery had urged Henry to take the bar exam in Maine, but Henry had no desire to stay.

He left Maine the fall of 1851. He had just turned nineteen and had a young man's lust for adventure. He traveled to New York where he boarded a steamer going as far as the Isthmus of Panama. The farther south they traveled the more Henry's lungs began to feel healthy. They had not felt this well since he had been very young. Henry looked up at the towering masts and remembered another day when he felt free and happy with no problems with his lungs.

That day the citizens of Addison were holding a "hauling bee," moving a huge fishing boat crafted by one of the farmers to the water, several miles, thrilling all the young boys. Henry, always the leader, ran ahead of the rest of the boys. They thought it exciting to see 76 oxen pulling together and the dozens of men driving them with others rolling the logs on which the boat had been placed. They yelled along with the men, one ... two ... three ... rolllll! Henry had noticed he could run and yell without discomfort in his lungs, and when they played hide-n-go-seek, he had out-foxed them all by climbing the highest mast he saw in the shipyard. He chortled with glee as he watched them search and search for him. When they lost interest and left to raid the food tables again, he had climbed down and joined them in their gluttony.

The ship's passengers consisted of mostly men, easterners and new immigrants wanting to try their luck in the California gold fields. There were few women on board, mostly young, and Henry could not ignore the interested looks he received. He returned none of them, feeling he had no prospects or heart to offer.

Henry had struggled to control his emotions as he said good-bye to his family but wept bitterly as he hugged them all farewell for he knew he could possibly never see them again. He respected his older brother Moses and knew he would miss their talks. He wished his brother well in his upcoming marriage to Mary Nash. He thought him a lucky man for making such a match and knew Moses would never lack in love or financial security.

Bidding adieu to Annie's girls broke his heart. Both Abby and Beth reminded him so much of his mother, but parting with Natty was the most difficult. They had become very close when he moved back home. She bolstered Henry's perseverance of grandmother's disapproval by giving him smiles and winks when Elizabeth would tear into him with her sharp tongue and evil looks and sometimes would even hush their grandmother's ranting tongue.

Grandmother was another good reason to leave the family nest. She had taken to calling Henry names such as Nancy or Nancy-boy, which meant she considered him effeminate. She berated him time and time again for never courting a young woman. Henry would respond with, "Grandmother, when I have better prospects and I see a young lady that interests me, I will court her. It just hasn't happened."

She retorted, "Well, Henry, if you'd quit acting like a lick finger, hanging around that law office and that stupid man, Jeffery Stinson, you perhaps would have better prospects. That clerk's job you have is worthless, just like you."

Henry had kissed his favorite sister goodbye with a heavy heart, but his grandmother, he never cared to see ever again. He had said his farewells at the gravesites of his beloved mother, his grandfather, and his two sisters, Rose and Emily, who had died from tuberculosis when he was just four. One of his earliest memories would always be that of their funeral and the confusion he had felt at leaving them in boxes buried in the cold, springtime earth.

Henry welcomed the heat that swept over them as they neared Panama but hated the swarms of insects that filled the air. He found a room in an awful hotel in Chagres and then three days later crossed the swampy jungle either riding on the back of a stubborn mule or paddling in a dugout canoe, his only conveyances to the other side of the isthmus. He thought the mosquitoes would carry him away all the while sucking him bloodless, and he prayed that they wouldn't infect him with malaria, dysentery, or cholera. When they reached Panama City, Henry quickly secured passage on a steamer, the Golden Gate, heading for San Francisco.

The Golden Gate, carrying twice her limit in passengers, rife with humanity of all sorts, offered Henry many observations of mankind and several lessons bringing him further into manhood. Henry discovered that he attracted quite a lot of female attention. The young, fresh, innocent maids peeked at him coyly from underneath their sweeping eyelashes and would blush when he caught them staring at him. He saw their mothers looking him over but dismissing him when they noticed his clothing and unkempt hair. He couldn't wait until his facial hair came in enough to grow a handlebar moustache. Moustache or not, 'professional' women just plainly gave him open, inviting gazes.

One day Henry walked into one of the gambling dens on deck. Learning to play faro cost him most of the money he possessed. He had also indulged in his first use of alcohol and stumbled to the railing retching. Henry felt embarrassment enough when he was finished but when he looked up into the face of the most beautiful woman he had ever seen, he felt mortified. She made light of it by asking if he suffered from seasickness or bad food.

Henry shook his head. "It's my own stupidity that's making me ill. I just lost most of my money gambling and drinking, the fool that I am." Henry looked sideways at the handsome woman who he knew instinctively had at least ten or maybe even fifteen years on him. "You don't need any menial chores done for you, do you?"

She laughed and held her hand out to him. "Consuelo Huevartes and you are?"

Henry smiled, green and ashamed, and tipped his hat to her. "Henry Plummer, at your service, madam."

She smiled and asked, "So at what game did you gamble away your money, Henry. Let me guess. Faro?"

"Yes, faro. Looked easy enough. Guess I am just not that lucky."

"Let me take you to dinner, get some nourishment back into you, and I will also fill you full of hints and warnings about faro as well. You look like you have a good mind and memory?"

Henry nodded, "I can remember anything and did well in school but just don't have good sense, it seems."

Consuelo hooked her arm in Henry's, guiding him to the elegant dining room, saying, "Well, first Henry, don't ever drink and gamble at the same time. You may have a drink or two to be social, but don't get drunk. Keep your wits about you or you'll come out a loser every time. You've got to stay alert because losing is not the only concern you have when gambling. If you're a steady winner, which I will make sure you are, some men will want to kill you or at least rough you up."

After eating, Consuelo gave Henry money, and he sat down at a different faro table where he again tried his luck. By following Consuelo's advice, he was able to more than regain his losses, and he was hooked. As he counted out the money she had lent him and stuffed it into her hand, he didn't know what to say. He felt almost as inexperienced and vulnerable as a fourteen-year-old.

"Consuelo, you have saved me. I really can't thank you enough. You'll never know what a pleasure it has been for me to make your acquaintance and to have you help me out like this." Henry awkwardly gathered both her hands in his and gently lifted them to his lips, softly kissing the top of each one.

She looked up at him and winked, "Well, now, didn't you say something about doing some menial chores for me?" She put her arm around his slender waist and led him through the winding passages to the door of her cabin. When she opened her door, Henry felt a sudden wave of awe. Her cabin's elegance was nothing like he had ever seen, and his mind registered the significance of entering a strange woman's room.

Henry stood near the door speechless while taking in the fine wood that lined the walls, the thick carpet, and the four-poster bed made up in a rich, green velvet spread, piled high with lacey pillows. He felt that he should bolt out the door and down the hall to the safety and sanity of his own sleeping berth in a room four times as small and shared with eleven other men.

Consuelo wasted no time and pushed a button, which brought a maid immediately to the door.

"Miss?"

"Good evening, Anna. Could you please have a bath poured for me? And, please bring me my favorite wine and some brandy for the gentleman. Thank you."

Henry stared at her a few moments more and blurted. "You're rich? You are, aren't you? You're a wealthy woman. Are you married, widowed?"

Consuelo laughed. "None of those. I am a working girl. Not married, never have been and probably won't be for some time, if at all. I do okay. I am what they call in California, an entertainer."

"An, an entertainer?" Henry stuttered.

"Yes, I amuse men."

"Amuse men?"

"I am a prostitute, Henry, high class, but a prostitute. What do you think about that?"

Henry stood, twisting his hat around and around in his hand. He was intrigued; he had already fallen for her charms, her generosity, and good looks. He shook his head in wonder looking at her as if she couldn't really be standing there and telling him this with no reluctance, no shame.

He cleared his throat, nervous, and smiled a silly grin. "I need to give it some thought. I am sorry, but back East, in Maine, I never …"

"You've never seen a prostitute, have you Henry? Haven't ever given it a thought, have you? The sale of sex because there are hardly any women there. I make hundreds of dollars a month in this madness, this crazy search for gold that has brought every kind of man you can imagine to California. I can spend a night with a man, have no contact with him at all, no sex, and he'll still pay me well just to have dinner, wine, and a conversation with him. Other times, I find it necessary not only to have intercourse but also do other things I'm sure you could never think of in your wildest imaginings. Do you have fantasies, Henry? Stay with me and I will try to fulfill them."

Just then a troop of women trailed in with buckets of hot steaming water, which they poured into a metal tub. A waiter opened the wine and then quickly left. Henry looked longingly at the tub.

"Go ahead, Henry. I ordered it just for you," Consuelo said as she stepped up to him and pulled off his jacket, which she tossed carelessly aside. She began working on the buttons of his shirt, and when she went for his trouser buttons, he stepped back.

Henry stood quiet, still unsure. How did this fit into his morals, especially what his mother and grandmother had taught him about women and how they should be treated? But when Consuelo took up the task of unbuttoning his pants again, he allowed her.

The water felt amazing. Henry lay back, and when she offered him a snifter of brandy he took it.

"Just sip it, Henry. Let it warm in your mouth before you swallow it." She walked to the armoire, pulled out a dressing gown and slowly undressed, unabashed, and stood before him. He didn't know if he should look, but finally he did. He drank in the beauty of her body, noting the glowing olive skin; long, slender legs; and tiny waist, along with her beautiful hair she had just unloosed from its black net. When his eyes rested on her breasts, he went hard and groaned.

She chuckled as she walked toward him and asked, "Still thinking, Henry?"

He only nodded as she began to pour water over his head and began washing his hair.

"You need a haircut young man, and a shave," she said as she rubbed her hands softly over his face. When she finished scrubbing his head, she went on to his body. Henry groaned when she began washing his manhood and yelped when he came. He blushed hotly and groaned again, remembering another embarrassing incident that happened to him when he had lived with the Hamlin family in Bangor, Maine while he attended The Hampden Academy for Boys.

They employed a young, black cook, Alamina, who also served them their meals. Henry thought her to be the most beautiful girl he had ever seen. She had a lovely face and a tempting body that could not be hidden by her domestic garb. She had a bosom that stood out proud and inviting. One night, Henry could see the outline of her nipples through her uniform. He became so hard he squirmed, and when his seed spilled out, he moaned. Everyone stopped eating and Mrs. Hamlin exclaimed, "Oh! Henry! What is wrong? Do you feel ill?"

Henry had responded with, "Yes, I'm sorry! Please excuse me." Henry remembered how he had pushed his chair back and ran from the room to the sanctity of his own bedroom. He wished now that he could run away, he felt so ashamed, but being that he was completely naked that option was out.

"Sshh! It's okay, dear. Here, stand up and I'll dry you off."

Consuelo led him to her bed and tucked him in as if he were a young, sweet boy. "I think that's enough for tonight, Henry. Now sleep. You've had a big day." Henry slept, innocent, while Consuelo watched him, drinking her glass of wine, trying to decide what kind of a man he was and would be, if she had her way with him.

Henry woke the next morning sure that he had had some fantastic dream. But when he looked around and saw Consuelo sleeping next to him, he knew his reality. She was just as lovely in sleep as she had been last night, and he noticed that she wore no night clothes. He nestled closer to her and began kissing her throat just where he could see her pulse. Soon he went lower with a trail of kisses and rested his lips on her left nipple. When it hardened he was equally so.

She was awake and when he said, "May I?" She threw the covers aside and offered her body to his, saying, "By all means."

Consuelo taught him how to make love, asking him to do this, and then that, guiding his hands. Henry was as much a virgin in love-making as he had been in faro cards, but he learned the art of love-making as quickly and was equally infatuated. Consuelo used her mouth and every feminine trick. Outside of shooting his gun, Henry had never felt so much power and satisfaction at the same time.

Consuelo bought Henry a set of well-fitted clothes and had a barber cut his hair. She shaved him herself each morning. Now, when Henry walked the deck everyone took notice of him and he realized he was a handsome man. He had never felt better. He discovered that he did, indeed, seem to have inherited his forefathers' seaman's legs and belly. Not feeling one bit seasick, Henry thrived; and with every mile between him and the cold Atlantic breezes, Henry's lungs healed and he nearly lost his chronic cough.

Consuelo also made sure Henry ate well and offered him fine fruit, breads, and cheeses. She introduced him to aromatic, tasty wines and brandy. Henry could feel his slight, five-foot-ten-inch frame expand and strengthen, and he walked the decks sure-footed with head held high. His golden hair had been clipped to perfection and the soft sea breezes and the sun had replaced Henry's ashen skin with color, and he looked devastating.

One night after making love, Henry asked Consuelo why such a beautiful, educated, and promising wifely prospect like her had become a prostitute. She explained to him that her father, a wealthy ranchero, had raised cattle for years just south of the San Francisco bay and had owned thousands of acres of land. When gold had been discovered in 1848 and life as they knew it disintegrated into madness, he had sold his land and had relocated just south of the Mexican border.

"My father," she explained, "had always been very traditional, patriarchal, and has attempted to have me marry a number of men he deemed perfect for me and his plans. I have no other siblings, no brothers to whom he can leave his fortune and land. My mother died when I was young. I have been my father's only hope in continuing his dreams and in keeping the family tradition and wealth."

Consuelo went on to tell Henry that she had tried to convince her father that none of these men would be trustworthy enough for such a favored position, and she had refused to move south with him to his new properties. He had disowned her. End of story.

"I like my life because of the freedom it gives me. I can dictate what I do, with whom, and when. Like now, here I am with you, no strings attached, right?"

Henry didn't know so much about that. He reminded himself he should put his heart away. He certainly had no future with her; she had made that clear. Still, he couldn't help but ask, "But when you have a powerful, successful, demanding client, who really does the dictating when he is paying you? That's not freedom when you must do some of those strange things some have had you do."

Consuelo turned her head away from him and said, "Oh, Henry! Do be quiet. Sometimes you think too much and too deeply.

CHAPTER 2

1852-1854

When the Golden Gate reached San Francisco, Henry and Consuelo went their separate ways, but she did give him a card with the address of the 'house' where she lived and worked. Henry found a job as a bookkeeper and a room at Bessie York's boardinghouse the same day. He decided to settle into San Francisco life, saving his money for a later move north and east to gold country.

He found his relationship with Consuelo different and disturbing when he went to visit her. She had many admirers who competed for her with great determination and money. Finding that he could not compete, and because Consuelo's 'house' proved to be one of the more expensive ones, Henry roamed the streets until he found a 'house' fitting to his taste and his pocketbook.

Henry soon realized that he could easily enhance the weight of his pocketbook at the faro tables; and in short time had discovered his favorite gambling joints, saloons, and bordellos. Spoiled by Consuelo, Henry went from woman to woman, practicing his skills but never finding one who pleased him. Henry also learned that gold mining in California had become a real, laborious job. Most miners now worked for wages performing back-breaking work to extract the gold from rocks and graveled earth. Henry did not want any part of that and put off his move to the gold fields.

Henry continued to work as a clerk for a construction company that nearly worked around the clock. San Francisco, suffering from fire after fire, losing homes and businesses, alike, rebuilt constantly and began urging builders to use brick for walls and metal for doors, window frames, and shutters. Henry's employer paid him well due to the company's lucrative earnings. But, Henry still liked the thrill of playing his hand at the faro tables, where he usually won more money than he spent.

One night he had been playing at the table having a great evening. But for a dangerously drunken man, he would have pushed his winning streak even longer. The man jealously sat watching Henry's every move with slit eyes. Every so often, he would curse at Henry, especially when he had another winning card. Henry finally lost his patience with the man and decided he had had enough. Just as he went to scoop up his chips, the man accused him of cheating. Henry laughed and easily said, "Only the banker can cheat at this game." Henry saw a flash of silver and suddenly he had a knife grasped in his left hand. Henry looked down at his bleeding hand and couldn't believe it. The man had thrown a knife directly at him, and he must have instinctively reached out and caught it. The faro dealer looked at Henry in wonder.

"Good reflexes, man. That was close. You'd better git now. Don't want any more trouble."

Henry finished wrapping his hand tightly with his handkerchief and picked up his chips. He felt lightheaded and a little sick. He turned once more to look at the man as he pocketed the knife, shaking his head in disgust. The man had passed out cold and lay like a puddle at the table. His hand began to ache, and Henry wished the crazed man had passed out sooner.

Just as he reached the door, an older gentleman stopped him. "Hey there, son, let me look at that hand. I'm a doctor and have an office just down the street."

Henry looked at the man, distrustful, but he was well-dressed and had a pleasant aurora.

"Let me see your hands," Henry ordered.

The gentleman held them out for Henry's inspection. They were finely made, small, and very clean. Henry nodded and the man laughed a genuine laugh which wrinkled the skin around his eyes. Henry looked into his eyes and only saw honesty and kindness. Henry held his hand out to the man who gently unwound the kerchief and clucked his tongue as he examined the wound.

"Come with me lad, you're going to need stitching up. My office is just around the corner."

He introduced himself as Charles Peabody, M.D., and Henry thought the name sounded familiar.

Henry held out his good hand. "Henry Plummer, sir." And they walked down the street.

"There it is."

Henry looked up at the sign, yes, *Dr. Charles Peabody, M.D.* He had walked underneath that sign many times. His boardinghouse was just up two blocks on Bush Street.

Henry smiled. "We're almost neighbors. I live just two blocks north of your office."

The doctor chuckled, "I can tell you come from a small town, thinking like that. This place isn't too neighborly in my estimation because ugly things happen constantly to good people. Don't trust a soul, Mr. Plummer. Despite the vigilance committee and their doings a year ago, crime still rules."

"Vigilance committee?" Henry asked as the doctor ushered him into his office, which took up the front three rooms of his home.

"Well, let me explain some things first," Charles said as he rolled up his sleeves and began scrubbing his hands with strong-smelling soap. "San Francisco has grown by the thousands, tens of thousands, actually, in the last three years. All different people of various races, cultures, religions, and beliefs have moved here because of the gold rush. Greed has motivated most of them. When you think of all the differences, the greed, men out numbering women eight hundred to one, the gambling joints, bordellos, peep shows, and saloons, it's no wonder we have so much crime."

Henry winced as Charles cleaned his wound and began stitching. He concentrated on the doctor's lecture to get through the pain.

"Some of these sorts were not too wholesome to begin with, coming from Australia as ex-convicts, criminals then and criminals now. These people have been credited with committing robberies, rapes, murders, assaults, and starting fires just to plunder shops, businesses, and even homes. They have a name for themselves—the Sydney Ducks. San Franciscans have had to rebuild time and again because of these fires." Charles shook his head with disgust. "At one point, in only three months' time, over 100 murders had been committed with no arrests, no convictions, or executions."

Henry looked a little green, so the doctor paused to pour them a whiskey, which brought Henry's coloring back. The doctor shook his head again. "You're a pretty man, Henry, you must be careful. Many of these toughs and rowdies don't care for good-looking, refined men and think they can take advantage of them. Watch out."

The doctor applied salve on Henry's stitched wound and went on with his story. "So affluent men like Sam Brannan … have you been to the Cliff House for supper yet? Nice place, Sam's. Men like him, hundreds of them, got together and organized The Committee of Vigilance to fight back and eliminate crime, vice, graft, and corruption. Last year, alone, they lynched eight men, ran hundreds out of town, mostly immigrants, especially the Irish, and forced the most unsavory, corrupt officials out of office and out of the city."

"But that's unconstitutional to take the law into your own hands!" Henry protested.

"Unconstitutional or not, it has proven to help. Criminal activities have greatly decreased since then."

"It's still not right," Henry interrupted. "They held no trials, called no witnesses, nothing legal?"

Charles looked thoughtful for a moment and then said, "Well, yes and no, there was a trial of sorts, you know, a quick review of the facts, sometimes witnesses were called, and then usually a declaration of guilt, and then the hanging. Vigilance has kept the criminal-minded out, or at least lying low. Our violent crimes have been less. You know, Henry,

California just became a state, and people aren't accustomed to thinking about the constitution or federal law, I guess."

"But really, how could people do that to other human beings? They must have had a strong, overwhelming build-up of hate and disgust for them. Unbelievable."

Charles laughed, bitter. "San Francisco's a strange place. Our city hall sits next to, is actually dwarfed by, the largest, wildest gambling den in the city. You need to come back tomorrow and a few days after that to have me put new dressings on this, son."

Henry yawned and stood, unsteady, after Charles finished bandaging his hand. He thanked the doctor, paid him, and walked home to his room and bed, glad of his room's proximity. But as he waited for sleep, he could not stop thinking about The Vigilance Committee and how they seemed to him just as murderous as those they had put to death.

He thought about his discussions with Hannibal Hamblin when he had been his understudy and assistant in his benefactor's law office. When Hannibal left for Washington D.C. to perform his duties in the Senate, Henry met with Mr. Hamblin's clients, acting as a go-between, exchanging letters with him to keep his clients happy and their cases as current as possible. Henry would also meet with prospective plaintiffs, becoming caught up in their grievances and wondering about the law.

One day upon Hannibal's return, Henry bombarded him with questions, asking first, "How do you know you are following the law when helping your clients? Where does the law come from?"

Hannibal, more than pleased to discuss law, answered, "Well son, the law comes from several sources. Here in the United States we follow much of the old English code called Common Law. We also look to the Bible, as well as the wise and ancient Greek and Roman philosophers at times, and most importantly, we rely on the Constitution of our country as a guide. The Constitution has become the main instrument we heed when deciding cases, especially the sticky more difficult ones."

"We also heed the idea of 'Live and let live' a code taken from the Bible. When Jefferson swore us in as new Senators he pretty much said that we should always remember the principal laid out in the Declaration of Independence, which states—that all men are created equal, that they are endowed by their Creator with certain unalienable rights, which are life, liberty and the pursuit of happiness, pursuit of happiness meaning we should be able to follow our dreams and passions when making a living for ourselves—when living out our lives. After which, he asked us to remember always and to ask ourselves when making decisions 'would we be taking any of these away from our neighbors—would we be right to take their lives, their liberty, and their livelihoods at any time?'

Henry interrupted, "But sir, what about the slaves? They have none of those. How can that be?"

Hannibal smiled a smile without it reaching his eyes, "Son, that is one of the greatest questions and imperfections of our nation, as I see it, that our country faces. We, as a nation, have only been able to stand up to this problem by asserting that slaves aren't quite human—we count them as partial human beings because of the Three-Fifths Compromise. When we count population for apportionment purposes in elections, they are considered 3/5 of a person even though they will never vote. We don't allow them to vote for obvious reasons, of course."

Henry could only shake his head and say, "It's not right. None of it is." And thinking of beautiful kind Alamina, he shook his head again, thinking, she's as human as anyone I have ever known.

After that, Hannibal had Henry read and study the Declaration of Independence, the Bill of Rights, and the Constitution, which he did as faithfully as he had the Bible and just about as many times. By the time he was fourteen, Henry had read the Bible seven times about which his grandmother loved to brag, until they had their disagreement, naturally.

Henry kept the knife and purchased a dart board, spending hours throwing the knife. He had gone faithfully to Dr. Peabody's for new dressings and discontinued his nightly visits to the faro tables, for a time. He and the doctor became friends and would sometimes eat supper together. Charles took him to the Cliff House one evening where Henry discovered he loved the Pacific Ocean as much as the Atlantic. After that, he often walked down to the beach for nightly walks, and it occurred to him that he should do something about self-protection besides the knife.

Henry possessed an awful yearning to see Consuelo. But, he couldn't afford her and save money at the same time without sitting down at the faro tables. He began frequenting the gambling halls again and regularly came away with heavy wins. He tried to find joints that catered to the more refined. Charles continuously warned him to be careful and suggested that he buy himself a six shooter—the revolver of choice in California. But Henry shied away from that idea thinking that he would never wish to shoot another human being. He did purchase a new knife more to his liking. He now carried a sheathed, double-edged, boot knife with a five-inch fixed blade.

Henry would sit in his room with his small table set up next to him as it would be at the faro table. He pushed it close to his dart board, which he had lowered to where a man's torso would be in the chair opposite him. He practiced reaching stealthily into his boot, pulling out his knife and throwing it across the table at the board. He never told Charles about this or his plans to continue gambling.

He experienced bad luck at the tables one night and decided to leave early. Before he left, he walked up to the bar and ordered a drink. Two men with whom he had been at the tables before on different occasions stood at the other end of the bar. He nodded to them and they acknowledged him. Soon they sauntered over to Henry and asked if they could buy him another drink. Seeming in a friendly, carefree mood, they asked how his night at the tables had been.

Henry, prideful, just shrugged his shoulders and said, "Not bad. How about you?"

"Oh, we ain't playin' now. Had so much hard luck that we're plum outa funds. Can't even play one game."

"Yeah," the other man agreed. "Tough, tough luck lately. Guess we'll have tuh go out and find ourselves some real work for a while."

Henry just nodded and said, "Yeah. Real work's what keeps you honest, I guess."

"Well, now," spoke up one. "You sayin' we's dishonest or sumpthin?"

Henry chuckled, "Heck, no! Just what a friend of mine keeps telling me. That's all. Nothing meant."

The three stood there quiet for a few minutes and then Henry offered to buy them a drink. He noticed that when he took out his money, they took a healthy interest in his stash. Henry became nervous and decided to call it a night.

"Speaking of that friend, reminds me that he wanted me to stop by tonight. You two have a good evening." Henry paid for the drinks and left. The wooden walks were full of people, which made Henry feel better. But his scalp still crawled when he thought of the two men and their demeanor.

Henry stayed away from that house and soon forgot about the incident. He still took his walks down on the beach, hardly seeing anyone most nights. He guessed most of men spent their free time gambling or whoring. Some mornings he would walk down to the wharf to feel invigorated and freed by the fresh sea breeze and to enjoy the noisy squawking of sea gulls. He watched dock workers as they, bare-chested, unloaded and reloaded ships and steamers. He admired their muscled chests and backs, their flat hard bellies, and the round, jumpy muscles that bulged from their arms. They made him feel like the effeminate clerk he was, unfortunately.

Henry continued going to the faro tables at least once a week. He steered clear of the brothels and bordellos, saving his money, and himself, for Consuelo. His nest egg had increased to the point where he knew he could comfortably spend the money for a couple nights with her and still have funds to explore the gold fields.

But gaming was in his blood and he had trouble thinking of life without the thrill and heart-pounding excitement he felt when he chose to engage in cocking at the tables, venturing both his stake and wins. Henry also liked to triple his stake, risking it all again, to win seven-fold, which not only made his heart race but also made him sweat. Henry usually succeeded in punting because he always remembered which cards had been played and how many times.

Henry decided to try a new joint in late October when he had been in San Francisco for almost a year. He had begun to feel comfortable and at home. He loved the ocean and the temperate weather, not too hot and not too cold, perfect. His lungs could even take it when the weather did turn nasty blasting the coast with cold winds and rain. He walked into a den, studying the bankers at the different faro tables, hoping to choose one a bit more honest than the others.

He found a man with the right look to him and sat down. It wasn't until Henry began playing that he noticed two of his fellow players were the two men who had boldly showed interest in his winnings after he bought them drinks. He gave them a little nod and then settled his mind on the cards.

Henry had a good night, couldn't seem to make one bad move, and decided to quit early. He walked out of the joint and smelling the sweet scent of the ocean, decided to take the long way home. The night sky was dark with heavy clouds cutting off the moon's glow. As he walked down the wooden sidewalk, he decided to visit Charles instead, since it was still early.

Henry, anticipating Charles's rich brandy, slipped into an alley to take a short cut. Just as he was about to step out of the alley, he felt someone grab him by the coat and flip him around. His two 'friends' had decided to make their move on him. Henry had no chance to reach for his knife or defend himself. One man held him while the other sucker punched him several times, and once he was down on the ground, he knew he was in for a beating. The last thing Henry remembered was a booted foot kicking him in the head.

Henry woke up. At first, he thought he had gotten by easy, but as he became more alert, he could feel a huge, swollen, bloody lip throbbing and a searing pain in his side. He had blood seeping down into one eye. He struggled to get on his feet and once there, headed for Charles's house just blocks away. He felt like howling when people met him and simply crossed the street to avoid him and his mess. He, for sure, was not in Addison any more.

Charles clucked his tongue when he saw Henry and the condition he was in. "Young man, I told you to be careful, and for God's sake, buy a gun. No sane man walks these streets any more without protection."

Noticing Henry's blood-soaked shirt, he said, "Oh, for Christ's sakes, Henry, they tried to gut you."

"My knife, check for my knife."

Charles got him laid out on the examining table and pulling off Henry's boots, found no knife. After removing Henry's trousers, Charles realized Henry's money was gone, also. Henry passed out when Charles took off his clothes, and Charles gasped when he saw the gash in Henry's side. Thank God they hadn't gone deep enough to hurt much more than skin and muscle. Charles went to work cleaning and stitching as rapidly as possible before his friend came to again.

Henry woke up stiff, hurting everywhere, and he was sure even his toes had been injured. Charles helped him sit up enough to get some water and some medication in him to help him sleep. He helped Henry down off the exam table and walked him slowly to a bed into which Henry sank, falling asleep instantly.

When he woke, Henry could tell it was early morning by the way the sun shone in the window. He could hear the street coming to life with people bustling down the walk and the whinnying of the horses pulling the break-of-day delivery wagons. Charles looked in and saw he was awake. He told Henry he would need to move around to avoid stiffness and to keep healing blood flowing through his injuries.

He helped Henry up and into the little house out back. Henry couldn't stand long enough to pee like a man and slumped down on the seat and did it like a woman. He looked down and saw that, yes, the bastards must have stomped on his feet because his toes were turning black and blue. He groaned and Charles stepped in to help him back into the house.

"They really did you good, son. They weren't just happy to take your money. No, they must have tried to break every bone in your body by the looks of it."

Henry shook his head in bewilderment, "Didn't do one thing to them. Must be pretty miserable to want to do such a thing."

Charles had Henry drink more water, medicated him, and helped him into bed, muttering the entire time. "Crazy no-good-for-nothings.

Like to break every bone in their bodies. You just sleep, now, Henry. Next time you wake up, we've got to try to get some food into you."

When Henry woke again, night was approaching. He felt much better and got up to go to the john on his own. Charles sat him up in a high-back chair in his parlor and went to fix him some soup. Henry sat thinking about his situation. He hoped he wouldn't lose his job, not showing up at work like he had. He wondered how soon he would be able to go about his business again. He loved Charles but certainly didn't want to live with him or have him play nursemaid to him for too long.

Charles brought Henry noodle soup in a heavy mug. Henry found that he was hungry once he began eating, and his appetite improved even more when Charles told him that he had stopped by his work and explained what had happened.

"I told them you'd probably be back in a few days."

"Really, I'll heal that fast? Good. Thank you for everything, Doc. Make sure you bill me." Henry laughed and asked for more soup.

"Just promise me I won't have to do any more stitching on you, son. That's all the payment I need."

Henry went back to work, and three weeks later walked down to the docks and hired on as a part-time worker. At first, he suffered from constant pain, his overworked muscles feeling as if he had been beaten again. But in time, he began looking forward to the hard labor and felt better than ever. He had always been afraid of overexerting himself because of his lungs. In the beginning they did act up some, but now he hardly coughed and could take a deep breath without a wheeze and the usual catch in his breast.

Charles helped him buy a pistol, a six shooter, and then took him out into the countryside where he could target practice. He found Henry to be a natural at handling the gun and was amazed at how quickly Henry became a dead-on gunman.

"You've got great reflexes, Henry. And, your eye-hand coordination is outstanding. I believe you are becoming quite dangerous, my boy."

Henry bought another knife and a new board. He drew the silhouette of a man on the board and practiced his throwing. He looked in the mirror and saw a changed man. He seemed taller, with broader shoulders and arms with muscles like rocks. He proudly splayed his hands on his tight, flat belly rippling with brawn. He couldn't see his back but could feel the tight ridges of muscles. Now his upper lip grew enough hair for him to fashion a nice-looking handlebar moustache. His face and arms were tan, and he decided that come warmer weather, he would go shirtless like the rest of the men who worked on the docks. He was ready to visit Consuelo and spend a glorious night with her.

As Henry approached Consuelo's house of business, he stood outside and collected himself. He had an itch and it needed scratching because he had not had a woman for nearly a year. He knew he was as fit as ever, more appealing than before with a tan, a moustache, and a new suit of clothes. His inner voice warned him that she may not be available for the evening, despite that he had made sure he would be there before any other clients; it was only five o'clock. He took a deep breath and walked up the steps and used the door's enormous, brass knocker.

At his third attempt, an older woman opened the door and looked him up and down.

"A bit early, aren't you?"

Henry cleared his throat, "I am hoping to spend the night with Consuelo. I have money and assume she is not yet engaged for the evening."

Henry's earnestness must have reached the madam's stony heart because she invited him in without hesitation. Henry glanced around and saw two women lounging in the parlor. They gave him a good once-over and then one of them sauntered over.

"I'll take this one, Amanda. Looks like fun."

Amanda gave her a stern stay-in-your-place stare and told her to go sit down. "I'll handle this, Betsy."

She turned to Henry and said, "Consuelo doesn't work here any longer. She went back home."

"Yeah," called out Betsy, "the high-horsed, Mexican bitch went back to her rich daddy and husband. Good riddance, I have to say!"

"Hush!" the madam admonished sternly. "Behave or you'll be sitting out the night. Go upstairs and take off some of that face paint. You've used too much again."

Betsy sulked off and took her time going up the stairs, then she turned and said, "Perhaps, Amanda, you should just tack a sign on the door that says, 'Consuelo don't work here no more.' Be easier than giving the sob story to everyone that wants her."

Amanda lifted her eyebrows and turned back to Henry. Something about this young man made her think he wasn't the typical John. "I'm sorry, sir. Is there anyone else that will do?"

Henry shook his head, and then asked, "Could you please tell me where she is?"

Amanda searched Henry's face for a moment. "You know, I do believe you are the young man she told me about. From the Golden Gate?"

Henry nodded his eyes wide. "Yes, that was me. Why?"

"Well, Henry, that's your name, right? You are one of the reasons she left this business. Something you said to her. Would you come with me, please?"

Amanda ushered Henry into her office just off the parlor. She asked him to sit down and poured him a brandy. She sat down across from him and told him Consuelo had left him a note, but that she wouldn't tell him where she lived, now, again with her husband. Henry nodded, feeling deflated.

Amanda opened a safe and handed Henry a note. He could smell Consuelo's scent on the envelope and took a long, wistful whiff before he opened the letter. It was short and to the point. She thanked Henry for her time with him on the steamer and for him being so honest and open, and for saying something that brought her to her senses. She had felt changed after her time with him and found it difficult to go back to her former ways.

"I'm sorry for my lies to you Henry, and I'm sorry I cheated on my husband. I hated how he and my father attempted to bully me and order me around, so I left them because of my foolish pride. You were the best experience of my rebellion. Have a good life, Henry, and forget me. Consuelo."

Henry looked up at Amanda and asked, "If she worked here, why was she on the Golden Gate?"

"We knew her family was about to find out where she worked, so she went to Panama City for a time. She's actually a very good person, Henry. Most of her time here she spent pleasing men with only her personality and grace. They were satisfied with her companionship and nothing else. I'm going to miss her, and I'm sorry you cared for her. Just go on with your life. You'll find someone else."

When Henry walked past the parlor, there were more women sitting there. They all seemed bold and lewd except for one youthful and innocent looking girl. Henry felt sorry for her. She looked like a sweet flower among the cactus and in his heart, he secretly wished her luck.

Just before he left, he turned to Amanda and asked, "Why would they take her back? Her father and husband, I mean. Why would he want her back in his life?"

Amanda smiled and asked, "Wouldn't you?"

Henry walked down the street and into the next saloon, ordering a drink. He stood at the bar, trying to push the image of that sweet young girl out of his mind. He threw the drink down his parched throat and walked back out into the street, striding purposefully back to Amanda's. He walked in and when he met her questioning eyes he asked how much for a night with the youngest girl there.

Amanda laughed and said, "Quite a lot, my good man. She's a virgin and will bring much for the first time, even though most men don't want those sorts of inexperienced goods."

Henry grimaced at her words, making the girl even less than a slave—three-fifths a person. "Well, I want her any way. What's her name?"

Her name was Callie, which fit her perfectly because she was, indeed, beautiful and lovely. He would tell her about her name and where it came from—that it was Greek and what it meant, perhaps that would help. Her hair was a pale blonde but her skin tone, a creamy golden brown, showing that she was quite fresh—off a farm most likely,

Henry thought. He shook his head sadly as she led him to her room. He imagined her a year from now, the pasty skin, shadowed eyes, caked with powder, rouge, and heavy lines of black to liven her up—making up for the freshness long gone. Henry shuddered and wondered if he should do something.

Henry left early the next morning and without knowing why, he paid Amanda a huge chunk of money, saving Callie, making her his for the next month. Amanda made him a good deal since she was so naïve and fresh, hoping Henry would teach her a thing or two before he got over her.

Despite his best intentions, Henry did return almost every night that month. The evenings he stayed away, his soul would be a battleground between evil and good; at least that is how he saw it. The baseness of his body craved her but his moral inner voice would tell him to do the right thing, make her realize that prostitution would kill her—spirit and soul, at the very least.

After that first night, even though he had been worshipfully gentle with her, he had seen some of the light go out of her eyes, and that tormented the good side of him. But that wantonness wickedness in him, what he envisioned as a black dog with eyes full of depravity, yelping out its insane base reasoning, told him repeatedly that she had chosen the life of a whore and that he shouldn't worry about her and just use her.

He felt justified in that every time he made love to her his good side would at least make him try his best to make her feel something, if only extreme pleasure, but much like what Consuelo had done with him, he was truly using her. They developed a friendship and only that—there was no passion or love between them. They were worlds apart. She was just off the farm, so to speak. She and her family got by as fruit pickers. Her father was a drinker and sometimes, not often, yet frequently enough, would physically attack all whom he loved, blaming them for his lowly station in life.

Callie knew enough to realize that he would most likely always be that way and had left her family. Becoming a prostitute had seemed the only possibility of making a livelihood. But, she was no Consuelo.

Henry found her sweet but very uneducated and definitely not knowledgeable about life. She looked at the world through ignorant and unquestioning eyes and that bothered Henry. He found it difficult to carry a conversation with her, and because he had been so capable a teacher in love making, she craved it as much as did his evil side.

One day as Henry walked to work, he noticed a sign in an elegant women's boutique announcing a position open for an assistant seamstress, stating that the owner would be willing to train that person as a seamstress. Henry recalled the night when they did have a decent exchange, that when Callie's family had lived somewhere long enough for them to call a town home, living there for almost a year, she had worked for a tailor who had taught her the fundamentals of sewing.

She told him that her time there had been the most satisfying in her life, bringing home substantial contributions to her family and finding peace and satisfaction the art of sewing. When she couldn't sleep in like the other girls at Amanda's, she would stitch away, embroidering something of a trousseau for herself. Henry, remembering the talent exhibited in her work when she had shown off her delicately embroidered under things and linens, felt relief. He had found an answer to his dilemma that would please the saintly side of him.

It didn't take much to persuade Callie to apply for the position. Henry took her shopping for a nice, attractive and yet proper, set of clothing and upon meeting her new employer, Mrs. Howe, a refined English tailor, Henry knew he had done the right thing. The two women seemed enamored with one another immediately.

Henry would keep his relationship with Callie, never going back to their former relationship again, but they did become dear friends. Henry escorted her often to theater productions after a fine dinner at one of the many fine restaurants sprouting up in San Francisco, and when Callie found the love of her life and married, Henry stood as her best man, while Mrs. Howe, Katherine, attended as her a lovely matron of honor. Because Callie married a young and decent railroad baron, he knew she would never want for anything, especially love and honor. She had become, under Mrs. Howe's tutelage, a proper young woman with a mind of her own. Henry's soul rejoiced at his triumph in this entire affair but that malevolent black dog of his, hounding him constantly, had some devilish plans for Henry's vengeful side.

Henry's yen for adventure in the gold fields began to bother him, but he had one more thing to accomplish before leaving San Francisco. He knew that the town had lost much of its appeal because Consuelo was gone and because of his misgivings when buying sex from Callie. He swore off women completely and never patronized another brothel or bordello again in that burgeoning city.

He went out and purchased two sets of handcuffs and told Charles his plan. Charles thought him crazy but still allowed Henry to practice cuffing him over and over until Henry felt he could handcuff a person in his sleep. He continued to go to the gambling dens but became more careful in taking away winnings. He kept a low image but was always on the lookout for trouble. Three times, he needed to pull out his gun, threateningly, to avoid injury. Those times, his speed and deadly aim scared off his confronters.

Henry continued to work part time on the wharves; and when he went to buy new clothes, he found that he had grown some in height and a lot in breadth. He and Charles continued with their suppers together, and Henry became something of a connoisseur of fine food, especially in fresh fruits and vegetables. After growing up in Maine, he couldn't seem to get enough of California's fresh bounty.

One night when gambling, the opportunity for which he had been waiting arrived. He had had a prosperous night and was about to leave when he looked up to see his two attackers from two years before. They leered at him, and he played the weak victim, acting a bit nervous and remaining subserviently amiable. When he got up to leave, their appraisal of him made the hairs stand up on the back of his neck.

Henry left and walked rapidly down the street slipping into an alley waiting for his prey. His heart beat crazy, feeling like it was in his throat as it drummed loud in his ears. The adrenaline in his mouth tasted like bile, and he spit. He detested that taste and spit again just as the two men turned into the alley. The first man didn't know what hit him as Henry attacked him with punches anywhere he could land one and he could smell that his quarry had urinated in his pants. Henry then quickly handcuffed the man's wrists behind his back and turned to face the other opponent.

This man was much more difficult to best. He struck Henry a good, hard blow to the jaw and Henry could see stars floating around him as he stumbled a little and then came up with his fist cuffed and gave the man the same treatment. Henry tasted blood from his split lip and remembered his pain from these toughs' former beating. The man went down and Henry stood over him and picking him up by his shirt, punched him twice in the head and once in the stomach before letting him go. Henry watched him fall to the ground and when he had him handcuffed, he dragged him next to his partner. He administered swift hard kicks to each man, not caring where they landed and when his anger had been spent, he looked down on them, satisfied, at last.

Henry pulled down each man's trousers and took out his knife. He left them both lying in the alley with their pants down with a large X carved into each of their butt cheeks. "An eye for an eye, so to speak," he whispered softly. He laughed to think of how each time they sat down they would think of him until their asses healed. Henry wondered what sort of story they would tell any woman who saw their behinds. Henry was now ready to move on. He had sickened of San Francisco.

CHAPTER 3

1855

Nevada City lay 166 miles northeast of San Francisco and as California's third largest city, was home to more than 20,000 people by 1854. Henry had stopped in a saloon when he first arrived and an old miner told him how things had changed. "Yeah," he said, "in 1849 when gold was first discovered here, miners could pull a pound of gold dust each day from the creek. But, by 1850, that easy gold panning had become a thing of the past. They had to rely on organized mining when the Empire Mine developed, and miners began to work for wages instead of the easy pay dirt."

Henry decided to ranch with a partner, a man names Stephen Grey, in Nevada County a few miles north of the city, raising beef. The life was full of hard work but quiet and too peaceful. Henry missed the city and did not care for the dirty, manual labor. Henry knew the isolation helped him keep his resolve to live clean, to steer clear of gambling and women, but he couldn't help but wonder if he couldn't accomplish that in the city. Despite his wish to live a decent life, Henry continued to hone his skills with weapons, deeming them necessary for any occupation. The incidents at the faro table and in the alley had destroyed any trust he had ever entertained for people. He now carried his six guns wherever he went.

In January 1855, Henry sold his half of the ranch and bought a little house in Nevada City. He found work at a local bakery as a salesman and by April had saved enough money to buy a partnership in the Empire Bakery. Nevada City, with a bustling downtown complete with multiple brick buildings, a theater, a Wells Fargo bank, saloons by the score, and of course the usual girly houses, made life more of what Henry expected. He hadn't gambled or drank, but it helped to know it was all there.

Henry and his partner began a catering service out of their bakery, which became an overnight success. Henry's acquired taste for fresh foods and California cuisine served them well. They delivered food to the wealthy for their parties and to saloons and brothels, allowing Henry entrance once again into these establishments. Though he never became a client, he did establish many friendships with the owners and their patrons as well. Henry brought in good profits, saved his money, and decided it was time for him to establish himself in the middle class. He was only twenty-one and felt as if he owned the world.

Henry's advertising slogan for the bakery, "Live and Let Live," not only portrayed his innocence about people but also pointed out his political ignorance. He wanted to be counted among the middle class but knew nothing about how to play their game. His belief in tolerance would plague him. In northern California, people who called themselves Democrats were usually of the lower classes, the laborers, miners, immigrants, Catholics, and liberals. Henry knew and understood these people best and joined the Democratic Party. He didn't realize that by becoming a Democrat he would make his middle class dream a struggle and that to be considered bourgeois he should have been conservative, Protestant, and not friends with barroom owners and brothel madams.

Henry had met a girl from a well-established family when catering a party for her parents. The George's lived on a hill overlooking Nevada City in a Victorian mansion, a large, opulent home even by San Francisco standards surrounded by beautiful grounds. Henry loved the setting because it had trees. The people of Nevada City had been so anxious to build that they had almost eliminated every tree in the area.

Emily's parents put her in charge of the catering arrangements. Henry, not realizing she was the coveted daughter, became familiar with her. Emily, accustomed to being treated with kid gloves by former beaus, was completely charmed. He admired her openly with enigmatic eyes and ravishing smiles. When she signed the bill and Henry realized who she was, he blushed, doffed his hat, and swept her a low bow saying, "Thank you, very much Miss George." Her laughter pealing out over the hillside was the last thing he heard as he jumped on his wagon, cursing himself for his stupidity.

Then, Henry completely ruined his chances at bourgeois status by becoming a deputy police office after he and his partner failed in their business. They had sold their bakery and had moved into a new, bigger building not realizing that the new owners at their old site would keep their former customers. They found that Nevada City, despite its constant growth, did not need a second bakery. After a few months at their new location, they went out of business.

As a new deputy, Henry was frowned upon by his two bosses, Marshal David Johnson and Sheriff W.W. Wright, both supporters of the Know Nothings who hated Democrats and liberals. Henry, in high standing with the Democrats and praised by Tallman Rolph, the editor of the *Democrat*, decided to run against David Johnson for the position of Marshal. Henry easily defeated Johnson and was now Nevada City's new marshal.

Henry could not stop thinking about Emily even though he tried, knowing that her class kept her out of his range. But as marshal, he was invited to join the city council. He looked at it as another chance at respectability. Introductions were made at his first meeting, and he blanched when they attached the name of Cyrus George to the tallest, most dignified man present. Ironically, Henry's quiet, thoughtful pose due to intimidation compelled Cyrus George to become even more interested in the young man.

At the next council meeting Henry remained quiet except to suggest the city consider planting trees to replace the ones cut down earlier. He asserted that Nevada City, though still a beautiful place, would be more pleasing if again populated by trees. Henry finished by suggesting that some floral gardens wouldn't hurt either. After the meeting, Cyrus invited Henry to dinner at his home the next Sunday evening to further discuss his ideas.

When Henry arrived at the George's he looked handsome in his new suit and stark white shirt. The only outward sign of his nervousness was a slight cough, which he lost as soon as he realized that Cyrus George sincerely respected and liked him. What would happen when Emily appeared, he did not know. But, it did reassure him to know that the older, established man took him seriously.

Emily, charming and beautiful, immediately began flirting with Henry. Dinner was pleasant, with just the four of them. Henry could tell by Emily's high color that she felt just as excited as he did for this serendipitous occasion. He enjoyed her teasing but found it difficult to keep a serious conversation with her father when her light-hearted taunting gave him a constant hard-on.

She would run her soft, leather covered foot up and down his leg. Every so often she would drop something and lean over to retrieve it and Henry would get a good look at her cleavage. She licked her lips so they were constantly wet and Henry didn't know if he liked the wetness or the licking most.

Emily continued her coquettish behavior and earned a startled look from her mother, who, though lovely and cordial, looked as if she would have preferred a less high-style life. Henry perceived that she sensed the connection between her daughter and him, immediately. Cyrus had no perception of what was happening and continued talking about his pet plans for the city.

The next time Henry saw Emily was at a Christmas dinner at her home for a small group of what appeared to be mostly dear friends and acquaintances. Henry counted his blessings to be among them. Emily, inviting with her auburn hair swept up high, her brown eyes warm and lively, and her lovely décolleté driving Henry crazy, appeared much soberer and more serious than the previous dinner, displaying her best behavior, it seemed.

Dinner, pleasant enough, became somewhat awkward when Emily began placing Henry in the center of attention with her questions. "So, tell me, Mr. Plummer …"

"Call me Henry, please?" Henry intercepted.

"So, tell me, Henry, what do you like about being marshal?"

Henry drew a long breath, not expecting this question. He thought a moment and then answered, "I like the people I see and meet and the idea that I am hired to protect them. I appreciate the respect they, most of them, give me. I enjoy going out early in the morning when all is quiet and watching the city come to life, and then late at night when I watch people disappear for the evening and it becomes still again."

One of the other guests, a stingy looking man with a pinched face spoke up. "Yes, tell me Henry, do you really like interfering in people's, shall we say, conflicts, really? What about the incident at the Foaming Tap? How could you allow the quarrel to end up in someone's death?"

Henry, upset, cleared his throat after a short coughing fit. The man referred to a recent night when Henry had let his guard down and accompanied a friend into a saloon for a brandy after his shift. He had left his gun at home and had only his night stick. His friend, drunk, picked a fight with the bar owner. When his friend began rocking the bar and breaking things, the bartender pulled out his gun and fired a warning shot into the ceiling.

Henry promised the bar owner he would arrest his friend and jail him for the night, but the man refused. "I can protect my own property!" By then, Henry's drunken friend had his gun in hand and shot at the barkeep, wounding him in his arm. The wounded man spontaneously shot back, killing Henry's friend.

Because of that event, Henry learned several valuable lessons about being a lawman. Henry found that he could trust no one's behavior, not even a friend's. Furthermore, a gun would not have helped that night. Henry decided that, as a lawman, what worked best was to use his charm always, to soothe drunken, heated men and to talk them out of hotheaded, violent acts.

"Sir, I was not armed and will try to do better with diplomacy in the future. Someone would have been shot whether I had a gun or not.

I just didn't talk fast enough or say the correct things to break up the confrontation, and for that tragic, needless event, I'm sorry."

The other guests graciously moved on to a new subject, but Henry still left the party as soon as it was polite with his pride stinging. Emily ran out onto the porch to tell him good-night and that she was sorry about Harry Whitehead. "He's such a bore," she asserted, attempting to placate Henry.

Henry bowed to her and kissed her hand saying, "Goodnight, Miss George. I suppose I'll never see you again after Mr. Whitehead's remarks about my failures, but it was lovely knowing you." He walked out into the night for his long walk home. He really wanted to stop at a saloon for a drink but did not.

Henry did see Emily again and became the proper suitor with her making the first move. Henry received a hand-delivered note from her in his office on January 5. The invitation written in her small, spidery hand stated that she had two tickets to the theatre and wondered if he would care to escort her. Emily's feminine scent of wildflowers wafted out from the paper, and Henry smiled thinking about the last perfumed missive he had received.

Henry responded with his own brand of seduction. He dressed in his best clothes, bought a bouquet of wildflowers mixed with red roses, and walked up the hill to the George mansion. Emily answered the door herself and seemed genuinely surprised by Henry's gesture. She clasped her hands and sang out, "Why Henry Plummer, I didn't know you were a romantic. I thought you more a rake and the kind of man accustomed to girls falling all over you without your encouragement." Then she paused, smiled, and became sincere. "These are lovely, really, Henry, just beautiful. Thank you." When she finished praising him, she pecked Henry on the cheek, and he returned the kiss by picking up her hand and softly brushing his lips on each one of her knuckles.

"Oooh, Henry, you're giving me the shivers. Does this mean you'll be my escort to the theatre on Sunday evening?"

"Yes," Henry answered, "and I was hoping you would do me the honor of having supper with me before? May I come for you at six?"

Emily sighed and said, "That sounds wonderful, Henry. I'll be ready."

"Until then, Emily," Henry said, bowing and sweeping off his hat.

Henry's evening with Emily was satisfactory and yet disappointing. Their buggy ride into town was pleasant apart from Emily's constant teasing and coquettishness. Henry wished she would stop performing her young-maiden-with-not-a-thought-in-her-head pretense. He sensed that there was much more to her than she let on. Her endless, silly giggling quickly became quite bothersome.

Supper went much better. Emily seemed to have perceived Henry's feelings about her attempt at lightheartedness. They discussed each one's educations, and Henry was surprised to discover that Emily, under the guidance of a female tutor had read many of the classics including the Greek and Roman philosophers. Their discussion of natural human rights allowed Henry a glimpse into the true nature of this young woman.

"I have resigned myself to my fate as a nineteenth century woman but will not back down when I have my own daughters. They will be able to make many more decisions on their own about their lives. I will make sure of that. It's too late for me, now, but for them, it will be different."

"Why do you think it is too late for you, Emily?" Henry asked, with a puzzled shake of his head.

Emily shrugged and said, "It just is, Henry. Let's talk about something else."

Henry, thinking of his chances of wedding a girl such as Emily with her social status, asked her "What do you think of my running for the lower state house next year? I will be going to San Francisco to talk it over with my good friend, Dr. Charles Peabody this coming week."

Emily looking troubled, bit her lip and said, "Oh, Henry, I, too will be leaving next week for St. Louis to stay with my grandparents for a spell. My parents want me to meet my relatives and to acquire more sophisticated social graces." Emily finished her announcement with a small, ladylike snort, and Henry smiled inwardly to know she could be genuine.

Henry's only response was to lean across the table, brush his lips across Emily's fingertips, and say, "I will certainly miss you."

When they returned to Emily's home, she went in to ask permission to entertain Henry on the porch for a while and then came out to sit with him. She allowed him some kisses, and when he reached down and captured a breast with trembling hands, she shied away like a young colt, whispering, "I can't. I just can't," with a sob catching in her throat. Henry knew she had liked his kisses and cursed silently as he bid her good night. He yearned for the open and honest sex that he had had with Consuelo. All he wanted was a real woman who would love him with no strings attached.

Henry felt relief to be with a good, trusted friend again and poured out his frustrations with life and politics in Nevada City to Charles. But, they both decided that it would still be the right move on Henry's part to run for office. Charles believed that politics in California should be more balanced by young, progressive, and liberal-minded men like Henry. He thought the conservatives, especially the Know-Nothings, had been allowed to go too far in acting on their beliefs because they, once again, had organized a second vigilance committee in San Francisco and had hanged two prominent men. Henry listened quietly as Charles told him of the latest events. First, he told the story of Charles Cora and how he came to kill Marshal William Richardson.

"On November 15, last fall, Charles Cora and his longtime girlfriend Arabella Ryan, the most famous and expensive prostitute in the city, attended the opening play at the American Theatre. Sitting in the first balcony seats, they caused quite a stir being the most noted prostitute and gambler in town. This offended the wife of Marshal William Richardson, and the marshal attempted to have the notorious couple thrown out. The manager refused to do so since the two had become regulars at every opening night, reserving the costliest seats in the house.

"The next day, still stinging with indignation, the marshal went from saloon to saloon looking for Charles Cora. When he did find him, they drank together, seeming to mend their differences with friends of both encouraging this conciliation with rounds of drink and good cheer. The following day, they encountered one another in a saloon and began drinking again. Somehow, no one really knows how or why, they ended up on Clay Street with Cora shooting Richardson dead.

"Cora was arrested and tried with the trial ending in a hung jury. Opponents of Cora accused Arabella of bribing witnesses and jurors. Many people believed the hung jury came about because of the defense attorney's, Colonel E.D. Baker's, comparison of Arabella to Mary Magdalene. Cora remained imprisoned while waiting for his second trial, with Arabella's lifestyle and occupation seemingly still on trial. Emotions and politics heated the situation with the conservatives reestablishing another vigilance committee, which hoped not only to rid the city of open vice but also take control from the liberal Democrats."

Henry couldn't believe the ominous tone of Charles' story. "So, why did they hang the other man? What did he do?"

Charles went on. "James King of William, a severely insecure man with a failing newspaper, had decided to begin a crusade against the corruption in San Francisco to increase readership. He hoped to capture the interest and support of the many conservatives in town by raging against the liberal standards supporting vice. He published an editorial that exposed another newspaper editor and a liberal, James Casey, and his criminal record in New York.

"On May 14, James Casey challenged him to a duel and won, shooting King dead. That is when the vigilance committee organized again with more than 6,000 strong. They have an arsenal of weapons, a central headquarters with assembly halls, a prison, an infirmary, reinforced with cannons and gunnysacks nicknamed Fort Gunnybags. The vigilantes marched on the jail where Charles Cora and James Casey were being held and demanded that Sheriff David Scannell turn them over. The sheriff, in the face of so much power and strength, could do no more than to give up his prisoners to the committee.

"They quickly held a second trial for Cora and a first for Casey, choosing their witnesses and jury from their own ranks. The men were convicted and sentenced to be hanged the next day. Arabella and Charles Cora married just two hours before the men were summarily hanged. Since then, the vigilance committee has dissolved again after ridding the city of many other questionable people. They now have full control of San Francisco; they have taken all power from the Democrats and christened themselves the People's Party. The first thing they have done is to outlaw dueling, and they have also rezoned the city, placing all brothels and gambling joints into their own section of town."

Henry sat speechless, shaking his head back and forth. "Those goddamned vigilantes. It's not right, just isn't, and it sounds like it could be dangerous, being a Democrat, I mean."

Charles agreed saying, "Yes, Henry, watch out. I want you to stand up for your values, but be careful! The conservatives, especially the Know-Nothings, cannot be trusted."

Henry felt relieved to leave San Francisco because the city just wasn't the same. He missed the old, wild way each street could be home to so many different and varied entities. Now, the harlots and gamblers, did indeed, have their own subdivision without benign businesses to offset the dangerous undertones and the hot, steamy, wicked feeling of those gambling halls and brothels. Prostitutes had taken to walking their streets, becoming more visible and aggressive, and Henry, a fetching man, was approached many times as he made his way into the seedy district. He would tip his hat like any gentleman but pretend to not hear their invites.

Henry, itching to gamble as an anonymous person without the constraints that came with being a marshal, entered the sinful part of town. Here, in San Francisco, no one would know who he was unless he murdered someone or they killed him; then, and only then, would his identity be known and people would shake their heads at the incongruity of it all—a marshal in the unsavory segment, gambling at the faro tables.

Sometimes Henry did feel like a counterfeit lawman; he understood the other side of things so well. Hadn't he committed an awful crime when he had cuffed his tormentors and carved X's into their asses? What kind of a person did that? Not someone expected to uphold and keep the law. Not a decent person.

Henry cursed himself for his vengeful act against those men that had beaten him to a shred. He felt quite confused and his cheeks burned when he thought of his argument with his grandmother, Elizabeth. Tough, mean woman that one and he did not want to become her, ever. She had been giving him his weekly Bible lesson, and they argued over biblical the concepts such as "an eye for an eye" and "turning the other cheek." He couldn't help it and blurted out the Bible seemed full of contradictions and so did she.

"I don't understand, Grandmother, why does the Old Testament talk about it being fine to enact revenge for a wrong, "an eye for an eye," when in the New Testament, Jesus preaches about "turning the other cheek? It's just plain silly."

His grandmother simply looked at him, hate and frustration in her eye, and said, "If you're so smart, feel this and figure it out!" as she brought her hand up and slapped him as hard as possible on his right cheek, eyes gleaming. Then a few seconds later, she demanded, "Turn the other cheek!" and when he defiantly did so, she slapped his left cheek as hard as she could and stood up, screaming at him, "Think about what you're saying before you make an ass out of yourself. The Bible always tells the truth and should never be questioned!" leaving him with his cheeks burning but with dry eyes though he cried inside, wishing his grandfather still lived. Two weeks later, Henry moved in with the Hamlin family in Bangor, Maine, thinking that being away from his grandmother by only 60 miles wasn't far enough.

Henry won big. His fall from grace had paid off, and he would have a little nest egg once again if he should decide to pack it in and leave Nevada City. For what? What could he do next? Why did these thoughts creep into his mind? Shouldn't he be happy to stay where he was and remain a stable, settled citizen?

Henry walked up the hill to the newest residential development. He marveled at the grand mansions clinging to the hillside. He couldn't imagine ever owning one of those. He knew instinctively that he would never be the sort of man who could build such a home. He was not a business-minded man, and that's what it took to live in that part of town. He had done okay with the bakery and catering business but had been quite relieved to escape from the day-to-day worry about financing and making the right decisions. Henry shook his head, regretful; he guessed that easy winnings at the tables had spoiled him.

Henry returned to Nevada City with ambition in his head and a new concept of self. On his journey home, he determined to work hard at becoming a moral, genuine marshal that thought only of the safety of the people he was to protect. He would court Emily when she returned and perhaps marry her. He would run for office if the Democrats nominated him next August, and meanwhile, he would become the perfect citizen and dedicated lawman.

Henry ran for marshal again, defeating David Johnson, this time by only seven votes. Sheriff Wright, due to his dislike of Henry, hired Johnson as deputy only to torture Henry and to attempt to thwart Henry's authority. When jailed suspect, James Webster, escaped from the city's flimsy jail, Henry dutifully tracked him and brought him back to his cell. Webster dug himself out of his confinement and escaped again, this time with two convicts known as the Farnsworth brothers.

Henry then had to handle a vigilante situation when Sheriff Wright and Deputy Johnson organized their own posse with which to pursue the escaped man and his accomplices. They had several men waiting with them out in the woods surrounding a cabin in which they thought they had entrapped their prey. One of the men, jumpy, began shooting, and soon it was apparent to Henry that they were shooting at one another.

He yelled, "Stop! Wait! You're shooting at each other!" Unfortunately, it was too late. One man died of a gunshot wound inflicted on him by his own friends. Webster and the Farnsworth boys, nowhere near the cabin, had successfully gotten away. There was a coroner's hearing in which Henry was cleared of any misconduct but he was still stigmatized.

From then on Henry kept things to himself and quietly went out and tracked many a man and brought them to justice. He had the jailhouse built properly so men couldn't dig out any more and took personal pride in escorting these men safely to San Quentin himself. He stayed away from the brothels and the saloons unless he needed to be there officially. He improved his little home and frequented the library often in search of interesting reading material.

CHAPTER 4

1857

Emily returned home in time for the Harvest Ball. Henry donned his best suit and walked to the George mansion, anxious to see Emily and wondering if she had changed. They hadn't seen one another for nearly nine months. She had never answered the three letters he had sent her, and he gave up writing to her. Henry didn't know what to think of that. He did know that Cyrus George seemed to shy away from him when attending city council meetings, though he still offered him friendly greetings.

Henry planned to ask Emily to the dance and hoped that she had at least gotten rid of her habit of hiding behind the silliness of being a proper young lady. Henry noticed tables, tents, fountains, and floral arrangements being set up on the south lawns and wondered what event would need such elaborate arrangements. He breathed in deep to calm his nerves and smelled the wonderful aroma of roasting beef and other delicious, tempting odors and recalled the first time he had met Emily. She had captured his attention with her warmth and joy of living. He remembered her hearty laughter and her merry eyes and lost his insecure feelings at seeing her again after such a long time.

Henry knocked at the front door three times before it was opened. Emily frowned, deep at seeing him and took a deep breath as if she had bad news for him. She made him feel that he should not have come. Henry smiled and simply said, "Emily."

"Well, hello, Henry," she said as she quietly shut the door behind her. "What brings you here so early in the day?"

"Well, to see you, of course. It's been months. How have you been? You're looking very well."

"I am quite fine, Henry, uh Mr. Plummer." Emily hesitated and then drew a deep breath and said, "Henry, I have something to tell you. While in St. Louis, I became engaged to my second cousin, William. We will marry this afternoon and then return to St. Louis. William runs a large textile factory there, and that is where we will make our home."

Just then a large, red-haired man with icy blue eyes stepped out onto the porch. He looked Henry up and down, making Henry feel like a pinned specimen. After a few moments, Henry stepped up to the homely, unfriendly man and held out his hand.

"You must be William, I assume."

"Yes, I am and you must be the beau Emily has told me about." William, never offering his hand, voiced the word "beau" as if it were the most absurd word ever used in the English language and as if it were past tense, and Henry understood what his demeanor and manner of speaking implied.

Henry took his hat off and swept a bow before Emily as if she were royalty and said, "I'll be leaving now, Miss George. I wish you a happy marriage and a good life."

As Henry turned to go down the steps he heard William say, "So that's him, huh, well it's obvious he has no prospects. I can't imagine why your father allowed you to think such disillusioned thoughts about the man."

Henry heard Emily begin to speak and then William hushing her. "Just be quiet! I don't want to hear anymore about him. Is that understood?" The silence hanging in the air broke Henry's heart. Emily had been completely cured of her prima donna behavior and had been silenced in her own opera.

The morning's revelations made Henry feel sorry for Emily and even William. Like so many middle-class people of ambition, they had been thrust together only for the sake of keeping wealth in a family. He wondered if was all worth it, feeling remorse for his own ambitions. His disappointment in recognizing his courting of Emily as grasping at becoming middle-class made him ill. He went about his duties with a feeling of regret but also relief. As if he had escaped something. But now his mind filled with jumbled thoughts. By evening he looked at his plans, so sure and heady that morning, as nonsensical. The uncertainty Henry felt about his future and what he wanted drove him to a saloon.

The more Henry drank, the angrier he became. Trouble was he wasn't quite sure what to be infuriated about. He was furious at Emily, not that he had ever really loved her, but he felt disappointment in her for succumbing to her woman's fate that she knew was not just. He felt resentment toward her for playing him the fool. Most of all, Henry felt a helpless rage at discovering that middle-class status, its values, and wealth, a wonderful life did not make. He felt lost with all his dreams washed away—swept away by none other than a good dose of reality, a truth that left him hopeless and adrift.

Henry had become drunk enough at the end of the evening to want a woman. Why not, he thought. I'll never be able to escape who I really am—a man with a gambling habit and who needs to make love to a woman. Why deny myself? Henry walked around the corner to a brothel owned by a discreet and warm-hearted woman named Anna Beth. She wouldn't tell a soul about his becoming a customer, and he knew he could count on her to match him up with the right woman, one who would be as circumspect as she.

It was late, and Henry walked into an almost empty parlor.

Anna Beth stood to greet him. "Henry! What brings you here?"

Henry smiled and tossed up his hands. "Just what you're in the business for, Anna Beth. What do you have for girls tonight? I need a woman, bad!"

Anna Beth looked at the only girl sitting in the parlor. "Well, I have Pauline. But, but she's only got one leg, Henry."

Henry turned to look at the young woman. She sat there, pretty in Henry's estimation, and returned his stare unabashed and yet, Henry could see her fear of rejection. Henry held her gaze. She had large brown eyes that a man could easily get lost in and long, golden hair. She had a lovely nose, almost patrician, but small enough to not make her appear too regal, and her chin jutted out, proud over her beautiful neck and décolleté. Henry would never know what affected him most, her eyes, or the pride that made her stare him down.

Henry walked over to her in three long strides and picked her up, carrying her up the staircase. "Just tell me which door it is miss, and we'll be in business."

Henry carefully laid her on her bed as if she were a bird with a broken wing. She laughed bitterly and said, "You know, I won't break. You can handle me like you would any other woman."

Henry smiled as he removed his jacket and hat and tossed them onto a large wicker chair, "This is how I treat any woman."

Henry undressed, taking his time while Pauline watched. She thought him positively beautiful. When he finished removing his clothing, he sat on the bed and gently began dispensing with Pauline's many layers of dress. She assisted him only when it became necessary. She braced herself when he reached the last of her underclothing. Most men, when they got this far, either fled in revulsion or simply asked that she use only her mouth, as if it was the only part of her body that was good enough.

Henry stood up to pull her final underclothing off and when finished, studied her body with eyes hooded with desire. Pauline took the look as rejection and sat up to cover herself saying, "Yes, sir, you can go ahead and leave now. Most men do. Or, I can …"

"Henry. Call me Henry."

Pauline lay down again and allowed Henry to finish his appraisal. She saw him rise and knew then that he was different. Henry loved her body. She had high, rounded breasts with nipples a delectable red, her waist was tiny and her hips splayed out in perfect proportion to the rest of her body. Her one leg was long, shapely, and slender. She wore a black stocking over her stump.

Henry leaned down and began kissing her on her mouth and as he moved his kisses downward, he said, "I think you are gorgeous. You remind me of a Greek goddess. I think you are perfect in every way."

When he noticed her tears, he placed his kisses on them and said, "Ssshhh, you needn't cry."

Pauline opened her arms and pulled him to her. When Henry entered her warm, wet, welcoming passage, he sighed with satisfaction.

Henry went back to Pauline the next night and the next and the next. He began going to her almost every evening just before Anna Beth closed her house. Henry loved sex with Pauline but enjoyed her heart and her mind more. He had found a friend, a person he could trust, like Charles, and surprisingly, a companion that had been finely educated and could discuss the many things he had studied and read. They would talk about books and about subjects such as the idea of free will and determinism, which still had Henry pondering.

One day Henry gathered enough courage to ask Pauline how she lost her leg. She had told him that it still "pained" her and that she was grateful that she had no memory of the surgery to remove it.

Henry had to ask her a second time, "How and when did this happen to you—a beautiful, sweet woman?"

Pauline sighed. She sat up and leaned her head back against the headboard of her iron bed. She closed her big, beautiful eyes and began.

"You know about the Kansas-Nebraska Act? The one that states popular sovereignty should decide whether or not slavery should be legal in those two territories?"

Henry nodded. "Yeah, the one that's got everyone rushing to Kansas or Nebraska to settle and fight for the right to be pro-slavery or anti-slavery? Stephan Douglas, the Democrat from Illinois, angered every anti-slave person in the country because this act has opened the question of slavery after it had been outlawed by the Missouri Compromise. I've read all about it. It's making things violently crazy in both territories, especially along the Missouri/Kansas border where men fight and kill one another and vote on both sides hoping to win their cause."

Pauline sighed, long, hard, and sad. "Yes, it's a deadly situation and can cost a nineteen-year-old woman her leg."

Tears rolled down Pauline's lovely face as she struggled to overcome the lump of bitterness rising in her throat. Henry gently kissed the salty wetness on her cheeks, waiting for her to continue.

"I'll start from the beginning and tell you how I came to be in Lawrence, Kansas, when it was sacked on May 21. My father is Eli Thayer, an educator, a lawyer, and a Massachusetts legislator. He founded Oread Institution in 1848, a school with the same studies as Worcester Academy for men but only accepting girls and young women. I studied there for two years. My father is also an abolitionist.

"As an abolitionist, he helped organize the New England Emigration Aid Company. He and his co-founders wanted to provide affordable transportation for New Englanders who wished move to Kansas to take their stand as anti-slavery and free-soil people. The NEEAC gave them not only money to get to Kansas but also funds to build homes and sawmills. The company has financed several newspapers to promote anti-slavery ideals and morals.

"When studying at the Oread Institution, I met John Brown, who taught at the institute."

Henry interrupted, incredulous. "John Brown was your instructor, really?"

Pauline snorted acrimoniously. "Yes, he was my teacher and my indoctrinator of, shall I say, obsessive abolitionism. I went wild with my passion to do something about slavery. I decided to follow him when he and his boys moved to Kansas to fight for a free state. My father told me that I would do better by staying in Massachusetts, settling down, and raising a family of my own abolitionists. I refused to listen to him and before leaving, secured a position at the Free State Hotel working for one of the newspapers. My father basically disowned me, telling me that if I left I could never come back no matter the circumstances."

Pauline shook her head, swallowed hard, and went on. "So, I was there, in Lawrence, Kansas, when the Kickapoo Rangers, pro-slavery Missourians, decided to sack the town. They had a cannon, which did nothing when they fired it at the Free State Hotel. The building had been staunchly built out of brick, and the balls just seemed to bounce off. So, they set fire to the hotel and then ran through town looting homes and businesses."

Pauline turned to look Henry in the eye. "That's when I lost my leg. I had been in the Hotel when they set fire to it. They threw me into the street, literally, and just as I landed in the street, someone took off with the wagon carrying the cannon. The cannon did not have enough ballast to send heavy enough balls to destroy the hotel, but the weight of it was sufficient enough to ruin my leg as they ran over me."

Henry, stunned, took gentle hold of her hand and ran his fingers softly up and down her arm, digesting what she had shared with him. Here she was, having just lost her leg in May, going on with her life, he thought. Incredible. He didn't approve of her new occupation, but if not for that, he would have never met her.

"I woke up two days later. I guess I had been awake off and on before that but not enough to realize my fate—that I had lost a leg. They put me in the care of an elderly couple who contacted my father. He sent money for my medical care but said nothing of me coming home to him, and I was too proud to ask. Everyone agreed that I had a remarkable recovery, but I had lost my zeal as an abolitionist and just wanted a new start somewhere else. As soon as I learned how to get around on one leg, I left my kindly caretakers and took a very long painful stagecoach ride west with the money left over after paying my medical expenses. Anna Beth joined that stage ride, and that is how I came to be here."

Henry sat up and stared at Pauline. "Why didn't John Brown come to your aid?"

Pauline shrugged her shoulders, stoic, and said, "John had other things on his mind. After the sack of Lawrence, Charles Sumner made his speech, *The Crime against Kansas,* in which he ridiculed the southern pro-slavery people, especially, Senator Andrew Butler. As everyone knows, on May 22 Preston Brooks nearly caned Senator Sumner to death while a fellow southern senator, Laurence Keitt, held those who would have stopped the assault at bay with his pistol. Thinking that Sumner would die, John Brown led a revenge-driven raid on pro-slavery settlers May 24, killing five of them."

"But, two of John's sons were captured, and on June 2 John led another attack on Henry Pate, who held them prisoner at Black Jack, Kansas. Then on August 30 his son, Frederick, was shot down while defending Osawatomie, Kansas, from the Border Ruffians. By

September 13, when my father's money had arrived and the Battle of Hickory Point occurred, I had decided to leave Kansas. Until you came along, my earnings here were nil, but Anna Beth's kind heart forced her to keep me on and for that, and for you, I am till-I-die grateful."

Pauline turned and looked intently into Henry's eyes. "This is the first time I have talked about it, and I feel as if a huge weight has been lifted from me. When I first realized my misfortune and heard that Senator Sumner might die from his injuries, I wished I had had the same fate. I felt envious of him. But, now, I feel bad for him since he still suffers from horrific nightmares and severe headaches. They don't know if he will ever be the same again. I have been much luckier."

Henry rearranged himself on the bed and began slowly and gently removing the black silk stocking from Pauline's stump. She gasped and then stilled, holding her breath. When Henry had removed the stocking, he began a series of wispy, velvety kisses up and down Pauline's still angry-red scar, then he reached up and clasping his hands around Pauline's tiny waist put her gently into a prone position and proceeded to make love to her.

He began at her lovely widow's peak with more feathery, delicate kisses and after spending some time doing satisfactory service to each of her nipples, he trailed his lips down her belly and ended up where he later buried his swollen self, grateful that he could comfort Pauline this way and that she had been able to keep her sensual self intact.

Henry continued to see Pauline, making the trip to San Francisco several times, once before Christmas and twice in January, to see Charles and to sit at the faro tables to collect enough money to keep Pauline in style and to repay Anna Beth for her generosity and kindness.

He and Pauline began to make plans to leave Nevada City, to marry, and to start over somewhere else. Henry planned to run for the state legislature the next fall, if nominated, and thought he could serve his time there as a representative and still have the time to study law and take the California bar exam.

CHAPTER 5

1858

Henry now spent every night with Pauline at the bordello, and when he heard that a young couple was looking to rent a small house in town after selling their little farm, Henry gladly leased his little home on Spring Street to them. Once Henry met them, he could see why farming had not suited them. John Vedder appeared weak and self-centered, and Henry could not imagine him ever putting in one day's hard work ever in his life. He stood tall and had a brawny, muscle-bound physique that could have easily handled his farming tasks, but he came off too arrogant to do such humble labor. He had taken a job dealing cards in one of the town's many gambling halls.

Lucy Vedder, on the other hand, appeared to be the brains of the family with a bearing that was, at once, both meek and steely. She had the look of a frail, delicate, petite woman that seemed easy to manage until one looked into her eyes, which glowed with fierce determination and strength. Henry stood only five feet ten inches tall and she only came up to his shoulders. Her hair was flaxen blonde, and those eyes of hers were a shrewd, penetrating blue that softened only with laughter. Their child had just turned one and appeared burdensome for Lucy to hold and carry. Henry admired her looks but preferred Pauline's warm, golden coloring.

He was not surprised when neighbors began complaining about the Vedder's noisy and heated arguments. He could well imagine Lucy standing up to that brute husband of hers with her back rigidly straight and her chin up, defiant. Vedder was not that well liked as a card dealer and more than once had been caught cheating his tables. John's reaction to his being exposed caused him to create such a silly charade of indignation and rage that everyone would get up and leave his table. It's a wonder he's not let go, thought Henry with a disgusted shake of his head.

Henry had no intention of becoming mixed up in the Vedder's affairs but began to be swept up in them because of his friend, a lawyer and fellow Democrat, David Belden. When John Vedder nearly lost an eye when struck by a bottle rocket on the Fourth of July, he immediately hired David to file a civil suit. Henry thought that perhaps he only wanted to bring some extra money into their family's finances. Lilly, their tiny daughter had suffered from pneumonia in June and had remained sickly and needed medical attention continuously.

Henry had stopped by his house several times to pick up some of his things, and his heart went out to Lucy and her child, who she constantly nursed, taking special precautions to make sure the little girl could work the phlegm out of her tiny lungs. Henry knew just how little Lilly felt, as she struggled for breath. He hoped for Lilly and Lucy's sakes that something would come of the lawsuit. Despite that Lucy spent her every effort and minute of the day to recover her child's health, rumors spread that John, jealous and insecure, had his wife followed, so afraid he was of her having an affair.

Henry steered clear of them as much as possible. He had his own ambitions to look after since he had been nominated by the Democratic Party to run for one of the eight representative positions in California's lower house. He and Pauline hoped for success so they could carry out their plans. But, sadly, he was severely defeated September 9 when the electorate voted in a conservative candidate. Henry had developed some enemies as a lawman, especially newspaper editors who sympathized with the Know-Nothing Party.

The *Sacramento Union* had published an article that accused Henry of taking money and orders from a Nevada City brothel. They pointed out that he ran more with gamblers, brothel-goers, and idlers—the wild crowd instead of with the decent and respectable crowd. Someone had passed out handbills accusing Henry of planning to vote against the interest of the miners and mill workers, supporting wage cuts, and advocating foreign ownership of the mines and mills. These bills ridiculously accused him of hoping for heavy and early spring rains to stop the efforts of creek and river prospectors in the surrounding area.

Henry felt impotent rage over his misfortune, and both he and Pauline felt devastated in not being able to make the new start they had planned. They needed to think of a different means to leave the city but now felt hopeless. Henry determined to go to San Francisco more often to increase his nest egg which was now dedicated to his and Pauline's move and new life.

By September 17 Henry had become deeply embroiled in the domestic disputes of the Vedders. Lucy had had enough of John's having her followed and one evening made her arguments to him about such silliness. John didn't care for Lucy's accusations or her audacity. She had taken him by surprise, and he reacted violently, pulling out his Bowie knife and holding it to her throat threatening to kill her.

The next morning, Lucy sent for Henry, the city marshal, and requested his protection. She also told him that she planned to divorce John. Henry sent for his friend David Belden to consult with her. After David spoke to her about the proceedings of the divorce and they had discussed custody of Lilly, Lucy began weeping, claiming that she still loved her husband but that they both had horrible tempers, which made it difficult for them to ever work things out. Both Henry and David encouraged her to reconcile with her husband if she truly felt that way.

After Lucy spoke with John about their marriage and the visit from the city marshal and his lawyer friend, John only became more aggressively angry, threatening to kill Henry. Lucy gave up and moved into the Hotel de Paris one block from Henry's little house. She would keep house on Spring Street during the day and after serving John his evening meal would go back to the hotel with their daughter. Since John continued making threats against Lucy and Henry, Henry felt obligated to rent a room across from Lucy in which he and his deputy, Pat Corbett would take turns sleeping to ensure Lucy's safety. Lucy was to yell and scream like hell should her husband come visiting and threatening.

The entire situation frightened Pauline to the point that she encouraged Henry to resign and leave town as they had planned. Henry refused, saying that the divorce would soon be final, Lucy would move to Sacramento, and that these circumstances would then be resolved. Pauline accepted his decision gracefully.

Little did she know, or Henry for that matter, that the gossips of Nevada City had begun spreading the rumor that Henry and Lucy were lovers and were at fault for the Vedder's marital problems. The fact that both Henry and his deputy slept every night across the hall from Lucy, with Pat acting as a chaperone, did not lessen the tension between husband and wife or quiet the false reports about Henry's and Lucy's relationship.

John continued to threaten Henry's life with talk around town that he planned to kill him using only his knife. Henry laughed at his boasting and asked if any one, seriously, thought that Vedder's fulminations frightened him. He inwardly congratulated himself that now Vedder seemed bent on threatening him and had forgotten about including Lucy.

But by September 30, John had increased the ante, taking his daughter and secreting her away at their former farm under the care and guard of the new owners. He warned them to not allow Lucy and Plummer to take his child. He also borrowed a Colt pistol from a friend. Henry responded by simply saying Vedder could find himself arrested for kidnapping his daughter, and that he was keeping a vigilant eye on him and had no intention of allowing the man to draw one drop of blood from him, by knife or bullet.

On October 1 Vedder visited Belden's law office, saying he needed divorce papers drawn up, served, and recorded as soon as possible, acting as nervous and aggressive as a cat at dusk. That afternoon they went to the house on Spring Street to have Lucy sign the papers. John promised his soon-to-be ex-wife that he would return Lilly to her that evening if she would sign them. Belden told Vedder to stay away from Lucy now; he had no legal right to see her again until he returned with their child.

That night, after Lucy had packed her bags and bought train tickets to Sacramento, she returned to the Spring Street house to wait for John and Lilly. Henry and his deputy had decided they had better guard Lucy that last night since David had reported John's extreme agitation when working with him on the divorce papers. Pat Corbett took the first shift and then at nine o'clock, Henry took over.

Henry built a fire in the kitchen stove, and he and Lucy sat on either side of it soaking up its warmth and talking quietly. Lucy seemed restless and voiced her worries that John would not keep his word.

"Don't you worry, Lucy. John's gotta realize that Lilly's best off with you. He's not that crazy to think of taking your baby girl from you. No. I don't think he would even consider it."

"But why did he take her in the first place?"

"He knows he could never get away with it. Lucy, just think about it, everyone knows where your child is—that she's out at your old farm in good hands."

Lucy stood up and paced. "No, Henry, you don't know him as I do. He's got something planned and wanted the baby out of the way. Don't you see?"

Understanding dawned on Henry. Yes, he thought, that bastard has got something planned in his arrogant but stupid brain. Now that he realized that Lucy had a point, a damn good one at that, Henry began to perspire and moved away from the fire. He rubbed his chin and laid his gun in his lap. In all his months as city marshal, he had not yet had to use his gun to kill anyone. He had always proven to be quicker on the draw, staring down his opponents or nicking a limb until they gave up and threw their weapons to the ground.

It was dark out, pitch black, but, he reasoned with himself, at least Vedder would have to climb a flight of stairs to come up to the kitchen, and having the advantage, Henry formed a plan. When Vedder comes, if he has good intent, he'll make his presence known by yelling something. If he doesn't, I know where the stairs creak and he won't be able to sneak his way up them without divulging his location.

Lucy sighed. "It's getting so late! What time is it?"

Henry pulled out his watch and held it to the glow of the hot stove. "It's almost midnight." Henry realized then that things weren't right at all. Just then he heard the first creak on the stairs. He put his forefinger to his lips, signaling to Lucy to sit and remain still. He sat, silent, and but for the cocking of his gun, he made no move. Henry heard the second creak and knew exactly where Vedder was. Henry had only one more creak to catch before he had to make his move.

His thoughts raced. Henry remembered how Vedder had hurt Lucy from time to time. He thought, as he heard the last creak, this mongrel's planning to break the law because he's creeping up the stairs hoping to surprise us, then kill just me or both of us. Henry stood up and took three quick, long strides to the stairwell and began firing.

Henry heard Vedder's body tumbling down the steps. He stood on the top stair and yelled, "Vedder!" He heard only a groan and then silence. Henry took the stairs, two-at-a-time and stooped to look a moment at Vedder. The bright harvest moon shown in through the back-door window, and Henry could see a red stain spreading just above Vedder's heart on his left chest. Henry ran out into the street, blowing his police officer's whistle as though someone else had done the shooting.

Henry could hear Lucy calling, "John! John!" He heard a moment of silence and then Lucy yelling out, "He killed him. Henry Plummer shot my husband, dead!"

Henry stood in the darkness collecting his thoughts. He could hear the neighbors coming, and then Lucy crying out again. "He shot John. I think he's dead."

Henry felt sick to his stomach and leaned over, retching. Then, he firmed his shoulders and began to walk toward the jail house. When Henry arrived at the courthouse, he found Charles Van Hagan, the jailer, alone there. He awakened him and found him to be quite put-out.

"What do you want, Plummer, at this hour?"

"I've come to turn myself in. I've just been in some sort of mess between John and Lucy Vedder. I think I shot him. He may be dead. I had been sitting there all evening waiting with Lucy for John to show up with their child. She planned to take the five-a.m. train to Sacramento. Instead, of just coming in through the front door, he began sneaking up the back stairs. Because of all his threats, I became nervous. He didn't say a word as he crept up the staircase, and I knew he meant to kill me or, perhaps, both of us."

"He entered the kitchen brandishing a pistol saying, 'Your time has come.' I shot three shots and he stumbled to the stairs, rolled down them, and lay at the bottom. I'm not sure if I fired the first shot. I think he fired at me first."

Van Hagen took Henry into custody and as he did the paperwork Henry sat there berating himself. Why did I shoot and not talk to him first? I shot him down like a cur in the street. Oh … What trouble have I caused for myself? And, Lucy, why did she yell and scream about me killing him when I was there to protect her?

Henry felt shaken, but when he held out his hands, they shook not a bit. Henry, in his crazed state, saw that as a good sign. I did this to protect myself and Lucy. I am in the right—it was self-defense. All I need to do is to take the high-moral stance. Everyone knows he was out to get me. He had even threatened Lucy. Henry worried about Pauline and how she would react when she heard the news. This event would be highly publicized.

David Belden came to see him in the morning and agreed to represent him, trying to reassure Henry. But, the coroner's jury came back with bad news as did the autopsy report. Lucy had collaborated with Henry's story that Vedder had come into the kitchen and yelled, "Your time has come!" How she managed to match his thought-up words, Henry had no way of knowing. But, the coroner and his men could not find one ball in the kitchen, only finding one in the wall of the privy outside and the other in the wooden wall below the stairs. The autopsy showed that Vedder died of a fatal wound to his left chest and had another wound in his left arm, accounting for the other two shots, and they all appeared to have come at him from above.

The judge bound Henry over to the grand jury and set bail at $8,000. Belden paid his bond with money out of Henry's nest egg, and Henry was free. By the time he reached Pauline, she was a mess. She had read all the newspaper reports and was beside herself in grief and worry. She told him about how the papers condemned him despite that Vedder had been so threatening and had been an abusive husband. She told Henry that they had labeled him a seducer and that he had been having an intimacy with Lucy causing all this trouble. She quoted one paper word for word, 'A man who would steal another's wife and then shoot him should be hung."

Henry reached out to gather Pauline in his arms and became alarmed when she balked at the gesture. "Oh! Please! Not you too," was all Henry could say, and then she succumbed to his embrace.

Pauline wept and said, "We should have left when we had the chance, Henry. I told you these people were bad luck."

On October 15 the Nevada County grand jury indicted Henry for murder. He pled not guilty with his lawyer, David Belden, asking for a change of venue due to all the negative talk in the papers and the people of Nevada City accepting his guilt so easily. Henry could not believe his terrible luck. He, a man of the law, who worked so hard to be a good citizen and protector of the people of Nevada City, was now considered a murderer.

Henry went on trial for murder on Monday, December 21. It took three days to select twelve jurors who did not admit to or show bias. The papers had done a fine job in turning Henry into a seducing, husband-killing monster. They also linked him with the seedy world of bordellos and gambling dens. People had noticed Henry's daily visits to Anna Beth's and that was enough for them. It mattered not what woman or women he saw—a whore was a whore—they were all alike. What did it matter with whom he spent his time?

After having so much trouble in choosing the jury, the judge asked Belden if he still wanted to request a change of venue. Belden said, no because a juror had been chosen who was also from Maine. Henry's lawyer thought he would be likely to provide at least one vote for acquittal.

The trial began in earnest December 23 when the prosecution called its first witness who attested to the fact that Vedder had never fired one shot from his Colt revolver—their most important argument. The coroner testified that Vedder died from one fatal shot to his left chest and that he had also taken a ball in his left arm. One of the other two balls had been found in the privy wall out back, just behind the stairway, and the fourth ball was found in the wooden wall of the stairwell. All proved to have downward trajectory and had been delivered from above.

After the prosecution rested, the defense put Lucy on the witness stand.

"Please tell us, exactly, what happened the night your husband was shot," Belden asked in his kind, benign voice.

"Well, first Mr. Corbett came to sit a while with me as I waited for John to bring Lilly to me. I planned to leave early the next morning by train for Sacramento. After a few hours, about nine o'clock, Mr. Plummer came to relieve him. He started a fire in the kitchen stove, and we sat on each side of it just talking. Mr. Plummer tried his best to assure me that my husband would really bring me our daughter. But, I was losing hope when it became so late. I told Mr. Plummer that things didn't feel right. Why did John take my daughter away in the first place and why hadn't he been there sooner? It had become very dark by then.

"I think Mr. Plummer began to feel, like me, that something wasn't right. We both had become a little spooked by the time we heard footsteps on the stairs. He, John, suddenly was there walking into the kitchen. He stopped for a moment and then looked at Mr. Plummer saying, "Your time has come!" and fired his pistol. As he fired, Mr. Plummer stood and fired at him. John had remained just inside the doorway at the top of the stairs."

Lucy looked relieved to have given her testimony and began to sit a little taller in the witness chair lifting her chin a bit. But, then Prosecutor Henry Meredith began his cross-examination. Lucy wilted as he approached her menacingly and asked her in a very accusatory manner, "Didn't you tell your father-in-law, Vulcan Vedder, that you were happy with your husband when you went to see him October 11, just two weeks after your husband was shot? Didn't you admit to him that he had been a good provider? Did you not admit that Plummer promised to pay for your divorce so you could marry him? And, didn't you also tell him that Plummer wanted to put you up in a bordello so he could live off you?"

Lucy had, this entire tirade, shook her head "no" at each allegation. "No, no, no!" she exclaimed. "Mr. Plummer only said once, after my husband had hurt me, that if worse came to worst, he could put me and the baby in a bordello where we could hide and be safe for while until I could decide what to do about my marriage."

"But you did say those things to your father-in-law?"

"No, not exactly. He's twisting my words."

"Twisting your words!? How?"

"I don't know, we did have a conversation, and I did admit that John had made me happy in the past and that he did provide well. Mr. Vedder, my father-in-law, wants revenge, saying he would spend his last dollar and last drop of blood to have Mr. Plummer convicted."

The courtroom went wild after that, cheering on the older Vedder and his vendetta. After the judge quieted down the crowd, the prosecutor came forward with a document.

"Mrs. Vedder, do you recognize this?"

Lucy shrank back and sighed, "Yes, I do."

"And you signed it, am I correct?"

Belden stepped forward, "I object. This document was most likely signed under duress."

"Objection overruled."

The document admitted as Exhibit A was an affidavit that Vulcan Vedder had Lucy sign stating that she had told him nothing but the truth. She had been in Sacramento on December 4 when the older Vedder pleaded with Lucy to tell him "the truth about the murder of his unfortunate boy."

The prosecutor held the paper to Lucy and asked her to read her statement that she had signed. "I have told him nothing but the truth."

Next the prosecution put Vulcan Vedder on the stand and asked him to tell his story.

Vulcan Vedder began to speak after giving Henry a deadly look. "Lucy told me that the reason, he (pointing at Henry) was there was to sleep with her. My son was shot dead at the foot of the stairs before he even started climbing them. The object of Plummer killing my son was to get her (pointing at Lucy) into a bad house."

The courtroom went wild again, and it took the judge a while to regain order. Henry's lawyer got up to cross-examine Mr. Vedder.

"Mr. Vedder, you have had custody of Lucy's daughter the entire time since your son was shot. Is that correct?"

Mr. Vedder nodded, yes.

"Mr. Vedder, you need to speak out loud."

"Yes."

"Now, is it safe to assume that Lucy desperately wants her daughter back under her care?"

Mr. Vedder, smirked, "I suppose so."

"Have you talked about it, about her taking her daughter?"

"No, not really. She hasn't said one way or the other."

"Really? Why then did she steal her away from you as early as October 11, the first time she came to visit you after your son's death?"

"Well, I guess she was just lonesome for her."

"Is it safe to assume that the subject came up when you had her sign this affidavit?"

"If you're accusin' me of coercing that signature and statement from Lucy, yer wrong!"

"Really? The subject of Lucy getting her child back from you was never addressed?"

"Never," Mr. Vedder said, shifting in his seat, keeping his eyes on the floor.

The judge sent everyone home to celebrate Christmas and announced that the court would reconvene Saturday, December 26. Henry and Pauline spent a subdued Christmas. Despite Anna Beth's girls' attempts to cheer them, they could not lose the feeling of foreboding. Henry paced Pauline's room trying to think of a way out of this predicament, wondering why in the hell hadn't he used persuasion to talk Vedder out of carrying out his threats.

Saturday arrived and both sides made their final arguments. The judge gave the jury instructions and then sent them out to deliberate. The jury came back with their verdict at two the next afternoon, less than seventeen hours later. They pronounced Henry Plummer guilty of murder in the second degree. The judge set sentencing for Wednesday, December 30.

On Wednesday, before Henry's sentencing, Belden came into court and charged George Getchell, the juror from Maine, and two other jury members of bias against Henry before the trial had ever begun. The judge deferred sentencing. Henry's lawyer acquired affidavits from people proving the men's bias. One quoted Getchell as saying, "The people ought to take Henry Plummer out of jail and hang him."

After two weeks of deliberation, the judge sentenced Henry to twelve years hard labor at San Quentin but freed him on a $10,000 bail while his lawyer prepared and presented an appeal to the California Supreme Court. That same day, January 18, Henry resigned from his position as city marshal.

The California Supreme Court reversed the verdict with a unanimous opinion after a very short time and ordered a new trial to be held in a new venue. The justice writing the opinion had much to say about mob psychology and victims of vigilantism, a hangover from San Francisco's vigilante committees and their actions. He wrote, "The prejudiced jurors who convicted Plummer were guilty of an offense little short of murder itself."

The second trial held in January, only thirty miles from Nevada City, rendered the same results. They found Henry guilty of murder in the second degree. The judge sentenced Henry to ten years of hard labor at San Quentin. He was to report to San Quentin near the end of February leaving him two short months of freedom and Pauline.

CHAPTER 6

1859

The new city marshal, Edward Tompkins, stood in Anna Beth's lobby, waiting patiently while Henry said his final farewell to Pauline, who looked regal despite that she leaned heavily on a sturdy cane sporting an intricate brass head. She had no tears left to cry. Henry found parting difficult, hating to part with the one person, besides Charles, that had meant anything to him since coming to California, feeling guilty to leave this fine woman.

Henry swallowed over and over to keep the lump of emotion deep in his throat. His eyes pleaded with her once more to please forgive him for this trouble he had brought them. He had apologized time and again for his lack of judgment with Pauline finally telling him she did not want to hear any more of that. What was done was done, and they would have to live with things the way they now stood.

Henry promised her he would be the perfect inmate so he could be released early. Deep down in his heart, he could not see himself in prison for long. He had convinced his lover to believe the same. The stress of the trials and facing his prison sentence had sickened Henry's lungs once again. His cough was becoming worse, and he checked his handkerchief often for signs of the dreaded blood.

The hope for an early release was what made it bearable to part. Henry turned one last time. He memorized the vision of Pauline standing proud, her head held high, her beautiful brown eyes shining with unshed tears, her gorgeous hair down and falling to meet her beautiful bosom, which rose above her tiny waist and supple hips. They had made love often in the last months, and Henry hoped the memories of those passionate times would last him until he could return.

Henry was glad that it was his friend, Edward, who escorted him to San Quentin. But once there, he found their parting difficult as well. They stopped outside the immense gray walls. Henry looked up to view his new home and realized that he had never really thought much about the structure when delivering his prisoners to its gates. Now, everything looked different. The tall brick walls with their towers on each corner, topped with barbed wire looked ominous, like an ancient, Dark Age castle. Escape looked impossible.

The first thing Henry experienced was being stripped entirely naked and thoroughly probed and examined. Every orifice on his body was none too gently checked. He found it difficult to retain his dignity, especially when every part of him was described in detail for a clerk to record. They listed his two knife-wound scars and even the moles on his back. "Just in case you escape, and by the looks of it, 1573, you've gotten around plenty. Been in plenty of trouble already, eh?" Henry ignored them, thinking that escape was the last thing he would do. He knew how easily a man could be tracked, hunted down, and captured.

Henry received no prison uniform, only ragged pieces of clothing with the number 1573 painted on them. That is what he was now, a number, out of more than 600 men. He wondered what had happened to the other 953 men.

Next, he was taken to the warden for his indoctrination. The warden droned on and on with rules and regulations. The last thing the man said to him was, "Don't forget, Plummer, number 1573, if you try to escape you will be hunted, found, and returned. Your sentence will be doubled and you will receive twenty lashes at the whipping post. Speaking of which, you need to join the other prisoners to watch a flogging that should be starting about now."

Henry thought the next hour of his life to be the most barbaric he had ever lived. He was marched out into the yards where a man was being chained to a large, sturdy, cross-like structure. The men securing him to the post looked like brutes but nothing like the man who took up the cat-o-nines. His head was enormous, bald, and he looked out of beady, mean eyes that seemed to glisten with anticipation. His strangely muscled torso was bare and looked as if he had suffered, many times over, the same beating that he was about to administer. The midday sun had already brought a sweat out on him even before he dispensed one lash.

The men around Henry cheered and hooted, betting on how many lashes it would take to make the man faint away. Henry looked around him and did not see one quiet, empathetic man. Their clothes were so ragged they resembled street urchins, and they were not too clean looking. Henry shuddered. He felt as if he were amidst dirty, lusty animals instead of men. When the poor man's ordeal began, Henry retreated into his mind as far as he could. He kept his eyes hooded, just enough to look open but with his lids down far enough so he couldn't quite see. After the man's first yelp of pain, the other men began counting the lashes, and Henry forced his mind to hear only the ocean waves of his childhood and the cries of the gulls.

Supper that evening was so awful that Henry soon offered his tray to anyone who would take it. That move could have caused him much grief except that the doctor who had examined him came to his rescue. Henry left with him still receiving the jeers of his fellow tablemates berating him for thinking he was too good to eat the food. Because of Henry's lung condition, the doctor, Alfred Taliaferro, put Henry in the sick bay, which was on the ground floor instead of down below.

"This location should keep you somewhat healthy. You'd die soon enough down there with the rest. Now, if you prove decent, honest, and trustworthy, I may make you my assistant. You appear to be a well-mannered, educated, intelligent man."

"Thank you, sir, for that. I will do my best not to disappoint you. Thank you, again, Doctor. And, for the record, I have no desire to escape. Well, the desire is there, but I have no plans to do such a foolish thing."

Henry, feeling as if he had been redeemed somehow, slept well that night, the first time in months. Life went along well enough for Henry in his new situation. The doctor made sure he had good, healthy food to eat and had him doing tasks in the infirmary that made Henry feel as if he, once again, could do something to help others. The men there mostly ended up dying. That was the saddest part.

Henry became acquainted with them, discovering that, really, no man was all bad. They had hearts and souls that revealed themselves fully when they were so sick, especially when death came stalking. Most of the men died from either consumption, the dreaded tuberculosis, or from food poisoning. Henry felt justified in refusing to eat his meal that first night and felt awful that most of them had no other choice. They could refuse the food and starve or take their chances eating the putrid offerings.

Some men simply died because of being severely beaten or knifed by other inmates. Many these men suffered this fate simply because they could be bullied, because they couldn't fit in with those inmates who ran things their way in the prison yard, showers, and johns. Then there were those who couldn't control their tempers and ended up fighting to the death with someone who had crossed them.

Alfred, or Doctor Al, as Henry came to address him, admired Henry for his resolve to behave so he could leave early. He saw Henry's self-control as his saving grace in this god-awful hell hole and did his best to encourage him. Henry honored and respected Doctor Al and soon learned many of the simplistic medical practices the doctor used, such as keeping a man from burning up from fever, making sure he was well-hydrated, and using his natural charms to quiet down an agitated patient. Sometimes these convicts were their own worst enemy when it came to settling down and allowing others to help them. They had been so mistreated and battered.

Doctor Al had come to trust Henry enough to acquire passes for him so he could leave the prison and run errands for him. Henry always came back. He would send Henry out to harvest herbs and roots for some of his medicinal concoctions. Henry enjoyed these times and came back to the prison feeling as if his lungs would finally heal. One day Henry returned to find no doctor in the sick bay and soon found himself down in the dungeon, his ankles shackled in leg irons—for escaping.

The contractor who had run the prison previously had been given back control as warden and had fired everyone that his replacement had hired. Henry's fellow leg-ironed prisoners told him how bad things would be now that the wretched man was back. He had a brutal streak and was known for his money-making schemes. The food would be much worse and scarcer, there would be more beatings, and the most notorious cons would be able to buy their pardons through him.

Henry was left below for five days and his lungs went backward. Just as he began to despair, a big but bloodied man burst into their holding cell with a key. The men passed the key around, and they unlocked their shackles. It was May, and a number of the prisoners, it seemed, had suffered such a bad case of spring fever that they orchestrated a small but sadly, unsuccessful prison break.

The repercussions had no end. Henry, though, now relegated to a regular prison cell with three other men, looked upon this time as the most awful. Food of any kind was withheld from all prisoners until they became weak and as helpless as babies, and then they began hauling men out, by the scores, each given their turn at the whipping post.

Henry thought it ridiculous. Most of these pitiful victims passed out after the first several lashes and as the henchman continued their punishment, Henry couldn't help but think of the insanity of it all. Many of these men died, having no strength to fight their way to recovery. Henry knew this because the new warden had not bothered to hire any new doctors. Two guards came for him one day and marched him to the infirmary, ordering him to take over the duties there.

Toward the end of June, fifty inmates organized another insurrection, holding two guards captive. Life in the prison was so terrible, most of the inmates felt it would be better to escape and risk all that went with it rather than to remain imprisoned in such conditions. As the men were hunted and recaptured, the number of them needing hospitalization grew tremendously. Just when Henry felt at the end of his endurance, the warden recalled Dr. Taliaferro and another doctor, Theodore Burt

Heiry. The prison remained in lockdown for days after, but Henry felt safe working once again under Doctor Al.

The two doctors and several prison guards collectively wrote a letter to Governor Weller pleading for medical aid and for better food to be sent to San Quentin. They pooled together enough money to purchase a wagon load of fresh vegetables and beef along with a good supply of medicines. Doctor Al assigned Henry the task of riding into San Rafael, a short four miles away, to procure the supplies and food. Henry was to take his pass and a horse from the prison and ride into town to claim the stocked wagon and to return with it.

Henry felt relief and happiness as he mounted his horse to embark upon this mission. The horse, though, of bad quality, would only plod. Henry felt frustrated, wanting to feel the wind on his face and the joy of galloping free once again. By the time they reached town, storm clouds had filled the former clear blue sky. Henry hitched the horse to the wagon and knew it would be a slow, aggravating journey back. By the time Henry could see the corner towers of the prison, a driving rain along with an equally rambunctious wind slowed their progress even more. When Henry arrived at the prison, he was soaking wet and began coughing uncontrollably.

The guards at the prison gates looked upon him suspiciously and sent for the warden. Henry had a difficult time explaining his presence, an inmate, at the prison gates with a wagonload of beautiful food and a surplus supply of medical supplies. He was shown into the warden's office where he attempted to explain all he knew of the circumstances. After what seemed forever, Doctor Al and his associate appeared.

They explained their actions, their letter to the governor, and their own appropriation of food and supplies. The warden became furious and wanted revenge on someone. He dismissed the doctors and kept Henry confined to his office.

"I don't know what to do with you. Now, that the good doctors have alerted the governor, I must be on my best behavior but what to do with you, my son, I have no idea. What do you have to say about this?"

Henry cleared his throat, nervous, dry mouthed. He knew he wanted his say, but how should he deal with this crazed man? He thought of how and why he was here in the first place and decided to try reasoning with the brutish man.

"Sir, I was given orders by my boss, Doctor Taliaferro to go and fetch these goods. I carried out this task in the best of faith, and I returned. I have no plans of escaping, ever, and I know I have better circumstances than most inmates here at San Quentin. But, if I may say something outside of all this, sir, I think, as do the doctors, that you would not suffer so much insurrection if the men felt cleaner and were better fed. I don't think most of these men would be so desperate to escape."

The warden paced around the room as Henry shared his thoughts, slapping his hand with a riding crop the entire time. Henry could easily imagine the crude man using it on him. He would be helpless, his hands cuffed as they were. Henry felt a little frenzied with fear, trying to avoid thinking of the whipping post. He needed to please this man. He knew of warden's yen for gambling and had also heard he preferred the faro tables.

The warden stopped short in front of Henry and got down into his face to deliver his ultimatum. "You know the doctors have no way of defending you. You acted in defiance when going into San Rafael for their goods which they had no right to purchase. And, now, I'm in a fuss and am going to have to defend my ways with the governor."

The warden stalked around the room, circling Henry. "How 'bout this, I let you go back to the infirmary to do your thing, and I won't have you disciplined if you promise to discredit all that the doctors have written about me when the governor comes to call?"

Henry thought long and hard. He certainly didn't want to be at the mercy of this licentious man. He did not want to be beaten. That would surely kill him. But, he did not want to undo the good the docs had accomplished. He would never want to be traitorous to them and their moral standards.

Henry took a deep breath, and spoke very slowly, "How about you and I make a wager? You take me into San Francisco and we have ourselves a night at the faro tables. Whoever comes out ahead, wins. If you win, I will do as you ask." Seeing the warden's frown, Henry said, "You may even discipline me. If I win, I want you to give better conditions here a try. In other words, you will work with the governor and the California officials to improve things here at the prison and you will not take any action against me or the docs."

That brought the warden's pacing to a sudden stop. He stood there a moment, weighing all the possibilities. He loved wagers and had, at times, become bored with the usual ones easily found in the gambling dens. This young man offered him an exciting, different sort of bet and knowing how lucky he had always been at the tables, he decided to accept Henry's challenge. He stooped to remove Henry's handcuffs, and they shook on it.

"I'll send someone for you tomorrow evening," he said as Henry succumbed to a hacking, coughing fit.

Henry returned to the sick bay and was immediately put to bed by his doctor friends who did what they could to improve his condition. Henry's trepidation and anxiety kept his lungs worked up but his fever did break. Little did Henry know how exciting bits of information got around in the prison. He hadn't said a word about the bet he had made with the warden, but the doctors did hear of it. They said not a word to Henry about their knowing, but they did not trust the warden and sent word to the Governor.

The next evening Henry was summoned and the doctors put up a fight. Henry placated them and left willingly with the armed guard. The night was colder and darker than usual, and Henry suffered coughing fits the entire way to San Francisco. At first Henry lost miserably with the warden cackling his decrepit laughter all the while. Henry perspired and coughed and soon became chilled and feverish. Even the card dealer seemed to enjoy his discomfort and bad luck, leering at him from time to time.

About midnight, a posse of well-dressed men gathered around the table. Soon, they were hauling out the dealer, accusing him of cheating. Another man took his place and smiled, sincerely. After that, Henry won game after game. The ride home with the warden would have made Henry fear for his life but for the fact that the 'posse' of men escorted them the entire way back to the prison. Henry had won but now knew that if he didn't leave San Quentin soon, he would be dead.

The doctors kept Henry quarantined in the infirmary saying that he had a bad case of tuberculosis. Henry did struggle with chills, fevers and coughs but no sign of blood plagued him, yet. He did not know that his good friends, Doctor Al and Doctor T.B. had been at work requesting a pardon for him from Governor Weller. He also did not know that Governor Weller had known about his wager with the warden and had sent the 'posse' of rescuers. His pardon would only be a matter of time.

Henry, fretting day after day in the infirmary, fearing for his life, decided to take matters into his own hands. The doctors had been forced to remove the leg of one of the escapees from the June insurrection, which greatly affected Henry. He needed to get out of there and get back to Pauline. He needed his freedom, knowing that without it he would die of consumption, so riled he felt.

After bleeding a patient, the doctors had been called away to an emergency. Henry stole out of bed and soaking his handkerchief in the blood, smeared it all over his pillowcase. Once Doctor Al saw that, Henry's pardon was expedited, and Henry walked out of San Quentin August 15, then six months after entering.

Henry returned to Nevada City on August 23 so anxious to see Pauline he almost went immediately to Anna Beth's. When he first left the prison, he had gone to Charles in San Francisco, where he borrowed some money from his good and faithful friend. Charles assured Henry that he had done right in shooting Vedder—that it had been truly self-defense considering the facts. Henry bought a new suit of clothes first and then went straight to the gambler's section of town. He left for Nevada City three days later, with ample money in his pocket, a sizeable bank account at Wells Fargo, and his friend completely repaid.

Henry received a warm welcome from his lawyer and friend, David Belden and a job offer. His friends Pat Corbett and Edward Tompkins waited there to congratulate Henry on his pardon. After the other two men said their goodbyes, David insisted that Henry use the bath he had ready. Henry quickly bathed, put on his new suit for Pauline, and slipped the jeweler's box containing the diamond ring he had purchased in San Francisco into his pocket.

Henry stopped at the flower shop and bought a bouquet of red roses. He whistled as he walked the streets to Anna Beth's, thinking that soon his lungs would feel like new again. Henry debated whether to perform the ultimate, romantic proposal or to make love first and then offer the ring and marriage. Henry's manhood bulged so large he decided they had better make love first, and then he would propose. Henry lowered the bouquet each time he met a lady.

Henry ran up the steps singing a song he had heard in San Francisco. He had changed it from *The Yellow Rose of Texas* to *The Yellow Rose of California* as he pounded on the front door. "There's a yellow rose in California, that I am going to see, No other man knows her, no man only me, she cried so when I left her it like to break my heart. And if I ever find her, we nevermore will part." Henry stood there humming the tune as he waited for the door to open. He began pounding on it again just as Anna Beth opened the heavy, red, wooden door.

He reached down and grabbed her, giving her a hard hug, and then pulled back from her asking, "So where's my beautiful Pauline? Look see the flowers I've brought. They're just like her, soft, and lush, but sturdy and brilliant all at once." Henry's enthusiasm diminished as he observed the sorrowful demeanor of his friend's face.

He let go of Anna Beth's shoulders and stepped back. "Anna Beth, what's wrong? Where's Pauline? Why the gloomy face?"

Henry's heart stopped when Anna Beth said, straight and undisguised, "Henry, she's gone. She passed on five weeks ago giving birth to your baby. We tried everything, the doc and I, but we couldn't get the bleeding to stop."

Henry stood silent for a few moments, and then as the words registered in his mind, he yelled, "Nooo! No! She can't be gone!" And he charged up the stairs, taking two at a time.

"Pauauleeene! Pauauleeene! Where are you? I'm back. I brought you flowers and a ring! I want to marry you." Henry stopped short when he entered her room. It was just like it had been when he left six months ago. Nothing had changed except that Pauline wasn't sitting in her wicker chair where she usually sat waiting for him.

Henry turned to Anna Beth as she entered the room. "Where is she? What's going on? Where's my Pauline? Anna Beth, you gotta tell me straight, wherever she's gone, you must tell me. I need her. I need to find her. I want to marry her. Tell me, Anna Beth, where in the hell is she?"

Anna Beth took a deep breath and wiped the tears from her eyes, squaring her shoulders. "Come, Henry, follow me." She turned and marched down the staircase, leaving Henry with no other choice but to follow. Anna Beth opened the door, stepped out, and waited for Henry. They walked down the street, past Henry's former bakery, past the library, the theater, the Wells Fargo bank, down to the other side of town, and as it became evident that Anna Beth was leading him to the cemetery, Henry stopped and grabbed at Anna Beth, "No, no, no, nooooo. She really didn't die, did she?" His voice held a pleading quality that undid Anna Beth's resolve. She reached up and wrapped her arms around Henry and broke down, crying out her grief.

"I'm sorry, Henry; I tried to do right by her. First, I begged her to end the pregnancy, but she would have none of that. She didn't see why a one-legged woman couldn't have a baby as well as a two-legged. I had to agree with her. Then when she started showing a belly and the extra weight was there, she decided to have a wooden leg fitted so she could walk easier and later would be able to tend to her child."

"She was doin' great until one day, us girls, we had walked downtown to do a little shopping, mostly for baby clothes and such, and when we came home all excited, we found her lying at the bottom of the stairs in labor agony. She had that baby early, too early. He died right away. She named him Henry Eli, by the way. And, she died later, despite that the doctor tried everything to stop the hemorrhaging. The doctor said that bleeding to death after giving birth happens often, one-legged or two."

Henry shook his head still hoping to deny it. He unwound Anna Beth's arms from around him and gently pushed her away. He grabbed her hand and said, "Show me, my dear, where are they?"

Soon they stood in front of a fresh grave. A wooden cross had been planted at the head with both names painted on it. "Pauline Elizabeth

Thayer. Henry Eli Plummer." Henry's only thought at that moment was that he wished it said, Pauline Elizabeth Plummer. He had wanted to make her his wife so fervently; they would have been connected forever, sharing the same name. Henry laid the bouquet of flowers below the cross without shedding a tear.

Henry and Anna Beth walked home, silent. When they reached the bordello, Henry walked up to Pauline's room, entered it, shut the door, and locked it.

Henry remained in Pauline's room for two days. He lay on her bed, inhaling her scent, remembering her, her laughter, her deep understanding of life—of humans and their ways, her humility, her ability to forgive and forget, her sweetness, and the way she lived her life without pretension. She had steadfastly lived life true to her beliefs, swayed by no one or any principles other than the ones she had developed on her own in her short but well-lived life.

Henry sighed as he turned over and breathed in Pauline's perfume that had been so like her, alluring and yet not overbearing. He thought of how she had given up a leg because of her profound sense of justice and how her immeasurable courage and strength had allowed her to heal physically as well as emotionally.

He thought of her pregnant and hopeful. He knew that women, especially those in her profession, had ways to rid themselves of unwanted babies. But not his Pauline. She wouldn't do such a thing. He knew that she had wanted that baby perhaps even more than she wanted him, at least as much, he reckoned. As he lay there on the bed where they had lovingly made a new life, he let his mind fantasize about the life they had planned with one another.

Henry let out an animal cry of grief as the terrible realization struck him. He had ruined everything. He had lost the election that would have given them the reason to move out of Nevada City and become respectable, and he had miserably and completely failed and made a mess out of things when he shot John Vedder. Henry punched the pillow as he lifted himself up and off the bed. He began pacing, tearing at his hair, making awful, inhuman wailings, which did nothing to ease the hard, tight ache in his chest. He wished he could cry, but tears would not come. He felt dry, cotton-headed, and dead inside but for the pain and pressure that gripped his heart.

He walked back and forth and around Pauline's tiny room, inwardly ranting about his folly, those few moments in which he had been accuser, judge, and jury and had made the decision to take another man's life. He believed, he knew, that if he had been there for the birth of their child, Pauline would have survived, perhaps not the babe, but Pauline at least. Henry paced and lamented, tearless but tirelessly for hours, until at last, he fell across the bed and drifted into a dead sleep.

Henry walked in a beautiful, vibrantly green forest. All around him nature was at its best. Squirrels jumped from tree to tree chattering so contentedly that Henry couldn't find it in himself to lift his rifle to shoot them. A mother skunk trudged slowly up the path ahead of him trailed by three babies, their white stripes so clean and fresh that Henry found them adorable despite their pungent odor in the crisp, fecund air. A doe and her fawn raised their heads at him, staring as he walked past.

Henry gazed up between the pines and saw a brilliant, blue sky with a few clouds scurrying across it as snowy white as the baby skunks' youthful stripes. Mice and rabbits made their presence known with flashes of gray and long skinny tails dragging and in downy browns with floppy ears and bouncing tails. Henry felt the steady green-eyed gaze of an aristocratic mountain lion allowing Henry's passage with merely a bold look. Birds of every color, size, and species wove in and out of the branches overhead creating a wonderful background of music.

Henry stepped out into a clearing where a smiling sun beamed down on him, gentle, caressing. Wildflowers bloomed everywhere and berry bushes of all kinds hung heavy with colorful, fat fruit. Henry squinted into the bright rays that danced with dust motes and saw four women coming toward him, waving, smiling, and calling out his name as they danced to him. Henry recognized them and grinned back. He began to run to them, quickly closing the distance.

Pauline walked proudly to him, her body whole. She looked stunning in the brilliant sunlight, happiness beaming from her face. She held a little, chubby-legged, blonde boy with eyes as gray as his own. The two girls twirling around and calling out to him were his two long-gone sisters, Emily and Rose. They had grown into beautiful young women. Behind them came his mother, Nabby, her hair no longer gray and the worry lines erased from her face.

Henry and Pauline clutched at each other squeezing between them the small boy who squealed with delight. They kissed each other over the boy's golden head and stared into one another's eyes. Henry could see the love and forgiveness in his beloved's face, her entire bearing, and his stony, grief-deadened heart melted. Emily, now a gorgeously filled-out woman, no longer skinny, her hair a burnished copper, took the babe from Pauline's arms, and Henry scooped up his love, twirling her around, engaging her in a much more amorous kiss. Henry felt a tap on his shoulders and, reluctant, stood Pauline back down on her own two feet. His mother stepped up to him, also forgiving, and with loving, gentle hands began brushing his hair back off his face.

Henry woke up with a start, happy tears streaming down his cheeks. His mind raced back to reality, and he saw that it was Anna Beth brushing the hair from his face. He lay for a moment and then remembered his situation, his loss. Grief came barreling down upon him like the hurricane winds they had suffered on his voyage to Panama. Henry began sobbing as Anna Beth gathered him into her arms.

When Henry had spent all his tears, he gently removed Anna Beth's arms and went to find his coat. He counted money out into her hands, asking that she commission a gravestone to be made for his loved ones.

"I would like you to have them install a large, heart-shaped stone in marble, engraved with their names, also enclosed by a heart and with an engraving of a Greek goddess holding a baby boy. Could you do that, please? Oh, and have them make the goddess one-legged."

Anna Beth gulped back tears, "Yes, Henry, I'll have it done just the way you want. Meanwhile, you need to go out back. The girls and I have a tub ready for you. A nice bath should help you some."

Henry nodded, silent, and then counted out more bills into Anna Beth's warm hand. "Here. There's money enough, I think, to keep me in this room for several months. May I please call this home for while,

Anna Beth? I would sincerely appreciate it if I could remain here for a while."

"Of course, Henry, and whatever me and the girls can do for you, just ask. We'd like for you to stay on. It'll help us, too. Now go take your bath and take a nice walk out in the woods. You kept mumbling things about the beauty of the forest in your sleep. Maybe that'll help." Anna Beth patted Henry's shoulders before she left and gave him a quick, tight hug.

Henry did take a walk among the trees far beyond the city limits. He shook his head at the stupidity of the founders of Nevada City in erasing all signs of the forested beauty that once had been where the town now sat. As he walked, he looked for the wondrous elements that had been so vivid in his dream. The trees made a cool, green umbrella over him but lacked the peace and harmony. When he happened upon small, scurrying creatures, they fled his presence. He found no meadow in which he could even attempt to bring back the images and essence of his loved ones. He gave up and walked back into town, disheartened but deciding to ask his friend, Tompkins, if the job as constable was still available.

CHAPTER 7

1859-1860

Henry became part of the Nevada City police force once again, but felt lost, empty, and dead to the world. He made his rounds, polite as ever, tipping his hat and head to every lady he met on the street, his demeanor subdued. He did not step one foot into a bordello, except for the one in which he lived. He never entered a saloon or gambling joint unless his job called for it. And when that occurred, he became stiffly officious and handled things as benignly as possible. All who observed him thought it right that he be so chastened and well-behaved. They felt mistakenly proud about the ways of the law and the rebuilding of men's characters within the prison system.

Little did they know that Henry's behavior had been tempered by loss and his not knowing how to go on in a world without Pauline. As time distanced him from his wonderful dream, he began to feel more bewildered. Anna Beth and the others at the bordello were kind, but Henry needed more than kindness.

October came and Henry had a hard time with nostalgic melancholy striking when he least expected, reminding him how happy he had been a year ago with so many hopes and plans with a smart, lovely woman. No, he thought, no other woman will ever do. I'll be alone for the rest of my days. He continued his duties as a constable and despite that some people still grumbled about his being back on the force, an ex-con and all, he felt as satisfied with life as he thought he could, considering.

He made daily trips to the cemetery, walking through the woods to gather his floral offerings. Each time in the forest, he would try to recall every aspect of his dream and did the same as he went to bed at night. He yearned to experience that lovely scenario again. He thought about taking his own life but his religious training warned him that doing so would never get him back to his loved ones. He craved danger once more, hoping that his duties would provide enough where someone could put a bullet through his head or heart, just if it killed him.

The force had received word that "Ten-Year Smith, an escapee from San Quentin, was in the area and dangerous. Henry remembered him from his work in the infirmary. He had doctored him after an insurrection. Ten-Year had been so badly injured that he escaped a flogging. When he had finally healed, the prison officials seemed to have forgotten about punishing him.

Henry noticed him one day as he took his lunch in a restaurant just around the corner from the jail. Henry finished his own lunch and waited politely as Ten-Year ate his, remembering the horrible food that awaited him back in prison. When the convict left the restaurant, Henry was ready to capture him and had his gun out as he commanded him to surrender.

Ten-Year blanched at the sight of Henry and attempted to cajole him out of arresting him. When that didn't work, he pulled a knife and slung it at Henry. The knife lodged between Henry's chest and upper arm. Henry, determined to never shoot another man, told Ten-Year to drop the gun that he had just pulled out, all the while with the knife wedged just above his armpit. Ten-Year tried using persuasion once again, never dropping his weapon.

"Come on, man! You know what it's like in there. Don't do this to me. Let me go and I'll disappear. Never to be seen in these parts again."

Henry shook his head and said, "Give it up, Ten-Year."

Henry anticipated the con's next move and shot the gun out of the man's hand just as a bullet went whizzing by his head, shattering a street lamp's glass globe. Ten-Year then jumped Henry and pulling the knife out of Henry's body, began slashing it around attempting to get at Henry's throat. Henry had lost his grip on his own gun and struggled hard to overcome the much bigger man, eventually besting the escaped man. Adrenaline had set in. Henry could taste it as he got Ten-Year's strong arm twisted behind his back. As he cuffed Ten-Year's wrists behind him, Henry spit to rid his mouth of the acrid, metal taste of adrenaline. He had lost his chance to die honorably.

Marshal Tompkins arrived and took Ten-Year off Henry's hands, telling Henry to take the rest of the day off after getting his wound stitched. The life-and-death struggle had taken every ounce of Henry's energy. He felt weak and stunned and knew he would never forget the awful look on Ten-Year's face as Edward led him away. Henry felt so sick he needed to run to the nearest john to rid his belly of his lunch before he visited the doctor.

After his visit to the doctor, he wandered the streets aimlessly, thinking about what had happened. Why hadn't he just let the man go? He knew Ten-Year. He knew that the man had accidently shot someone and had gotten just as harsh a sentence as he had received. Henry's guilt drenched his soul when he realized that but for his poor lungs, he would still be in the same situation as the man he had just apprehended. Henry remembered wiping the stolen blood over his pillowcase to cinch his early pardon, and he winced.

He felt like a damn cur. When would he learn and be wise enough to live life the way he believed it should be lived, honest, forthright, and decent? He needed to remember Pauline's straightforwardness, her scrupulous need to be genuine and never artificial. Eventually, Henry's feeling of self-loathing and culpability led him into the nearest saloon, and that was the beginning of the end to his quest for respectability in Nevada City.

Henry drank whiskey that day and most every day after that. Each night after work he would wander into a saloon, any saloon and begin to drink. He liked the feeling of abandonment drunkenness gave him. He would forget his grieving, and he could even forget Pauline for a while but he could never rid himself of his self-hatred, and the more he lost his self-respect, the more he needed to drink.

He was a quiet drinker, going off to a corner by himself. If anyone would approach him and try to engage him in conversation or argument, he would just pay his bill and walk either to a different saloon or to his room at Anna Beth's, who did her best to reason with him about losing himself in drink.

One night when quite inebriated, Henry stumbled home and crawled into his bed passing out immediately. He woke up later that night needing to go out back to relieve his full bladder. He started when he saw the largest eyes he had ever seen staring up at him from the other side of the bed.

"What the hell? Who are you?" he yelled as he jumped out of bed, reaching for the lamp on the bedside table. He lit the lamp and stared back at the prettiest girl—woman—he had ever seen. She was exquisite. Pauline had been a beauty, an earthy one. This creature looked as if she had come from some other place. As he gazed at her, he thought of the legendary wood sprites he had heard of in Maine.

Her eyes were as big as the bottoms of his grandmother's finest, most delicate tea cups. But, instead of the color of bone china, they swam with liquid warmth and were the color of dark honey. Her hair was golden like Pauline's but swirled out around her face in long, curly tendrils. She had a strong, fine-looking nose without it being too long or too wide and with her nostrils now flaring in fright, she reminded Henry of a proud, high-headed horse.

She raised herself up and crouched on the bed ready to spring up and out the door at any moment. He could see her breasts, quite a bit of them, peeking out of her nightgown rising with each frightened breath. Her small delicate hands clutched at the bed clothes, and Henry could see that the skin of them was the same golden honey color as her bosoms. Henry wondered if she smelled like wild honey too, this tiny, tawny most decidedly woman-nymph.

"You takes one step towards me and I's kill you, I's weel!" she cried as she pulled a knife out from beneath the pillow.

Henry held up his hands in supplication. "I don't know who you are, or what you're doing in my bed. But, please, be assured, I have no intention of coming near you or laying one finger on you. Now, I'm going out to take a piss and when I return, you had better be somewhere else besides in my bed. You hear me? Now, skedaddle!"

Henry stomped out of the room and down the stairs, muttering under his breath. "God damn crazy world. Can't get a peaceful night's sleep one way or another."

When he returned he could not believe his eyes. The little wench had curled up in his bed and looked up at him with challenge shooting out of those huge eyes. Henry was not in any mood to put up with nonsense. He stood over her and quickly reached under her pillow to take her knife, but she had it in her hand and slashed out at him. He caught her wrist and twisted making her let go of it. She cried out in indignant pain and spit at him. She missed and was forced to raise her other hand to wipe her spittle off her own arm. Henry grabbed her hand at that moment and twisted both arms behind her back.

"Anna Beth tol' me I's could sleep in hira tonight."

"She did, did she?"

"Yes, sur. She said you mos' likely not be coming home tonight. Said you probly be sleepin' it away in some saloon."

Henry let go of her arms, stepped back, and crossing his, he stood looking at the creature in his bed. He stroked his chin while he thought of what to do, and just when he remembered the knife on floor, she did, too. She leaned down the same moment he stooped over, and their heads collided with a loud crack. Dazed, they both remained motionless with their only movement being only that of rubbing their sore heads.

Henry stealthily moved his foot out and reaching the knife, pulled it to him with his big toe. "Damn! That hurt," he moaned as he reached down and retrieved the knife. She looked up, and as their eyes met, they began laughing, and when they each observed the other's goose egg beginning to rise, they howled and chortled, pointing at one another's head.

Henry realized how good it felt to laugh. He believed it was the first merriment he had enjoyed since finding out Pauline had died. Then, suddenly he felt tired, as if he hadn't slept for weeks, which, he guessed he probably hadn't, really.

He left the room to dispose of her knife, and when he returned he became serious and asked her, "Do you have any other weaponry you want to use on me?" She looked up at him, shaking her head her eyes still mirthful, and Henry noticed her mouth. She had a wide mouth to match her eyes with lovely puffy lips. Henry stared at her beauty and just shook his head in wonderment but he felt so tired, weakly weary.

"Well, I'm not going to fight with you over this bed. I'm dog-tired and want sleep. So, I guess if we'll be sharing the same bed we should at least know one another's names." He extended his hand, "I'm Henry Plummer, at your service. That is, if you promise to cease threatening my life and well-being."

She offered hers saying, "I's Spooky. Spooky Hamilton. And, I's be a former slave. I's Negro. Just so's you know. I's free now, but I's pregnant with my last master's child. I's Spooky because of my eyes, you know, so big. When I's born my mama took one look at me and says, 'Gotta name her Spooky because she looks like she just see'd a spirit." With that informative introduction, she turned onto her side and settled into the bed.

"Night, sir, I means Mister Plummer."

"Henry, call me Henry, Spooky. Nice to meet you, I think. Goodnight."

Henry settled into his side of the bed, wondering why the hell this lovely woman, who was with child, a situation he couldn't even think about right now, was in his bed. Henry began to drift off to sleep but remembered his latest injury as his head throbbed. He felt for the bump, which seemed quite large. No wonder he hurt.

"Damn, girl. You sure do have a hard head for such a little thing."

Spooky smiled, flopped over, and nestled up close to Henry, throwing her arm around his torso. "You do, too."

Henry could feel her ample bosom pressing against his back and soon he heard her soft, even breathing and knew she slept. He sighed, deep, and thought, oh, it feels good to be held again and dozed off into a deep, satisfying sleep.

From then on, he and Spooky slept together. Henry never touched her. He refused to bed a woman with another man's child growing inside her. Besides, he couldn't forget Pauline. But he did begin to feel much affection for that little sprite. She certainly was beautiful and sweet, just like Pauline, and her mind seemed just as ripe and fertile as her body. Her speech about drove Henry crazy, but that, too, was beginning to grow on him.

Spooky had her own view of things. She liked this man so much. No one had ever treated her so fine. The only time he irritated her was when he corrected the way she talked. The first time he ever did so, she had turned her monster eyes on him and looked so puzzled that he laughed at her, and that made her mad. Nobody had ever told her she said, *I am*, wrong. But she felt proud because after the fourth time Henry admonished her, she never said *I's* again.

Another thing that both bothered her and yet pleased her was that he wouldn't bed her. It made her feel like she wasn't good enough for him, but at the same time, it made her feel that he honored her. She felt confused. Every man she knew in the past, if they wanted her, they just took her whether or not she wanted them.

Spooky smiled when she remembered how angry Henry became when she told him that her last mistress would always send her to her husband instead of going herself to his bed. Spooky shook her head in disbelief when thinking about Henry's reaction. He had called her former owners beasts. Instead of thinking of her as only chattel, he had considered them an inhuman species. Yes, she did like this man so much; it made her nervous. She had never been in love before, never had the chance. So, did she love Henry? She couldn't decipher that yet, but the thought both scared and pleased her.

The months went by quickly for Henry after Spooky came. She took his mind off his grief, especially when they would lay in bed and talk half the night. She was fun and amusing and made Henry laugh often, which at times made her angry but then she would soon get over it. She begged for him to make love to her but he refused, never touching her or acting like he wanted to, and that infuriated her.

"You just don't want me because I'm Negro."

Henry would softly laugh and say, "I just don't want to because you're pregnant, for one, and two, I'm still in love with Pauline. She is in me and I cannot escape her. It wouldn't be right to bed you when I still feel so much love for another. Soon you'll be so big with child and you'll be happy I feel that way."

Spooky firmly shook her head, no. "No, ever since I am pregnant, I want it even more. Don't know why? But, you white people, I don't know. You won't do it with me, and Anna Beth won't let me have customers until I birth this baby. And, I want it. I want it bad. I feel likes I got a huge itch inside of me that wants scratchin'."

Henry just sighed and turned over to go to sleep. His heart ached for the little temptress beside him. When she talked like that, he became hard. He would never let her know that, of course. His blood still boiled when he thought of the stories she told him about her sexual life. God, she had no idea what love and making love with someone was all about. Those people had treated her like an animal and that is the only way she conceptualized sex—it was all she knew, those God-damned people.

Before Henry realized it, months had gone by and it was May. Spooky would soon be having her baby, and he felt nervous for her and the babe. She was now so miserable and big in the belly that she had to sleep in the parlor in the largest chair with her legs and feet splayed out on an ottoman. He missed her in his bed.

He longed for her chatter that kept his mind off things, and now, it seemed, he had a lot more to worry about. It looked as though his friend, Edward, would lose his reelection for city marshal. Gossip, again, was working against him. Talk was that if Edward Thompson was reelected as marshal, he would simply resign so Henry could once more take that position. That was so far-fetched, it made Henry burn. He was thinking about leaving town, no matter if Edward won the election or not. But, he would not leave until Spooky had her baby.

He had reluctantly promised to be there when the event occurred. That really scared him, causing him to think about prayer, even though when he had prayed for help when Pauline had died it hadn't done much good. And then, it dawned on him, perhaps he should think of Spooky as an answer to those prayers.

So, he prayed. He prayed like hell, as he told his friends later at the saloon. The doctor claimed that Spooky's labor and delivery had been in every way normal and short. To Henry, it seemed like an eternity. Henry sat and held her hand, gently wiping her brow with a soft, wet cloth. He had been allowed to stay with her until it was time to start pushing that little life out.

When the doctor moved to usher Henry out of the room, Spooky between clenched teeth, yelled, "Henry stays!"

After Spooky gave birth to a fuzzy-blonde baby with deep blue eyes, Henry considered her as tough as any man he had ever dealt with in his life. Moaning had been the only sound emitted by Spooky except for a wrenching scream when the little babe came sliding out of his warm cocoon. Henry thought Spooky's quiet stoicism astounding. As he stooped to kiss her on the forehead just before she drifted off to sleep, she grasped his hand and asked, "Now will you make love to me?"

Henry chuckled and said softly, "We'll see. Now get some rest. You've done a fine job birthing this boy, and you deserve a good sleep."

"Henry."

"Yes?"

"I's, I am going to name him Henry Eli in honor of you and your passed baby son."

Henry could only nod because his throat had tightened into a knot that couldn't be swallowed down. Henry felt all-done-in after this momentous event and went to the nearest saloon for a drink or two.

Edward lost the election, but Henry stayed around after losing his job because he couldn't leave Spooky and her baby. The entire situation enthralled him. Spooky seemed to have grown up completely when she became a mother. He thought her the best mama to that babe that could ever be, except for Pauline, of course. Sometimes he would catch himself imagining that Spooky was Pauline and little Henry was his.

Spooky felt grateful for Henry's love and devotion to her and little Henry. She had never seen a white man carry on so about a baby and had certainly never seen one change a nappy or give a child its bath. Henry loved doing all he could to help her take care of the baby. But, he still refused to make love to her.

It was New Year's Eve, and everyone at Anna Beth's anticipated their celebration with which to usher in a new year. Spooky hoped Henry would become drunk enough for her to seduce him. He didn't seem to be drinking as much since baby Henry had been born. She knew he went to the gambling joints from time to time but just enough to make some good winnings since that was his only current income.

Henry came home early that evening. All of Anna Beth's girls were there with their favorite customers. Anna Beth had hired musicians, and had tables moved into the parlor, setting them with her best china along with candelabras, floral displays, and bottles of fine wine and champagne. The band played soft, classical music, which Henry greatly appreciated. The fragrant odors of fine food wafted from the kitchen. Henry couldn't distinguish what they promised, but they did, indeed, smell delectable.

Henry charged up the staircase to his room to change and found Spooky in the big wicker chair nursing baby Henry. She looked gorgeous with her hair up and dressed in a low-cut gown of pure white, which perfectly complimented her honey coloring. She smiled at him almost shyly and proudly announced that she had a big tub of steamy water waiting for him out back.

He looked at her quizzical and couldn't help but remember Consuelo's sensual invitation to a bath. How long ago was that? It seemed like forever yet not. He thought about how fast and intensely he had lived life since then. He should be grateful for the fullness of it despite the losses. He, upon ruminating, thought that he had been blessed with the finest luck of any man to have had wonderful experiences with such interesting, warm-hearted, and loving women and not one of them had ever really judged him, not one.

He felt confused as he awkwardly collected his suit of clothes for the night and went down to enjoy his bath. Here he was, now planning to leave a woman who truly loved him and this time it would be of his own determination—a first for him. He knew now that he loved Spooky. He still loved Pauline, but she was gone. Her tombstone was beautiful and thought provoking. He had heard it was the talk of the town these days. 'Such a thing,' they said. 'Why would anyone have a beautiful, one-legged woman carved into a gravestone?' Henry could only laugh, bitterly thinking, little did they know.

That was the problem: These gossiping busybodies couldn't ever imagine the love of a man for a one-legged woman. He had to leave such ignorance. Couldn't be helped. And, he knew he was falling in love with Spooky, her baby, and the whole concept of them being a family. He still felt like bad luck—a purveyor of calamity—to any woman he loved-- a purveyor of calamity and didn't want to bring any more disaster to such a beautiful person as Spooky. No, he had to leave before his legacy struck once more, and he sighed deep and heavy as he sank into his heavenly bath.

When Henry joined the party in the parlor, he noticed Spooky was alone and without little Henry. Spooky took note of his presence immediately and walked gracefully across the room to meet him.

"Where's Henry?"

Spooky smiled, a little ashamed, and told him that Anna Beth had found someone to watch him for most of the night. Henry knew that most of the night meant until dawn since the little guy had slept almost every night since he had been born from late evening until daybreak. All the women of the house had made a big fuss about that, telling Spooky how lucky she was to have such a good baby.

Music filled the room and Spooky, without a word, gathered Henry in her arms and began waltzing with him. Henry had tossed down several whiskeys in the tub and didn't offer any resistance. Henry appraised Spooky as they twirled around the parlor, thinking again, yes, he was a lucky man. He had lost his heart to three amazing women and had fallen hard when things hadn't worked out. He thought about how lucky he was to have spent time, though, with such genuine women and bitterly snorted when he remembered Emily and her insincere chatter and ways.

"What's wrong, Henry?" Spooky asked, leaning back, gazing up at Henry.

Her having to lean back to look up at him was one of the things that pleased Henry, of short stature, the most. He just laughed and said,

"Just thinking about another woman from another time and how she doesn't even compare."

"Compare to what, Henry?"

Henry smiled down at Spooky and said, "You." His answer gave Spooky a great deal of hope.

Supper that night was all its aroma had promised, utterly delicious. They had wild mushrooms, oysters, and exquisite cheeses and bread before the main meal which consisted of roasted duck, pheasant, and chicken dishes all complimented with wild mushroom and wine sauces and wonderfully prepared potato and rice dishes. The wines and champagne proved to be the best anyone could want. After dinner they indulged in liquors of all makes and flavors along with cigars for the men and small, thin cigarettes for the women.

Spooky did not wish to smoke, which pleased Henry since he never smoked. When the opium pipe was handed about, neither Henry nor Spooky indulged. After that, the party quieted down quite a lot leaving the dance floor empty for Henry and Spooky to enjoy.

Henry found Spooky to be a very accomplished dancer, and when he asked her about that she told him that she had often gone to parties that men attended with their favorite slave woman. Now, Henry realized where Spooky had acquired such dance skills and the finesse she had shown at the dinner table that night. He couldn't help but feel jealous of her former master who had shared not only the intimacies of lovemaking with her but also dancing and fine dining.

After the midnight ceremonies took place, Henry excused himself to go out back and use the john. When he returned, Spooky had disappeared. He decided to go up to bed and made his way up the stairway. He walked into the bedroom and found it pitch black. He slowly and quietly removed his clothing. He felt relaxed and a little drunk as he crawled into bed. Spooky was there, completely naked, and she held her arms out to him.

Henry nuzzled her neck and found it to be soft and lightly scented. She smelled of honey, yes indeed, and of wildflowers, and he remembered Pauline. But that reminder didn't stay him. He needed to make love to this beautiful temptress who had become his best friend and redeemer.

He loved her and recognized that she had brought him back from some dark abyss that had threatened to swallow him. He loved her for that and because of what she was, simple and sweet, complicated and smart.

Henry kissed his way from her neck to her breasts and began suckling one. It tasted sweet and then he remembered that this part of her body belonged to little Henry. He moved down and kissed her in the hollow of her rib cage and then ventured further down. She clasped his head in her hands and returned him to her breast.

Henry obliged and soon found her nipples hardened and no longer giving milk. She moaned in delight and began moving her hips. Henry reached down and found her warm, wet, and responsive. Spooky threw off the bed clothes and welcomed him by opening her legs. Even though Henry moved into her slow and gentle, she let out a small cry of pain. He stopped but she urged him on telling him that she had been told that after birthing a baby it would be a little hurtful. Soon they fell into a comfortable rhythm, and their bodies melted together in pleasure and became one.

Henry packed his bags the next morning, planning to move into a boardinghouse on the other end of town. Spooky watched him, dry-eyed but with a heavy heart. Little Henry as if sucking out her misery with his milk became colicky and would not stop crying. Henry barely spoke as he finished gathering up his possessions. He had spoke often of his uncanny way of bringing bad luck to his women and knew she understood.

Spooky, with her sixth-sense understood his motives, and her innately superstitious mind accepted this even though it pained her. Spooky understood why Henry would feel the way he did considering his past. She also knew that despite her love for Henry, she wanted a more stable existence in the future for her and her child. She had sensed Henry's restlessness, indecisiveness, and his reluctance to commit. He reminded her of a small, very thoughtful and intelligent boy not yet anchored to anything on this earth—someone who had not yet found their way—a lost soul.

When she compared her life to his, she realized that despite her former life as a slave, or, maybe because of it, she had had more success than Henry in knowing what she wanted and that to do so one must find a course and stay with it. Her main goal in life was to find a way out of being pushed about as if she meant nothing, and, mostly, she wanted to find a position in life that would secure her and her child's safety and a promising future. She needed to be her own person. Henry followed the easiest path life offered him. She refused to do so. She would make her own future or die trying.

When Henry came down the stairs with carpet bag in hand, Anna Beth raised a fit. "What in heaven's name are you celebrating?" she cried indignantly. "You're leaving us—me, Spooky, and little Henry? Why? Where will you go?"

Henry stopped, put down his bag, and gathered Anna Beth into his arms, giving her a warm lengthy hug. Then, pushing her away, he said, "I'm moving into Bennie's on the other side of town. I must go, Anna Beth, my heart's becoming too attached to Spooky, to Henry, to you, to everyone here, and I need to leave before I bring anyone else bad luck, and you know I still love Pauline." Bringing his voice down to a barely audible whisper, he told Anna Beth, "I just can't allow myself to love again, not yet. You understand?" he asked, searching her face with beseeching eyes.

Anna Beth nodded and swallowed hard as she stepped back. "We will sure miss you, Henry Plummer."

Just then Spooky came slowly down the stairs with little Henry in her arms her eyes begging him for a decent good-bye. Little Henry held out his arms to his surrogate father upon reaching the bottom, cooing his wish to be held by him. Henry, with eyes glistening, stepped close to them and kissed them each on the cheek, whispering, "You know I love you Spooky, and the boy, but I just can't stay. I'll most likely love you forever, but now's not the time. Take care."

Henry damned himself as he walked through the town. Oh! God! He wished he could stay with them and where he was known and loved. But he just couldn't, not with Pauline haunting him with her love, the memory of her catching at him at odd moments, always when he was at Anna Beth's. He had to leave to move on, to heal his aching and still partially empty heart. He needed time alone despite his love and attraction for Spooky and her never-ending positive view of life.

God, he wished he could be more optimistic like her. Why couldn't he? His life had been so much better than hers thus far. The only person in his past to mistreat him had been his grandmother, and that had been mostly verbal assaults besides the face slapping. Well, he thought, yes, there was also that damned mean teacher, Miss Prescott, who took joy in beating him with her buggy whip and then canes when he wouldn't rat on his fellow naughty classmates.

His first love making had been tender and instructional with gorgeous Consuelo while Spooky's had been a painfully forced event with her losing her virginity and part of her soul while some old white man, who considered her only part-human, raped her. He prayed, just as he had prayed for her safe birthing of Henry, that she would someday find a good man to love her and treat her with esteem. Henry turned and headed to the cemetery to visit Pauline and another little Henry's grave, hoping to find some peace and comfort there before moving into Bennie's.

CHAPTER 9

FEBRUARY 1861— APRIL 1861

By February, Henry had become deeply engaged in doing nothing but gambling and drinking. As much as he wanted to, he couldn't leave, thinking about Spooky and her son just blocks away, as well as Pauline and another child named Henry buried deep in the earth just outside of town. He had fallen into self-pity and did not know how to crawl out of it.

It was February 13, the day before Valentine's Day, and Henry had been feeling lost. He wondered if he dared visit Spooky and the baby. He had been so lonesome and missed them in the most awful way, feeling empty and purposeless. He gave in and walked to Anna Beth's, whom he also sorely missed. He knocked on the big red door and suddenly felt a strong sense of *de je vu* even before Anna Beth answered the door. She answered the door and sighed. Anna Beth had the same long face as before, and today it, again, revealed her reluctance to tell him something he didn't want to hear.

"Hello, Anna Beth, how are you?"

"Fine."

Henry smiled though sick in his belly by now. "I came to see how Spooky and little Henry are doing. Could I please come in?"

Anna Beth sighed, closed her eyes, and shook her head slowly back and forth with tears leaking out the corners of her eyes.

Henry rushed in without her welcoming and immediately demanded, "Where are they? I need to see them."

Henry waved around his bouquet of flowers feeling so anxious that he almost needed to run out back to the john. "Anna Beth, where are they?"

Anna Beth squared her shoulders. "They're in San Francisco, Henry. Spooky's former owners came and made her a proposition, and she left with them."

"What sort of proposition?"

"They offered to take her and her son with them to their new home. They ensured her freedom. They want to raise the child as their own but with Spooky first being his wet nurse, then nurse maid, and then, his governess. They offered her a cottage behind their mansion to live in and an education. After little Henry turns fourteen, she will be free to do whatever she pleases, but will have the right to see him any time even though the adoption will be finalized and she will legally give up all rights to him."

Henry stood still as death. He threw his head back and groaned. "Oh! God!"

Henry began tearing at his hair and pacing the parlor. "Does she trust them? How does she know they will uphold their end of the bargain?"

Anna Beth shook her head, slow and clucked her tongue. "They signed papers, Henry, with witnesses, three of them. I was one of them. Spooky made sure she had numerous copies and secreted them away at a bank, with a lawyer, and with me so there would always be proof."

Henry spun around on his heels, agonizing, thinking he would never see them again in his life. "Did they leave an address?"

"Oh, yes, Henry. Spooky left a letter for you and her new address. Let me fetch it."

Henry clutched the letter to his breast and kissing Anna Beth on the cheek turned to leave. Anna Beth spoke up, "Henry, she did the best she could, you know, under the circumstances. She told me to tell you that she'll never forget you. She said, 'Henry was the best thing that ever happened in my life. He taught me how to be free and to love myself and I want the same for my son.' She said to tell you to take life slow and to think carefully about what you do before you do things, and to always remember who you are."

Henry left with a feeling of complete abandonment. He felt guilty for not seeing Spooky sooner, but he knew it would not have been good for either one of them. He knew, as he had told her New Year's Day morning, that he was not good enough for the likes of her and he could never live up to her standards. He still believed that but found it difficult to accept her leaving.

Henry made his way down the street and felt the need for drink. The first place was a saloon and bordello called Irish Maggie's. He walked in and ordered, not a drink, but a bottle of whiskey. Later that night, he felt befuddled enough to go upstairs seeking female companionship, crawling into bed with a woman called, Jezzie.

She proved to be comely enough, not the quality of which he was accustomed to, but she would do for the night. He had just made his usual foreplay and was about to sink himself into her when a pounding could be heard on her door. Jezzie told him to ignore it; she had problems with that—so popular she was. Henry didn't like the intrusion at the door and certainly did not care for her boasting.

The man continued yelling and screaming her name and banging on the door. Henry jumped out of bed and ordered him to "give it up and to go away."

The crazed man continued pounding on the door only responding to Henry with, "Fuck you!"

Henry had enough. He stepped out of bed, throwing on his clothes, cursing at Jezebel calling her a bitchy, lying, boastful whore who wasn't worth a penny of what he had paid for her and her services.

"Your name certainly fits you, you mangy excuse for a woman. Get your ass out of that bed and answer your fuckin' door. You can lay with him tonight! I want nothing more to do with you. I've been spoiled, by good, decent women, and you, my dear, certainly are not anything like them and for that, I'm sorry for you."

Henry opened the door and the man all but fell into the room. He was none other than W.J. Muldoon, a person with whom the police force had had many problems. The man pulled himself upright and came straight at Henry with a knife. Henry had his pistol out and butted him several times on his head. The man fell to the floor bleeding profusely as Jezebel leapt from the bed calling Henry a bastard for hurting her man.

Henry knew there would be trouble after this and went storming out. He ran to Edward's house and beat down his door until he finally opened it. The next day, Edward came back with the news that it was doubtful that Muldoon would live, so Henry decided to leave town. He had Edward go to the bank and take out his money and get his horse, and when Edward returned that night, Henry left for the Nevada gold fields that night.

Henry rode the trail as far as Johnson's Ranch, where he spent time resting and buying supplies. He headed east across the Sierra Nevada mountains, hoping to reach Carson City and the Comstock Lode within a week. Henry burned to do some good honest work, anything but what he had been doing. He felt like a no-good son-of-a-bitch for his violent behavior but knew that he'd be dead now if he hadn't fought back.

What really made him angry was that he had been acting like a drunken fool, drinking too much and falling into bed with whores, truly loose women who didn't care for themselves or their clients. He vowed to never drink and whore again. That night when he made camp and had his fire going, he sat thinking about what a man could do in the Comstock Lode. He'd try mining first. People said there was a lot of gold to be found there and recently, they'd been finding this blue stuff that some said could be smelted into silver. All Henry knew was that he was sure to find some good honest work, and that's how he planned to redeem his sorry soul.

The west side of the Sierras grew thick with forests and all that went with them. There were ferns of all kinds, and flowers, too. Animals large and small scurried out of his path as his horse easily stepped along. Henry could see a mountain lion tracking him to his right but felt safe enough because of his guns. He had them handy and could reach for them within seconds. He had a rifle, too, which he used to bring down game for his suppers. Every so often the trail would take him out into a clearing much like the meadow of his dream, and his heart would ache.

Going down the east slope was another story. It was rocky, tough country with the trail barely there. Henry met mule trains loaded to the maximum with ore, he assumed. He felt sorry for the dumb sons-a-b's that had to whip those huge mule trains up that mountainside. Dead mules lay beside the trail and sometimes the stench made Henry want to retch. After five days on the east side, Henry thought he would starve to death. He determined to kill anything he saw that would work as food. He wondered if he could come across a mule, newly dead. His stomach rumbled as he ate his last cold potato.

It was late afternoon and Henry began to gather wood. Most of what he'd been using was chunks from abandoned wagons and furniture. Henry had leaned over to wrap his arms around a broken chair when he heard the rattle. He stood up straight and nearly stepped back onto a large rattlesnake coiling to strike. Before he knew it, it lay dead at his feet. Henry looked down at his hand where his six gun still smoked.

That night Henry cooked the snake and ate with it gusto. He had saved his last bit of coffee and enjoyed drinking it knowing that he shouldn't sleep anyway because where there's one rattler there's probably a dozen. Henry waited until close to morning to finally sleep, when it was cold enough to keep the snakes from moving around.

As Henry crested the last rocky outlook and began his descent into Carson City, he saw a settlement of tents. He couldn't help but think of the Israelites and their twelve tribes waiting for manna from heaven. When he began his slow ride through town, it proved to be anything but biblical. Tents were everywhere, serving as restaurants, stores, livery stables, saloons, dance halls, and bordellos; he could see the women outside of them crooking their fingers at prospective customers while up the street a fist fight ensued between two toughs. Up the hill there were small tents and shanties made of odd pieces of wood, canvas, and old boxes.

Henry tied his horse to the rail in front of a decent-looking restaurant and stepped inside and stood until his eyes became accustomed to the dim light. The smell of food pleased his senses and he couldn't wait to eat real, home-cooked food. Long, high tables lined the walls and ran in two rows down the center of the tent. Henry could see the temporary kitchen set up toward the back. For two o'clock in the afternoon it seemed busy, and Henry noticed several tempting looking dishes as he sauntered toward the kitchen.

Henry stopped and read the menu posted on the wall that enclosed part of the kitchen. The selection of foods offered seemed simple and yet unmistakably pricey. Henry chose bacon, eggs, and biscuits with gravy since it had truly been ages since he had eaten a decent breakfast, not since he had lived at Anna Beth's. He sat down away from other customers, preferring to be alone. A young man brought him his food and coffee, and Henry asked if he knew where a person could find work.

"Well, there's work to be had everywhere here, sir. But I'd start at the top. Everyone's that worked for George Hearst's been happy as pigs in a mud wallow. His offices sit just across the street next to the livery."

Henry thanked the young man who spoke with a dialect that he couldn't place and gave him a nice tip. His food tasted incredible, and Henry had to force himself to slow down and eat proper. When he finished, he gathered up his utensils and plate and took it back to where he'd seen a pile of dirtied dishes in a tub next to the kitchen. He looked up just in time to see the interested gaze of a fresh and fetching young woman. Henry turned his eyes downward; he didn't need any of that.

Henry took his horse to the livery tent and made a deal for them to keep his horse. He promised to pay by the week and paid his first week in advance. Next, he walked to the Hearst offices and entering through the first door he saw, walked in to a meeting that appeared to be full of influential, self-important gentlemen. Henry, embarrassed, felt travel-worn and realized he should have a bath and a shave before looking for a job.

Henry tipped his hat politely and asked if someone could please direct him to Mr. Hearst's employment office. He received the directions and left them to their business. Henry returned to the restaurant and walking back to the kitchen inquired where a man could get a bath and a shave. The pretty young lady shyly gave him the information he needed, and without directly looking at her, Henry thanked her and turned to go.

"Hey, sir? Do you have lodgings yet?"

Henry stopped short and pivoted around on his foot and answered, "No. Do you know where I might find some?"

"Well, me da's fixin' to rent out tents just around the corner and up the street. He's settin' them up as we speak. He's gonna have several john's there and enclose it all in a fence to make it more private-like."

Henry smiled at her colloquialisms and politely asked, "Well, Miss, who should I be asking for when I seek out your father?"

"His name's Tom O'Riley and mine's Bridget, don't you know."

Henry tipped his hat to her and said, "Thank you, miss. Have a good day."

"You's too."

Henry's smile broke into a whistle as he walked down to the bathhouse. He ordered himself a bath and a shave and a jug of ale; no more whiskey for him. The bath felt heavenly even though it was even more overpriced than his meal had been. Henry stepped into a partitioned dressing room and unrolled some clean clothes from his pack, dressed, and walked up front for his shave. When he strolled down the street he felt like a new man and went directly to the Hearst employment tent.

They hired Henry as a miner and told him where to meet his crew in the morning, where he would also find his tools, picks, shovels, and wheelbarrow. Henry then walked down the street and around the corner to find Bridget's father and hopefully his new landlord. Henry chuckled when he heard the commotion at the O'Riley's canvas tenements. And, he thought Bridget had an Irish brogue. Tom O'Riley stood giving orders, his face almost as red as his hair, swearing like Henry had never heard before. "Oh, for the love of God, man, Jesus, Mary and Joseph! You's gotta sit those braces right, you know, or the whole damn tent will fall on ye. See, watch me."

Henry watched with the others, and when it was apparent that Tom couldn't set the braces without another man, Henry stepped in and began to help. Soon he became a member of Tom's crew, and before long a dozen tents sat side by side in straight rows of six. Tom ordered the men to take a break and turned to thank Henry. Henry soon had a tent reserved and left with Tom to drink down a pint, as Tom referred to his ale.

"So's you's come to the Lode to do some prospectin' have ye?"

"Well, I just took a job working for George Hearst's company as a miner. I don't know much about mining. Hope to learn though."

"Well, you's come to the right place. Minin' both gold and silver here. Not much placer work though, not any more. Hearst just figured out the blue stuff when smelted sure enough is silver. So's, when do you's start?"

"Tomorrow morning at seven."

"Make sure you's come to the diner and eat yourself a good breakfast. We's open at five in the morning. Yous kin move into yer tent tonight. I's hopin' to get some cots in on the next wagon train; I ordered from both Salt Lake and San Francisco. They's sure make sleepin' better."

Tom sat quiet a minute, as if to catch his breath and then stood, pushing down his hat. "Best git back to my crew. Nice meetin' yous, and thanks for ye help, Henry."

Henry felt lonely and foreign after Tom left him. He decided to wander around town and see if he could find a few supplies for his tent. All he had brought with him were several changes of clothes, his Bible, toiletries, and the letter from Spooky, which he had saved to read later. He just couldn't quite get up the heart to read it yet. He still needed more distance and time away from her.

Henry walked past the Hearst tents and noticed the men whose meeting he had interrupted were just coming out. His eyes met those of a man who had seemed in charge earlier, and they nodded to one another. Henry felt the man's eyes on him as he continued down the street. Henry walked past a wooden stand where three Indian women stood. Two were frying something over a wood burning stove and it smelled so tempting, Henry stopped. He smiled at them and one woman pointed to the sign, fry bread-30 cents, with meat-50 cents. Expensive. But if it tasted as good as it smelled? Henry bought the regular fry bread, which wasn't plain at all after they showed him how to slather butter on it and then drip honey over it. Henry loved it and nodded his approval at them.

The food made Henry tired, and he thought about his sleeping needs. He found a stand where more Indian women sat weaving baskets and rugs. Henry stopped there and motioned to a basket, requesting its price. Twenty cents. He smiled. Cheaper than his fry bread. He bought the basket and a good-sized rug for sixty cents. Down the street, he found another vendor, an old shriveled-up white man who sold him a jug for water, a basin for shaving, and a soft wool blanket along with a pillow. It was all he could do to carry everything.

Henry settled into his tent and felt pleased at how homey it looked. He had forgotten about checking to see if there was any place to keep his money. Was there a canvas bank? And, if so, how did they keep the money safe? He decided he would worry about it later and keep his money on his person. He went to try out the new, tented john.

He had worried about how he would wake up in time to eat breakfast and get to work. But Tom told him they had a street crier at the Lode. He started yelling out the hours at five in the morning. He would cry out the time and then ring a loud clang for each hour. Henry didn't hear the cry but heard the bell well enough, five crashing sounds resounded, waking him up for good. He had breakfast and couldn't help but feel disappointed that Tom's pretty daughter did not work that early in the morning.

Henry walked to the south end of town where he found dozens of men standing around. Soon a short, squat man with legs so bowed it hurt Henry to watch him walk showed up and began reading off names in groups from his list. Henry saw that his group consisted of four white men, including Henry, and two small, wiry Chinese men. They were handed their tools and they all trudged up the hill behind Bow-Legs. The going was just as bad as the east side of the mountain Henry had come down, and he broke into a sweat before he even had a chance to swing his pick.

When they reached the mountainside, they stopped and were told to watch the procedure used by a group of men who looked like they knew what they were doing and who were filthy enough to prove they had been working at it for a while. They began with one man swinging the pick. Chunks of rock of all different sizes flew out after each strike. After a sizeable pile accumulated, three men worked to pick up the rock and throw it into wheelbarrows, which were pushed by two other men to a large wooden slide at the edge of the mountain and emptied.

Then, a rock-picker would become a pick-swinger. The two men with the wheelbarrows kept busy pushing them down to the large wooden chute that, in turn, dumped the rock into large wagons at the bottom. The men continued to rotate so they each would get a break from the grueling job of swinging the pick.

Henry's team automatically, without question, assigned the wheelbarrowing to the Chinese men since they were so much closer to the ground, so to speak. The two ponytailed men just grinned and nodded their agreement. Henry and the other three took turns swinging the pick, and Henry soon realized the necessity for the rotation system. Each time the pick he swung hit the rocky mountainside, his entire body felt an uncomfortable vibration. That evening Henry felt as if his shoulders and back would never be without pain.

The second day was almost unbearable for the first hour, but then the work seemed to loosen up his sore muscles. Henry, Big Mac, Jes, and Pete talked little while they worked, but during lunch they exchanged personal information. Big Mac's name fit him well. He was Swedish and stood six feet six and carried his weight on top, making the pick work look easy. He came from Sweden only six years before and still talked with a heavy accent. Henry loved how he referred to their team as *ve*, instead of *we*.

Jes was a small, tough Mexican whose muscles looked piled on because they were so thick. Henry reminded himself to never get into a wrestling match with Jes. Pete, a Frenchman from Canada, was small and slight like Henry. Henry didn't think he had remembered to get in line when they handed out smarts, but Pete was nice. The two Chinese men had just gotten off the boat from China and had come directly to the Lode.

The six of them got on with each other well and Henry was grateful for that. He liked his teammates, and they must have approved of him because when Bow-Legs told each team to choose a leader, Henry's group picked him. By the end of the week they had gotten six feet into their hole. They worked to keep it six feet wide, also. Big Mac would chip away on the top just so he could stand up straight when it came to tunneling in. Henry figured their tunnel was most likely seven foot something high just to accommodate Big Mac.

The other three took turns working on all sides. Henry didn't like how, at times, a chunk of rock refused to come down from above and then would fall unexpectedly shattering into small pieces. He worried about what would happen once they all stood inside their tunnel working if a big rock chunk came falling, or worse, several of them. What if the entire ceiling caved in?

Henry had been mining for nearly two weeks when he came home one evening to find that the contents of his tent had been thoroughly gone through. They hadn't left one thing untouched. The only meaningful things taken were some coins Henry had stashed away along with Spooky's letter, which he had not yet read. He hoped to God that whoever took those things couldn't read. He didn't need the entire camp knowing his business.

After supper that evening, Henry succumbed to his need for whiskey and entered the most decent looking saloon he could find. He saw the man from the Hearst office who always seemed interested in him having drinks with several others. Henry sat down and ordered his whiskey. He sipped it slow not wanting to become drunk. His neighbor began speaking to him.

"Haven't seen you before. Been here long?"

"No. Been here almost two weeks now, just working as a pick-ass miner. Never worked so hard in my life." Henry grimaced as he spoke.

"Yeah, tough work. See that man over there? That's George Hearst. I wouldn't have an ounce of admiration or respect for the guy if I didn't know he's put in many a hard day's work as a 'pick-ass,' as you say. Rich son-of-a-gun now, though, after years of menial labor and selling goods in his little store. Now he's gone and made $91,000 on his first silver mining prospect. Hear he's heading back home to bring back his new bride, one of those hometown girls, you know. Gonna set her up in a brand-new mansion in San Fran. Lucky bastard."

Henry turned to identify the man his talkative friend referred to and saw that he was none other than the man who always noticed him. Hearst noticed Henry's observation and took in Henry's presence, making Henry feel like a toy set out in a store window. He felt silly for feeling glad that he had bathed and shaved that evening and had put on his best suit before coming to the saloon.

Henry reluctantly finished his drink and stood up to leave. He couldn't help but stretch trying to relieve his tired muscles. As he turned to make his way out of the saloon, he once again felt eyes boring into him. He finally acknowledged the look and directly met Hearst's piercing gaze and smiled. As he began walking out, he saw the man motion to him—waving his arm with a come-here-I-want-to-talk-to-you signal. Henry turned and walked toward him, and as he neared the older man's table his three companions stood to leave.

Henry had Hearst all to himself and felt intimidated. As he sat down, he took inventory of the now-famously rich man. He had long, brown hair, that hung to his shoulders in loose curls; a full beard and moustache colored the same as his hair; high cheek bones; and intense brown eyes. He had a commanding demeanor, and those eyes of his demanded full attention.

He held his hand out to Henry and introduced himself. "George Hearst. I believe you work for me?"

"Yes. And, thank you, sir, for the opportunity."

"Yes, the opportunity to work your ass off, correct?"

Henry laughed, amused by this formidable man's assessment of mining. "Yes. The chance to work hard and to, perhaps, die young." Henry's response ended with a bitter laugh this time.

Hearst raised his eyebrows, "Your meaning?"

"Well, sir, I do appreciate the job, but every day that we go deeper into our tunnel and there is more fall of rock, I do consider quitting. I really don't want to die in the bowels of one of your mountains. No, sir, it's become quite apparent to me the risk that goes along with the hard work. The wages are fine, they're fair. But, this problem has me worried. You know, I think if we could figure out a way to predict these cave-ins, or to shore-up our tunnels better, it would be a little safer. I've noticed that when swinging the pick, if you hit right at those light veins, the ones that look like water between all the blue rock, things fall apart much easier and quicker."

Henry was poised to go on but Hearst held up his hands saying, "Got your point, son. I am aware of the problem. We lose too many men to cave-ins. Valuable human beings, all of them. I've been watching you and have questioned the head man in charge of mining operations. You're an intelligent, evidently educated man, someone who doesn't come along often in these mining camps.

"I have a proposition for you, Henry Plummer. I've been in contact with a German engineer from California, someone whom I hope I can count on to come up with a solution to our problem. Would you consider going to San Francisco and bringing this man back to camp? He's not too western, you know, and needs a guide and a babysitter. I would also like to hire you to do some purchasing for me and to secure a contract with a logging company to deliver the timbers I believe it will take to shore up our tunnels. These pine poles we use now break like toothpicks. They're not the answer."

Henry sat back, stunned. Thinking he could go to San Fran and see Charles. Should he see Spooky and little Henry? Henry's blood quickened at the possibilities.

"Yes, sir. I would be happy to do such a mission for you. Yes, indeed. When would you like me to do this?"

"The sooner the better. Philipp Deidesheimer, our engineer, says he is available as soon as I can send for him. I'll get everything firmed up. Why don't you come by my office next week, say Wednesday? We'll find a replacement for you, and I'll make arrangements for your stay in San Francisco. In the meantime, please don't die on me, son."

Henry nodded and stood, offering his hand to this man who trusted him with so much responsibility. He felt as if a huge weight had lifted from his chest, and no longer felt like a total failure and he determined to do his best for this man who had made him feel confident once again.

Sunday was Henry's team's day off. Henry slept in, surprised that the crier's bell hadn't woke him. He stretched and rubbed his still sore muscles. He felt pleased to feel bulging, tight cords lying across his shoulders and down his arms. He stood up and felt around on his buttocks. Yes, they too had tightened. Henry thought about his lungs. They hadn't bothered him since he arrived here.

Henry dressed and since his stomach wouldn't stop rumbling, went to O'Riley's promising himself one of the largest breakfasts they prepared. He sat down after ordering, dismayed that Bridget was nowhere to be seen. There were few women in the camp except for the dance hall girls and prostitutes. Shortly after Henry began eating his breakfast, Big Mac and Jes joined him. They talked Henry into going out into the countryside to see if they could do some prospecting. Henry humored them but knew that the one-man or even three-man prospecting days were gone in the Comstock Lode.

It was April, and even in this desert-like land flowers bloomed and a few tufts of Indian rice grass peeked out from between rocks and boulders. Henry noticed a few trees here and there among the thick covering of flowering sagebrush. It made Henry happy to see that despite the lack of wooden, permanent buildings in Carson City, someone had been planting trees and keeping them watered. Henry knew trees could grow there because around the camp there were several growing naturally.

The men walked back to camp anticipating a hearty dinner. They planned to stuff themselves and then indulge in a long afternoon nap. As they neared town, they heard a commotion on the other end of the main street. Men had gathered around one of the few trees Henry had just been thinking about. Shouting and cheering erupted from the crowd from time to time, and when Henry's group approached the scene, they could see that a rope had been looped around the tree's one sturdy branch.

The other end of the rope was attached to the neck of a man who looked frightened and couldn't stop babbling, "I's pay it back. Jus' let me go. I's pay it back." He repeated this over and over until a group of men began pulling on the other end of the rope, finally lifting the man off the ground, leaving his feet dangling just inches from the surface. His face became intensely red, and he grabbed for the rope, attempting to reach his hand in between his neck and the rope.

The men let him down and someone tied his hands behind his back. They hoisted him again, and this time his face contorted so horribly, they let him down and someone fetched a pillowcase to cover his head so they wouldn't have to watch him as he struggled for air and life. They began hauling him up again, and this time they were able to hold him up, just inches above the ground, but enough that one could see by the kicking of his feet that he would die from strangulation.

Henry couldn't stand watching this horror any longer and pushed his way into the crowd yelling, "What in the hell's wrong with you people. Haven't you ever heard of the due process of law? Damn you? Did you even give him a fair trial?" And, with that he stepped up to the rope and cut the man down earning the complaint that, "God damned it!! Now we gotta get a new rope!"

The crowd went wild, and several men went after Henry. A huge burly man captured Henry and held him by the arms pulling them back until he stood helpless as two other men took turns belly punching him until he couldn't breathe for the pain. Suddenly they stopped. Henry had never felt so happy to see anyone than when Georg Hearst stepped up to them and ordered them to stop.

"What's going on here?"

"We were in the middle of hanging this damned thief when this wise guy interfered, shouting about due process and a trial. We's already held the trial, he's guilty, and gonna hang for it."

Henry by now could stand up straight and catching his breath, motioned his head toward the tree and said, "Vigilante group hanging some man. It appears he stole something, and now they've gone ahead and decided to hang him for it. No judge, no jury, unconstitutional, it is." Henry kept shaking his head, showing his disgust as George pulled him away, holding him under his protecting arm and shaking his head.

"Yes, these camps are tough. They go from complete lawlessness where everything goes and then swing the opposite way when the vigilantes gain control and hang men for sneezing the wrong way."

Hearst shook his head in regret and said, "Can't wait until we gain statehood here in Nevada and can once again live and work under law and order with trials, lawyers, judges, and juries. You should have seen it just two years ago, men quibbling over claims would just simply shoot one another. The quickest and most accurate gunman won the claim. But, my dear man, you need to let your standards go on this until that happens. Just mind your own business no matter how things bother you."

Henry shook his head once more and declared, "I was going to indulge in a big dinner and a nap, but now I think I'll go buy myself a drink. Would you care to join me, sir?"

George smiled and said, "No. I have got a lot of paper work to do this afternoon before I can indulge in anything comforting. Oh, by the way, I've got things in order for your trip, and Henderson hired a man that worked as miner here before to replace you. I would be very pleased if you could start out tomorrow."

Henry nodded. "Will do, Mr. Hearst."

"Call me George. How about you come meet me at my office at, let's say, nine. That way you can get your affairs in order before we meet."

Henry held out his hand and said, "Sir. Thank you once again for this opportunity." They shook hands and Henry, elated, sauntered into the nearest saloon thirsty for his drink.

Henry was so lost in thought that he didn't pay any attention to the man he had sat next to and as he pulled out his money, the stranger stilled his hand and said, "Let me get this first one mate. I's celebratin' today and want to share some of my happiness."

"What you celebrating?"

"Well, first off, have you ever heard of the Bushwhackers over yonder in Missouri?"

"Yes, a little from the papers," was all Henry would admit. He thought of Pauline and he began to feel a little hot around his neck as he loosened his shirt.

"Yeah, well, I was with the Bushwhackers many times as they did their raiding n' such. Got shot up once, too, and after that I just hung around and listened ta people. I heared many plans those God-damned pro-union Kansans made and would alert my side. I's ruined many a plan those Kansans cooked up. But, the Missourians never respected my help as much as my shootin' up people and their things, so I headed out for here. Gonna jus' look out for meself for a while, heal up, and make a little money prospectin'. How about you?"

Henry shook his head at the man's ignorance about things, especially Carson City, and his stupidity in talking politics, bragging about his raiding, to someone without ever feeling out their sentiments. Henry instantly detested the man and stood up to go.

"Thanks for the drink, but next time if I were you, I'd keep my mouth shut before I boasted about being one of those murdering, thieving, looting, and plundering assholes from Missouri."

The former Bushwhacker stood up, blubbering his indignation in his strange drawl, but Henry kept on moving and once out the door, looked back, thankfully the ass had not followed him.

Henry was glad to leave the next morning; he certainly hoped the ignorant Missourian would be gone when he returned. Henry's trek back down the trail toward Johnson's Ranch seemed to go much quicker than his trip to Comstock Lode. He stopped there, stabled his horse, and walked the little distance to town to catch the train to Sacramento and from there took another train to San Francisco.

He took a hack to visit Charles and explained all that had happened to him since they had last met. Henry knew that telling Charles about his sad events and disappointments would help him feel better and not so damned. Charles once again stood by his friend's decision to fight for his life at the bordello and urged him to shed the guilt he felt about the other man's demise.

Henry, while grateful for his friend's view, explained that the guilt came mostly from the fact that he had put himself in these deadly situations because of poor judgment and by living a reckless lifestyle. Henry regretted his reliance on the bottle to escape his pain and told Charles he vowed to never do so again. Then he asked Charles what he thought of him seeing Spooky again.

Charles chuckled and said, "Henry, only you can make that decision. What would you gain by seeing her if you can't ever be together?"

Henry smiled, rueful, "Just need to see her one more time, I guess. Make sure she made the right decision."

Charles wrapped his arm around Henry's shoulder, "Come on, let's go down to the Cliff House and have us a nice meal and some good wine. You'll figure things out; I have no doubt. Just empty your mind and enjoy my wonderful company and supper on me."

The next day Henry went to see William Benson, the logging contractor with whom George wished to do business. Benson wanted to sell the timbers by the foot, just as George wanted to buy them, except they were five cents apart in price. At first Henry didn't see that as much of a problem, but when he figured the many thousands of timbers needed for the Hearst mining operation, the difference did add up, indeed. Henry decided he needed to meet with the other contractors on George's list before making any decisions.

He met with two other men but couldn't get any better bid than Benson's. The last man on the list was out of town, and Henry would need to wait a few days until he could meet with him. He contacted Philipp Deidesheimer and explained the delay to him, promising to contact him as soon as their departure became more feasible.

It was Thursday, and Henry did not have any more appointments until next Monday. He took advantage of this free time to venture into the gambling district and take his chances at the faro tables. He did well, as usual, but became bored and decided to walk down to the wharf and then along the beach to think about Spooky. He knew he needed to see her. He must. He worried about her well-being and wondered if she had put herself into a safe situation. If there was one thing Henry had learned in this world—it was that you couldn't trust anyone, not really.

The Hamilton couple could just simply eliminate her from their lives and they, then, wouldn't have to deal with her or share the boy with her. They could sell her to someone that would take her far away, so far away that Spooky would never be able to make her way back. They could kill her. They could arrange for some horrible accident. Henry shuddered when he thought of all the ways a rich, powerful family could realize their dreams by simply doing away with her, his beautiful friend and one-time lover.

Henry had committed to memory the address Spooky left him and decided to walk up the hill to the newly developed wealthy section of town. His body ached for activity after working so long and hard in the Lode. The long walk did wonders for Henry's mood and his apprehension for Spooky. He took his time and began examining the fine, massive homes on the hill.

The hustle and bustle of the city had been left down below. Up here it was tranquil with only a few ladies walking the streets with their parasols and soft chatter. Several dandy young men stopped at one house and went bounding up the steps to a porch where three dewy-eyed misses waited. A lovely young woman with a baby carriage came around the corner with her beautifully coifed head held high, almost stepping along with a man's easy saunter, and singing, her clear lovely notes ringing softly through the air.

The babe was a boy; Henry could tell by the little cap on his head. He sat up clinging to the sides his conveyance acting as if he'd rather walk. The woman seemed to sense this because she stopped singing and came around to the front of the carriage and stooped to pick him up. Henry could see that she had a wonderful hour-glass figure with a tiny waist and a lovely, full bottom that the layers of fine cloth couldn't hide.

She put him on his feet, letting him grasp each one of her forefingers, and guided and half-held him up as he slowly made his baby steps down the walk.

"Oh! Little Henry, you're doing so well, today. I believe you'll be walking by your birthday."

Henry heard her voice and the name Henry and looked more closely at her. He couldn't believe his eyes. It was Spooky. She was right there before him, gorgeously attired, looking so finely kept, and with baby Henry, who was almost walking. Henry's first thought was to run to her and the boy. But then, he stopped, thinking, she looked well and even happy. He could save himself the heartache and go back down the hill and never worry about her again.

But Henry couldn't do that. He wanted, desperately needed, to see someone who cared for him, maybe loved him. He had to know if things had worked out the way she wished. Why she had bargained with their lives the way she had? What made her think this arrangement was safe?

Spooky's face filled with astonishment, and then when she fully realized it was truly Henry, there in the flesh, it lit up like a street lantern at dusk. She didn't say a word; she just came to Henry as fast as her dainty, richly shod feet could bring her. They embraced with little Henry becoming indignant at the squashing he received. Henry couldn't help but be reminded of his dream when he had met Pauline in the clearing. He stepped back out of Spooky's embrace and openly admired her appearance.

"Man, Spooky, if you aren't a vision. I've never seen you looking so good, and I surely like your taste in clothes. Everything is fine, then?"

Spooky smiled and said, "Yes, Henry, all is well." Henry noticed that her diction had also improved in the little time they had been apart.

Henry asked little Henry if he remembered him and held his hands out in an offer to take him from his mother. He smiled and almost jumped into Henry's arms.

A very pleased Henry exclaimed, "I think he remembers me."

Henry's happiness vanished when he remembered the circumstances that brought them to San Francisco, who Henry's actual father was, and what he was—a very wealthy, successful business man who had the money to buy his son and to clothe his mother so finely.

Well, he thought, that's not going to stop me from enjoying Spooky or her son. Henry settled the soon-to-be one-year-old boy in one arm and wrapped his other around Spooky as they walked up the hill to where she had left the baby carriage. Little Henry put up a fuss when they neared it, so Henry put him down between him and Spooky and each one of them took a hand, letting him walk his funny baby steps as Henry pushed the buggy with his other hand. No one spoke; they were satisfied to just be together.

Henry couldn't believe the size and elegance of the Hamilton mansion and its grounds. Six men of Mexican descent worked together planting bushes and flowers, and he thought of how different it must be for them to have to pay for that service now. When they reached the gate Spooky picked up her child, and Henry followed with the carriage.

Spooky took the walk that led to the back where her cottage sat—a fine accompaniment to the larger structure. Each house had been sided in white with brickwork adding a tasteful accent. The black roofs matched black shutters. Spooky proudly pointed out her flowerbeds, which she had planted herself. Henry could see her vivid personality in the riotous collection of annuals and perennials.

The elegant furnishings in Spooky's house pleased Henry almost as much as her attire. He wanted to ask her if she had chosen all her new and fine things or if the Hamiltons had been involved as well. Her home felt cool and was extremely clean with not a thing out of place. Henry started when Spooky ushered him into her parlor and he saw a much older version of her sitting near the windows.

"Henry, this is my mother, Ella."

"Mama, this is my good friend, Henry Plummer."

Henry walked to where Ella sat, and gave her a low bow, and accepting the hand she held out to him, kissed the top of it. "I am pleased to meet you, Ella."

She responded in the same lilting voice as Spooky, only hers was much deeper and had a soft melancholy sound to it, which told Henry she had learned to accept her heartaches and tribulations years ago. They still lay deep within her soul, but she had been able to lose the bitterness through the years, replacing it with wisdom. She seemed, to Henry, more than anything, sage—and her eyes, which examined him all the while she welcomed him, were discerning.

Spooky motioned to her mother and said, "Like I told you in my letter, she is what makes me know this deal is safe for little Henry and myself. The Hamiltons finally brought me my papers declaring me free, and they freed my mother and little Henry, too. We have many copies filed and secured in safe deposit boxes. And, hopefully if there is war and slaves are emancipated, none of that will be necessary any longer."

Henry nodded, wondering how they had found Spooky in the first place.

As if she read his mind, Spooky explained that when Anna Beth had purchased her from Madeline Hamilton, they couldn't finalize the paperwork until Henry Hamilton would give his consent. And, that is why the Hamiltons knew where to find her and that she had given birth to Henry's child. Henry raised his eyebrows, jealous to realize that Spooky could have been naming her son after his father.

"Henry, huh? So, did you really name the baby after me and my son, or did you have him in mind? Do you love him?"

"Henry! You know me better than that! I really didn't think I'd ever see them again, and no, I certainly do not love him."

"Then why all this?" Henry asked, motioning to all the fine things and Spooky's lovely house. "Why all this generosity and change of heart? I don't understand. Someone stole your letter from me so I never was able to read it."

Spooky and Ella burst into laughter as if they had some private joke, which they did. "Weel, it seems that Madeline Hamilton has Negro blood in her. She probably be's more Negro than I's or my mama." Spooky declared, falling back into her old speech pattern, which Henry knew so well. Spooky went on to explain, speaking carefully again, "Yes, her great-grandmother, on her father's side, lived to be ninety-seven years old. On her deathbed, she confessed that she had had an affair with a young, Negro buck when she was about sixteen and the result was a baby boy who grew up to be none other than Madeline's grandfather, raised white."

Henry had just taken his first swallow of lemonade offered him by the two and began sputtering, almost choking.

"Yes," Spooky went on, "that revelation changed Madeline's heart and whole idea of things. I am forever grateful to that old lady because I want my Henry to enjoy his true place in life—to become as wealthy and powerful as his own daddy."

Henry watched as little Henry, clinging to furniture, walked to his grandmother, Ella. When he attained his goal, he simply laid his head in her lap signaling that he was ready for his afternoon nap. Ella gathered him into her arms and stood to take him to the nursery. On their way, they stopped near Henry, and he reached over and ruffled little Henry's blonde curls and kissed his cheek. Yes, Henry thought, I want that for you too, Master Henry Hamilton.

Henry took Spooky out to supper that night, and Spooky finished telling Henry things she had written in the letter. She told him that she had agreed to give up her child, in name only, when he became a teenager, and that until that time she would not take up with another man or marry. Henry raised his eyebrows at that disclosure, and Spooky hurriedly told him that Henry's receiving his rightful inheritance and place in life would be worth that sacrifice.

"'Sides," she said, regretful, "I am or will be happy to be left alone for awhile because ever since I came of age, men been pestering me and I am quite tired of it all. Except for you, of course." She looked up at him, coy from underneath her long eyelashes. "Henry, about tonight, I did tell Mama to not expect us until tomorrow sometime. I's hoping that you and I could be together one more time."

Henry reached over and picking up Spooky's hand pulled it to his mouth and gently kissed it. "Sounds wonderful, Spooky."

Henry took Spooky to a fine hotel and checked them in as husband and wife. They both looked wistfully at Henry's entry into the registry, "Mr. and Mrs. Henry Plummer" each wishing that things would have turned out different, that Henry still didn't pine for Pauline, and that Spooky could be entirely, completely free from her past.

They made love that night several times, slow and tender without lovers' passion, more to comfort one another than anything else—like old friends or a married couple so long together they did it just for old time's sake. They talked about how grateful they were to have had each other when life had been so irrevocably harsh. They laughed about their first meeting and shed tears when acknowledging that this would most likely be their last. Henry confessed that he thought about going back east where things were more civilized, where there were laws instead of guns keeping justice. Spooky admitted that she worried about being too old to find someone in ten years when she would be twenty-eight and free to marry.

Henry reassured her, "Look at me, I'm twenty-nine, do I look like an old man? Besides, look at your mother, she has aged very well and I'm sure you'll do the same. Right now, at this very moment, I swear you are the most beautiful woman in San Francisco. And, you know what's best about you? It's the beauty inside you, your fertile mind, and thoughtful ways. You amaze me because despite all that you have been through, all the abuse and disrespect, you know your worth and respect yourself. I admire that. I don't have any of that."

Spooky, naturally, protested. She reminded Henry how he had stayed with her and helped her through her pregnancy and birthing, and how he had loved little Henry from his first moment of breath and had helped her take care of him.

She slapped him on his chest and said, "You loved, love, a beautiful woman, a woman who many men would not even make love to because she had only one leg. You looked past all that and recognized her worth as a human being. You have seen my worth even though most people just look at me as a black woman slave only with the value as, what did you say, three-fifths of a white person? Yes, Henry, you need to look again and see that you are a worthy man who deserves respect, not only from others, but from yourself.'

Henry only laughed and began his love making with her for one last time.

He escorted Spooky home the next morning and despite that they parted without tears, their sadness made little Henry cry with concern. As Henry walked past the big house and down to the street, someone watched from an upstairs window of the mansion. He never did meet Madeline and Henry Hamilton but knew, somehow, that Spooky had made the right decision. Still, he wished life wouldn't be so complicated or difficult.

Henry hurried to wrap up his business in San Francisco, thinking the sooner he left the quicker he would recover from his parting with Spooky and her boy. The last contractor came closest to George's figures, and Henry made a deal with him. He bought up the goods the Hearst Mining Company needed and supervised the loading of four large wagons, making sure the supply train had plenty of mules and was well on its way before he contacted Philipp Deidesheimer.

He had supper one last time with Charles but didn't tell him of his plans to go back east; he couldn't bear another final parting. Henry cleaned out his bank accounts and hoped he was doing the right thing in carrying so much money. George had assured him that Carson City would soon have a viable, safe bank. "How could a city be built, especially such a rich one, without banks?"

Henry left the next morning with his charge who kept Henry entertained the entire trip. He made Henry's last days of sorrow and partings fade quickly with his antics and German ranting. He cursed himself continuously, "Ich bin eine dum kopf!" whenever Henry would point out to him it was his riding methods and not the horse's fault when things went badly for him on the trail. Philipp lost his seat often the first days, but by the time they reached Comstock Lode he could at least stay in the saddle.

The man was also quite the storyteller, and at night after a few stiff brandies, he would tell tale after tale and break into German when he became excited. Henry loved how he would slap his leg and chortle at his own jokes; just hearing Philipp laugh made Henry chuckle.

Henry couldn't believe what difference three weeks made in a boom town as they crested the hill overlooking Carson City. The main street was now lined with several newly built, wooden structures and many more were in the process of being built. The lumber they had waited for so long must have finally arrived. He and Philipp went directly to the Hearst offices.

Henry felt relieved when he reported his dealings in San Francisco and George seemed pleased. He laughed when Henry seemed apprehensive about the price he had settled on for the timbers and said that he had purposely set his offer low to see how well Henry could bargain. He had expected to pay more. George had someone show Philipp to his room he had rented for him in the new hotel across the street. Henry went along to see if he could also find a room; he was not looking forward to sleeping on the ground in a tent after the luxuries in San Francisco.

The hotel had been built by the O'Riley family, and Henry congratulated Tom as he checked in and paid for a room. Accommodations were minimal and the entire structure had a raw feel to it with much more finishing work needed. Henry left for a bath and shave and after that he removed his belongings from his former canvas home. The beds in the hotel were quite small but at least they had mattresses and seemed comfortable enough.

Henry returned to the Hearst offices where he was to meet Philipp and take him up to the mines to show him what they were up against with their tunneling. Henry felt ashamed when he saw the dirty, sweaty state of his former teammates after their morning's work. When he spoke with them about showing Philipp their tunnel, they warned him that it had fallen in three times since he had left and that they had lost Pete in one of the cave-ins. Philipp didn't have much to say after he examined of the tunnel and watched the labor-intensive process used to dig out the rock that would produce silver.

George invited Henry to the supper and welcoming party to be held for Philipp later that evening. Henry didn't quite know what to do with his free time so he went into a saloon and ordered a whiskey. Soon, he had been joined by several other men one of whom began talking about honeybees and how much money he could make since the new developing town was always short of sugar along with other food stuffs. Henry politely asked him what beekeeping involved and before he knew it, he and his new friend, Milt, were walking out to the countryside to see his collection of hives.

Philipp, out taking a walk before dinner, fell in step with them and the threesome made their way to Milt's bees. Milt had them put on veils, hoods, and gloves while he opened a hive and deftly reached in to pull out a comb, explaining the entire hive structure, the importance of leaving the brood nest alone with plenty of honey for their food and taking only the 'extra' honey they store in the combs. Philipp became fascinated with the natural structuring of the hive and asked Milt many questions.

At supper that night Henry could see Philipp excitedly explaining something to George while drawing out his idea on paper. In examining the beehive, he had discovered a bracing system to shore up the tunnels. He designed an interlocking frame with hefty one foot by two-foot timbers four to six feet apart on each side making a square set.

The Wells Fargo Bank, which Henry hoped to use to keep his money safe, had not yet been completed. George offered to keep Henry's nest egg in his safe until he could safely deposit it in the bank. George pleased with Henry's performance in San Francisco offered him more work as a purchasing agent. Henry told him he would need to think about it since he had been planning to go east to Kansas. George told him he needed a man to secure some contractual work from a brick company in Salt Lake.

He had decided to build his new office out of bricked sandstone. Henry told George he would come back tomorrow to give him his answer.

The next morning Henry met George and told him he would go to Salt Lake but asked if it would work out if he left for Kansas after he had completed his mission. George agreed and didn't ask any questions, which pleased Henry since he didn't know exactly what he really wanted to do in Kansas.

He went about town purchasing supplies and decided he needed a more substantial horse. He found a seventeen-hand thoroughbred, cut-stallion with some racing blood in him. He rode him, and once he knew he could handle him well enough, made an offer for him. The horse was jet black, and Henry thought the name Avenger would suit him well and would be symbolic of his not yet fully developed plan to avenge Pauline's loss of her leg and Spooky's treatment as a slave.

Henry finished packing his saddlebags with a good supply of food stuffs and much coffee. Someone told him he could most likely trade coffee for home-cooked meals from the settlers along the trail. He had also been told that most of the way he would meet wagon train after wagon train going west so great was the pull of promising opportunities in Utah, Oregon, California, and Washington Territory.

Henry ate supper and then stopped for a couple of drinks. The saloon buzzed with talk of civil war. Abraham Lincoln, promising to keep the country together, had become President of the United States, and by April, the Confederates demanded the surrender of Fort Sumter. Southern troops had been seizing the forts and arsenals located within their boundaries. Jefferson Davis had been inaugurated as the provisional President of the Confederate States of America in February. President Lincoln had ordered blockades of ports from South Carolina and as far as Texas, and the Federals had recently captured the slave ship, Nightingale.

Henry had problems finding a seat, so he stood at the bar to order his first drink. After a bit, he began to distinguish different voices and accents, many of them, he swore, sounded just like the man who had claimed to be a Missouri bushwhacker. Henry looked around him and listened to their conversations, hearing such oaths as, "Goddamned Yanks, think they can tell us what to do and how to run our part of the country. Yup going home and join the Johnny Rebs and fight those bastards." Yes, they were definitely southern and pro-slavery. Henry paid for his drink and left.

He entered a second bar and first off, heard a vicious argument between two men, each arguing a different side of the country's civil unrest, and when the men began to exchange blows, Henry left. The third saloon he entered seemed peaceful enough and he found a seat in the corner. He downed three drinks in little time, so engrossed he was in his own thoughts and indecisions.

Should he take part in the obviously, inescapable civil war and become a raider on the anti-slavery side? Or should he go all the way home and join the Federal forces? He wanted to do something on behalf of Pauline and her loss, and because of Spooky's unfortunate life experiences, feeling that he would never rest until he did. He never had sanctioned the institute of slavery and never would condone it. He also hated the idea that people, in the south, especially, wanted to split their nation into two different countries. Now, that was insane considering what the generations of Americans had gone through in the past, almost a hundred years now, to keep the country intact as one republic—one people.

Soon a flood of bushwhackers invaded the saloon. Henry wondered why they were in Carson City. Too chicken-shit to go to war, Henry figured, and perhaps things had gotten a bit hot for them on the Missouri-Kansas border. He decided to leave and looked up just in time to see the braggart that had bought him a drink weeks earlier bearing down on him. Henry stood up and tried dodging him.

The man, the Toothless Wonder, was all Henry could think to call him since he had hardly any teeth, came up to him and shoved him back into his chair. "I's thinking we should finish that **con**—ver-sa-shun we's having before yous up and left me before."

The crude was obviously drunk, Henry noted, and he decided he was not even worth the trouble to argue with or to placate. Henry stood up saying, "Let me buy you a drink and we'll call it even." He strode over to the bar, paid for his drinks, and ordered one for Toothless Wonder, motioning to him at his former table in the corner.

Pointing to the man now sitting at his former table, Henry asked the barkeep, "Here's an extra coin if you'd just deliver it to him so I don't have to put up with him any longer. Would you please?"

The bartender nodded, and just as Henry had reached the doorway, Toothless came behind him and said, "I's said we's gonna finish that talk," as he clamped his hairy paw on Henry's shoulder and spun him around.

Henry looked him straight in the eye and said, "Well, I have decided that I really don't wish to talk to you. Go sit down and drink your drink, not that you need another. Just sit down and let it rest."

Toothless reached into his boot, pulled out a large knife, and with one swipe, the drunken man slashed Henry's forehead. Henry could feel the blood pulsing out of his wound and running into his eye. Toothless stood back and laughed, "Now boy, you gonna talk or what?"

Henry turned to go and could feel the man's hand on him again, this time when he swung Henry around, he had his knife raised and was ready to stab. Henry could see he was going for his belly and pulled out his gun and fired. Henry stood, silent and stunned. Toothless lay sprawled out on the floor with a bloody hole in his chest. His eyes stared out into the world, sightless, as dead as dead could be. Everything was a blur after that for Henry, who now had blood running into both eyes. He felt someone pull him out of the saloon, guiding him, pushing and prodding him down the street.

"I had to get you out of there since the vigilantes are so rampant these days with their justice. I saw it all and I calls it self-defense clear and simple. But you never know. I'm gonna see if the man I work for is still around, and then, hopefully, we kin git you stitched up and hid."

The man took him to George Hearst, who still worked in his office. George caught one look at Henry and called to one of his men to go fetch the doctor. He emptied a desk top of maps and lay Henry out on the desk, ordering Henry's savior, William Jenkins, to go get a basin of water. George emptied a portion of his whiskey bottle onto a rag and began dabbing at Henry's wound asking what had happened.

George's ministrations hurt like hell, and Henry described the entire event between clenched teeth. George let the alcohol-soaked rag rest on top of Henry's wound and found a blanket to roll up and lay under Henry's head. Henry wanted to sit up but George pushed him down saying, "You've lost a lot of blood, and I don't care to be picking you up off the floor. Just wait until doc gets here and sews you up. My man, Mayfield, will take you somewhere out of the way where you can rest up a couple of days before you head out for Salt Lake City."

"You still want me to work for you? You don't think poorly of me, now? You know, that's the last thing I wanted to do. In fact, it just makes me sick to my stomach." Jenkins returned with the basin of water and as he set it down beside the makeshift operating table, Henry reared up and began retching into the basin.

"Oh Christ!" cursed Jenkins as he saw that he would have a mess to dump and would need to run for more water.

Henry lay back down and quieted, now that his belly had emptied. He settled down and concentrated on the pain in his scalp. If he kept very still it hardly pained him. The doctor arrived and began tsking immediately.

"Damned! That's one deep cut you've got there, son. What's your name?"

Henry didn't answer, not sure if he could trust the man, and George interjected, "Just sew him up, Doc, the best you can. I'll pay you well not to mention this visit to anyone. Jenkins, you stay here, too. I'll need to talk to you later."

Henry grit his teeth to get through the twelve stitches on what the doctor claimed was at least a three-inch slash. "I'm trying to do this as pretty as possible, boy, but you're going to have an ugly scar from here on out." Soon, they heard shouts up and down the street. Henry had become a hunted man.

George doused the lantern and ushered the doctor into the next room. Henry could hear murmurs and then George counting out money. "Now after accepting this bonus I expect you to keep your mouth shut. The man acted in self-defense and you could see for yourself the cut that n'er-do-well gave him. I'm going to show you out the back. Go quietly. I'm sure you'll want to keep all the work I provide you."

George returned and had his talk with Jenkins and Mayfield. Jenkins was to help Mayfield get Henry out of town without being seen or caught. "If worse comes to worse, create some diversion. Mayfield, when you get Henry secreted out in the cabin, ride back into town in the morning and report immediately to me."

Henry could sit up now, and as soon as it became apparent that he would be stable on his feet, he was whisked out of the back flap of the tent. He and his two guides walked slowly with even and measured steps. Henry wore a hat belonging to George, down low, and finished tucking in the clean shirt he had also provided. When they reached the outskirts of the camp, they found two horses waiting for them. They untied them from the railing and led them quietly out into the sagebrush flats just below the mining camp. Once a safe distance from town, he and one of the men mounted and rode out into the dark night.

Billy Mayfield had a cabin about twenty miles from town and by the time they reached it, Henry felt quite spent and put up no fuss when Mayfield had him pee and ushered him up a ladder and onto a mattress lying across the ceiling beams in the attic. Billy told him he would need to remove the ladder and replace the ceiling boards, just in case. Billy provided Henry with a jug of water, bread, dried fruit, and a pot to piss in.

Henry stayed up there for almost three days. The entire time he lay there he berated himself for once again risking his well-being by patronizing a saloon. He tried reasoning with his conscience but to no avail—civil unrest or no, he shouldn't go into a bar where trouble always seemed to find him. And, why did he have to talk so smart to Toothless in the first place? Because, you dumb ass, he told himself, you thought you'd never see the cur again. Henry vowed to never assume too much ever again and to always think as cautiously as possible. Easier if he kept his mouth shut entirely.

As the hours wore on, Henry became increasingly uncomfortable and felt as if he would lose his mind. His good side continued to chastise him for letting his guard down and going into a drinking establishment in the first place and then to continue to drink there when obviously there was unrest all around him. By the end of the second day Henry truly felt miserable, sweating until his clothes felt as if he just taken them off the wash board and put them on, and his pot stank so bad he wanted to dump it out over the side of the mattress in the worse way. Decency and gratitude for a place to hide kept him from doing that, but then the black dog began working on him.

His two sides continued to argue until he knew he was going mad. His skin began to prickle, itching in the oddest places, making Henry quite sure he had lice crawling all over him. When he attempted to fall asleep, the war in his mind wouldn't let him. Why didn't you stay out of the saloons? Because, I'm a grown man and if I want a drink or two I'll have a drink or two. But you didn't stop at two. How many did you have, making you so careless not to mention losing your infernal temper once again to the point of killing another person? Well, he brought it on, that ugly toothless braggart!

But why risk anything on such a person? You would not have done what you did if the whiskey hadn't taken over. (The black dog really became defensive after that declaration.) You didn't have too much of anything! You weren't drunk and after all, if you want to get drunk you can drink until you are because you are a man with free choice and determinism.

Henry had studied free will and determinism at Bangor. They had spent an entire week arguing and discussing these concepts, and Henry had come away more confused than ever. He had read the Bible enough times to pick up on the idea of free will and had been brought up worshipping in the Catholic Church, which supported the idea that man did indeed have free will offset or tempered with grace from God. Henry understood that he had free will and would make mistakes using it but the grace, the unmerited forgiveness of God and his own belief in him and his son Jesus, would save him from the clutch of the devil and ensure him eternal life.

Even in the Old Testament in which he found the troubling "eye for an eye", the authors of the Bible had included talk of the grace of God and man's free will in the same sentences, repeatedly. Proverbs mentions it, he remembered, preaching that men's hearts can plan their ways, but God ordains their way, something like that. So, Henry thought, forcing the saintly side of him and his devilish black dog to retreat so he could think rationally for himself, did he completely choose to kill Toothless, or was he an instrument of God's to get rid of a bad, horrible entity in the world. Had he gone into the saloon with the intent to kill someone? Hell! No! (Henry pushed the black dog back and said a quick prayer to God begging for his grace and mercy.) No, he did not plan or wish to kill someone.

Henry thought of the concept of determinism, deciding that free will had so much to do with God and his freely given forgiveness and mercy that he was okay there. After all, he did believe in God and his son Jesus. He had, like a good Catholic boy, memorized John 3:16, which promises eternal life to all who believe— "For God so loved the world, he gave his only Son, that whoever believes in him should not perish but have eternal life."

So, Henry thought, back to determinism, which people have argued about just as much as free will all through the ages. He found it difficult to believe that men supported the idea that if man had determinism free will was thrown out with the wash water. Why couldn't the two work together? He learned at his Bangor school that if determinism really exists, then all our actions are predicted and we are assumed not to be free, and then, on the other hand, if determinism is nonexistent, then our actions are random and we do not seem free because we have no way to control what happens. So confusing.

Henry's good side stepped in then and wouldn't be ignored. Well, Henry, you have free will because you are a human being and a thinking one at that, though sometimes I do wonder. Your obligation as a human is to use free will to make moral judgments. Remember, moral, doing the right thing? Since you do have moral responsibility as a man, you are responsible for your actions. Only you. Now think back to the other night, what would have happened if you had gone home and went straight to bed or stayed up reading, like you often do? Think about it.

I don't have to tell you that **nothing** horrible would have happened. You wouldn't be in misery up here in this attic on a mattress with only a pot to pee in stinking to high heaven. Toothless would be running off at the mouth and perhaps someone else would dispense of him or they would be simply ignoring him. Right? Remember the Biblical axiom— "Live and Let Live?" Henry's mind went around and around thinking about this conundrum, driving him crazy as his two sides continued to wrangle, but it did help the time go quicker and he did quit itching.

George personally came to let Henry out of his attic hideaway. He brought him his money and paid him in advance for the work in Salt Lake City. "Now, I've drawn you a little map of how to get from here to the Central Overland Route which will take you directly to Salt Lake. You'll be well away from Carson City but if you do see anyone, for God's sake, keep your hat on and don't say a word, or at least, as little as possible."

George sighed and went on with his instructions, "The government has worked on the trail all year and it should be easy going. You'll run into men along the way setting up telegraph poles for the Transcontinental Telegraph. You'll have to bank your money when you reach Salt Lake City; they'll have decent, safe banks there. Good luck, Henry, I wish we didn't have to part this way, but there is no way you can ever return to Carson City, not for some time. I hope that whatever you decide to do will work out well for you, son."

"Just to warn you, they've got an arrest warrant out for you, and the governor of California is thinking about rescinding your pardon. And, that damned Mayfield had a fatal run in with Sheriff John Blackburn over your whereabouts, and he ended up stabbing the sheriff and killing him. But don't worry, Billy certainly did not give him the information he wanted and the sheriff's dead anyway. Mayfield's on the run now, too, but I sent him in the other direction to Washington Territory."

Henry shook his head in regret. "Sorry about all this, sir. I really am."

"Don't worry about it, son, these are strange, volatile times we live in and I'm sorry to say it but I don't think it'll get any better until we have ourselves a civil war and when that happens, things will really be precarious for the whole lot of us."

Henry mounted his horse, happy to be out of the attic. He followed George's map and soon knew he was on the trail because of the telegraph poles along the way. Later he had to pay the toll for crossing a bridge and then again when using a ferry to cross another river. Henry kept his eyes down low and only nodded when someone talked about the good weather they were having for traveling.

Henry camped alone that night and several nights after. He enjoyed the peace of being alone but slept poorly, always listening for wild cats or bear. He could hear the wolves and coyotes howling in the distance. The fourth night Henry shot a couple of rabbits and enjoyed the hot, tasty, roasted meat. He took the rest of the remains, buried them far from camp, and kept a large fire going, sleeping well until he felt the light and cold of dawn.

Henry decided that he should push hard to reach Salt Lake in as little time as possible. It was May and the hours of daylight stretched out further each day. He traveled with the light, getting up at dawn and stopping just before dusk to make camp. He reached Salt Lake City June 1and eagerly checked into a hotel that provided baths in each room. Henry luxuriated in his hot, soapy water and then took a long, serious sleep in the big, fluffy bed.

That evening he went down to the dining room and ate a substantial fried chicken dinner accompanied by roasted red beets, potatoes, and kale. Thinking of the last time he drank whiskey, Henry ordered a glass of wine, instead. He topped off his meal with warm apple pie and went back up to his room and slept the night away.

The next morning, he went to the bank, started a savings account, and rented a safe deposit box. Even though the bulk of the money had been deposited into his savings, he felt better putting his gold and silver coins into the safe deposit box. He just needed to remember to keep the key safe and to not lose it. Next, he went to the barber for a shave and haircut requesting that his hair remain long enough to at least, partially, cover his fresh scar. When the barber commented on it, all Henry did was mutter something about civil war tensions.

After that, Henry went shopping for a new suit, a hat, and some other odds and ends. He liked Salt Lake and its extreme sense of organization. Everything was square, the spacious city blocks, the parks, and many of the buildings. The saltbox homes reminded Henry of Maine, and the streets had been built wide enough to make negotiating simple with large wagons easily making their turns in the streets. The walk ways were neat, clean, and amply wide. Henry felt safe in Salt Lake and noticed that men did not, openly at least, carry guns. Henry began leaving his guns in his hotel room.

Henry accomplished his errands in no time, and since he enjoyed the city, decided to stay on for a few days before heading east. They had just built a large, lovely theater and Henry attended three nights consecutively, visiting the new, well-stocked library during the day. By the time he left Salt Lake, he had decided to complete his mission in Kansas, then take a steamboat to St. Louis, Missouri, and take the train home to Maine. He yearned to live in a place where law and order made life peaceful and secure.

CHAPTER 10

JUNE 1861—AUGUST 1861

Henry left Salt Lake City feeling lonely and unsure but knew he wouldn't be satisfied until he did something to right the wrongs done to Pauline and Spooky. He still felt the sting of hatred when he thought of Pauline being tossed out of the Free State Hotel as if she were an unwanted piece of baggage, right into the path of that damned wagon carrying the pro-slavery raiders' canon. He became infuriated when he thought of all the people, like Spooky, considered to be nothing but chattel in the minds of pro-slavers.

The way was easy as he followed the meandering Haight Creek out of the Salt Lake valley. Willows and cattails lined the creek and he could see deer, raccoons, otters, and pheasants as he slowly made his way. He wouldn't have to worry much about going hungry if the entire trail was this verdant. Soon he entered Weber Canyon and was amazed at the sandstone formations, and when he got to what people called the Devil's Slide, he sat on his horse staring at it in awe. It looked as if God had painstakingly inserted massive crystals into the mountainside, which was otherwise green and lush with vegetation. The rock was limestone but sparkled. The formation was made of two rows of these wonders and came down the mountain hundreds of feet.

After that the trail became more difficult as it wound up the mountainside. Henry would need to follow this all the way up until he reached what had simply been named, Big Mountain Pass. He made camp that first evening just about half way up the western slope. He made sure he had plenty of wood because everyone had warned him of how intensely cold the nights would be. They told him to expect some snow though it was already June.

Henry caught two large rainbow trout and made his dinner out of them along with some potatoes. The night became frosty, so cold, that Henry ran out of wood. He decided to hit the trail even though it was barely dawn. There was a light snow falling as he left his first camp. It took him six days to cross that mountain, and each night it was the same—cold and damp. Henry got little sleep trying to keep the fire going to stay warm enough for some rest but found himself breaking camp early each morning before the sun even peeked out of the eastern sky.

Early one dawn, Henry had to stop and wait for a grizzly mama and her two cubs to vacate the trail. Salt Lakers had warned him about them, telling him to make plenty of noise because they were as frightened of humans as people were afraid of them. Henry began singing *The Yellow Rose of Texas* until his throat tightened up when he thought of Pauline.

He cleared his throat and sat on his horse with his wrists crossed over on his saddle horn as he quietly wept, remembering how Pauline would wake him in the middle of the night when she couldn't sleep and seduce him into making love to her. He had felt there would be no end to that and had felt so safe and complete as long as he knew she would be there for him. He would wake up the next morning and watch her sleep the deep slumber that only came from complete happiness. They had been so content being with one another. Why did she have to die? That certainly was not a product of free will. No. Had to be determinism acting on its own, and Henry felt the bitterness creep up his throat, forcing him to heave it out.

He didn't know how long he sat there, so silent on that tender, crisp daybreak but soon realized that his stillness had made the mother curious. She rose up on her hind legs pawing at the air with her giant, deadly claws making a low and eerie half growl half scream. Henry could feel each hair stand up on his scalp and felt a quickening in his bowels.

The female slowly fell back to the ground and began walking toward him swinging her head back and forth, threatening. Henry clenched his buttocks together to avoid messing himself and yelled out in his emotionally wrecked voice as loud as he could, "Get the hell out of my way, you bloody beast!" and began singing his song again, hoarse, but defiant.

Henry pulled his rifle into his lap, lifted it up, and just in case his human voice would veer her off the trail, he began cursing at her and her babies. "You God-damned bitch. Take your kids and get out of here before I have to shoot you. Git!! Go!! God help me I don't want to kill anything again!" She stopped, shook her massive head, and turned quickly, disappearing into the woods with her offspring following.

Henry moved his horse along the trail as rapidly as he could, trotting from time to time, and that evening when he made camp, he collected a massive pile of wood, enough to get him through the night. He planned to have such a huge bonfire that no beast would come within miles of him. Henry sat up all night, deciding not to even attempt sleeping. He still felt chills run down his spine when he thought of the grizzly and her menacing behavior and sounds. He guessed she, too, had been told by her kind to make noise when coming across a human.

Henry sat beside his campfire and drank cup after cup of coffee, thinking. He pondered the Mormon ways he had observed. He didn't envy the men and their multiple wives. It seemed to him that the competition and strife between the ladies was the only evident discord among those people. Life seemed so peaceful, organized, and rewarding to them other than that. And, ladies and gentlemen were they all, Henry thought as he remembered their polite, kind behavior toward him. He looked forward to spending time with Mormons again knowing he would see many on his trek to Kansas as they traveled west to Salt Lake City.

Henry broke camp early and started down the trail. He hoped he would be off the mountain by nightfall and looked forward to warmer nights. He would still keep a big and hot fire going, knowing that once on the high plains and the prairie he would still need to guard himself against wolves and bear, but at least not grizzlies. He finally saw other human life—surly, sluggish-moving, federal troops guarding and helping set up telegraph poles. Their sullen attitudes, he discovered, stemmed from resentment of having to babysit the telegraph out in the wilderness instead of fighting back East.

Henry knew he had reached the far western end of the Nebraska Territory when he saw the strange rock formation called the Needles rearing up before him. Like the Devil's Slide, they stood out, looking foreign in the countryside around them, as if they had been dropped down onto earth by some unknown hand. They were a dark almost black mass of pointy rock forms with one having an open space toward its top, looking just like one of his mother's needles he had seen her threading when he was young.

The air seemed much drier and grew warmer with each mile he distanced himself from the mountains. Different looking grasses grew in bunches as well as a funny, gray-green plant that smelled like Henry's mother's favorite seasoning for the fowl he used to bring home. It was sage, Henry finally remembered. This stuff grew in bush form and, next to the grasses, seemed the predominate plant in this steppe land he now traveled. There were also bushy, yet tree-height plants in bloom with tiny golden flowers, along with other flowering plants, all with some shade of yellow for their blooms. At times there were only brown patches of soil where nothing grew. But when Henry looked out over the landscape, everything seemed all green and golden. Every so often, Henry could see sand dunes where nothing grew but the bushy, short tree-like vegetation.

Henry soon entered a greener environment with many more trees, and he could smell water and wondered if he would soon be coming to the Bear River Crossing. Salt Lakers told him there would be a ferry there run by the Ute Indians who expected money in return for their services, and they gave this warning: "Don't try paying with anything else, and forget socializing with them. Just pay up and cross the river and be on your way."

Henry neared the water; he could see several tepees burning on his side of the river but didn't see any other sign of human activity.

Henry looked at the river rushing past and determined he could probably cross on horseback. The current sweeping by looked fast, but the depth seemed shallow enough. Henry could see smooth, glistening river rock lying on the bottom at least as far as his eyes could see through the crystal-clear stream. Just as he headed toward the river bank, he saw a shadow moving from tree to tree. Henry slowly inched forward toward the ferry and could feel eyes watching him. He made a friendly looking wave. Soon a Native stepped out of the trees and walked toward the ferry. Henry could see that he was Ute by his dress and waved again. The man walked toward him and said, "Ferry. Ten cents," holding out his hand.

Henry smiled and slowly reached into his pocket for the coins. As he handed the money over he asked, pointing to the burning tepees, "What happened here?"

The young man, angry, shook his head, saying, "Cheyenne. Arapaho. No good. Take horses, women, and Black Hawk."

Just then six more men stepped out from the woods and came to help the man set the ferry loose and guide it across the river with long, wooden poles. Upon arriving on the other side, Henry gestured goodbye and took off at a gallop down the trail. He hoped he wasn't too close behind the raiders and wondered what would happen if they discovered him, one lone man on his way east to begin a life of revenge riding a beautiful, strong horse named Avenger.

Henry made camp early that night, hoping to stay well behind the Indian raiders. He built a good-sized fire, roasted the fat rabbit he had shot, and finished off his supper with a celebratory cup of whiskey. He put more wood on his fire and settled down into his saddle, which he used each night as first a back rest and later his pillow. There was a soft, light breeze and because of its gentle warmth and the whiskey in his belly, Henry soon slept.

Henry dreamed. He was young and back at home with his mother and lay with his head in her lap while she gently smoothed away his hair from the now partially healed and but very apparent gash in his forehead. He could hear the soft whiny of horses and the creak of leather and low throaty laughter. Henry woke with a start and looked around. He had been surrounded by at least a dozen Natives who peered down at him from their horses as if he were an exhibit in some museum. A man knelt next to him, laughing as he pulled his hand away from Henry's forehead.

"What you doing here, white man? All alone. You know that isn't a good way to travel out here in the wilderness. Most people have at least enough sense to traverse this country in pairs."

Henry looked up at his humorous interrogator and said, "I'm traveling back east to fight in the war. What are you doing here?"

The man roared with laughter and said, "Well, soldier, I'm here doing some business, I guess you could say, helping my people retrieve what's rightfully theirs. Which side of the war do you wish to fight on, soldier?"

Henry sat up straight and leaning back against his saddle, gingerly scratching at his scar, said, "I'm anti-slavery so will be fighting on the Union side, sir."

"Sir? I've never been addressed by a white man as 'sir' before. I think you very polite, perhaps, too courteous. What are you really doing here?"

Henry shook his head. "I told you. I'm going east to fight in the war."

The Native's smile wasn't exactly sincere but wasn't all sardonic. Henry decided that he had better convince this man that he would soon be out of his territory and wasn't a threat. The man stood up and held his hand out to Henry. Henry looked at him briefly and then took his hand as the man said, "I think we need to keep an eye on you for a while until we find your true purpose for being here, alone on the trail going the opposite way that most people usually take. Come with us to our camp." The Indian man, though short and slight, easily pulled Henry to his feet.

Henry looked about his campsite helplessly as the natives quickly put his fire out, gathered his things, threw his saddle on his horse, and began leading it away through the trees. Henry had no choice but to follow.

The man who spoke perfect English held out his hand and said, "I am called Friday. I had been named Black Spot as a boy but now am Friday."

"Henry Plummer."

"Well, Henry Plummer, when we reach our camp, I want you to tell me your story and then perhaps I will understand your purpose and your character. You see, I too have a tale to tell and once I enlighten you, you will appreciate why I am so distrusting of white men."

Henry did not realize how his predicament had affected him until he began coughing his usual hack. The cold and damp had been troubling to his lungs but as soon as Henry had reached the drier and milder climate he could feel their distress lessen. Now, they couldn't seem to stop convulsing as his captor questioned him about his problem.

"I have bad lungs, been that way since I can remember, one of the reasons I left Maine and went to California."

"Why didn't you stay in California? I hear it is pretty country and full of nature's bounty."

"It's a long story."

When they reached the Indian camp, Friday led Henry to a tepee. He told Henry to follow him as he entered the warm, cozy environment. Henry could smell a strong scent of herbs and soon his spasms subside after he gulped in huge breaths of the healing air. He watched as a beautiful young woman fanned the small fire and then lay bunches of grass on it.

Friday explained, "That is wheatgrass, which heals many things. Its aroma helps people like you with lung problems. If you eat it, it helps many other functions within your body."

Henry nodded and asked, "Why is it you speak such perfect English?"

"I'll tell you later. But, first, your story, soldier."

Henry followed Friday's lead and sat next to him, cross-legged, near the fire. Another lovely young woman came in and handed them bowls of steaming food, which tasted as tantalizing as it smelled. Henry could not identify it but because he felt extremely hungry, he ate his in no time.

Friday laughed at his enthusiasm and said, "You've just eaten a buffalo stew with the seed of the wheatgrass in it along with salt bush, wild onions, and carrots. Good, heh? You ever been to Washington, D.C.? Bad food there. I asked, 'What is this?' They answered always with strange things like blood pudding, beef short ribs, beef wellington. Terrible! So much fat! We don't eat fat unless we have to. Washington, a strange, wild, confusing place. Too many people. The sewage in the streets, awful."

Henry laughed and said he had never been to Washington, D.C. "Never had a reason to. Why did you go there?"

"I was part of a delegation of Indians, with the Cheyenne, the Sioux, a few Oto and Iowa men, and of course, our people, the Arapaho. We went in November of '51 and left in January of '52. Met with President Fillmore who made sure we saw all the wonders of what he called civilization. Not my preference, very unhealthy there. Too wet, too many diseases, too many people living so close together. We thanked the Mighty One that we came back whole, and not sickly. That's one reason I cannot trust the white man—we never did reach a reasonable agreement between our nations and the U.S. government. Tell me why you want to go fight for that government."

Henry thought for a few moments. He shook his head, confused. Finally, he began, "I don't know if I truly trust my government, but I do believe that eventually right will overcome evil. I do not believe that humans should own other human beings. Our Constitution, our rules of governing, states that very same thing."

Friday nodded. "Yes, I studied the Constitution when in school. I know what you mean. But, unfortunately, the United States has its weaknesses, one of which is that the government cannot control everything or everyone. Bad people will do terrible things no matter what the rules. Some people use the government to do that very thing, take advantage of others and misuse them, kill them."

"Yes, but when people band together and fight for what is decent and moral, then some things can be made right. What else can a man believe?"

"I see you are well-educated, Henry Plummer. Do you think that helps? To be knowledgeable about what man has written down over the ages about things? I have had a fine schooling, too, you know. And, still, I prefer the Indian ways and view of things. We have more justice in our traditions with dishonesty usually becoming a death sentence. We do not put up with such things, we cannot afford to, especially now with your people moving out here, wanting our land, and destroying our ways. You will see tonight how we settle things. We can't even risk killing off our Indian enemies. We need all the red men possible to stand up for our ways, our land, and our right to live as we wish."

"Isn't it near dawn? I slept so long."

"No, soldier, we watched you all evening. You slept early. You slept hard." Friday pulled out a pocket watch and announced, "It is only eight o'clock; it stays light out a long time out here. We have the entire night to talk and work out things."

A third young woman entered the tepee and couldn't seem to keep her eyes off Henry. She did not appear bold, only curious, watchful, and measuring. Henry had taken his hat off because of the warmth of the abode, and she quietly stepped up to him and timidly put her hand out to push back the lock of hair that had fallen over his scar. His jagged wound still irritated him with an itch that couldn't be relieved. He knew it wasn't a pleasant sight. Many times, when it bothered him, he had tried to alleviate the discomfort by gently scratching it but to no avail. Henry shied away and she retreated by gracefully stepping backward until she could exit through the tepee's flap.

Friday laughed and said, "I think she likes you. You know, she wants desperately to give birth to a half-Indian, half-white child."

Henry stared back at him, speechless.

Friday chuckled again and proclaimed, "Now, soldier, it's time you tell me your story. What brings you to this country and why do you reek of such sadness. It oozes out of you even when you sleep."

Henry told him about his childhood and how his mother had saved his life many times because of her unending vigilance whenever his lungs failed him. He told Friday how he was beginning to think that he should have died during one of those crises and that his life seemed so unlucky, that he believed he really shouldn't be alive. Friday snorted his disbelief.

Henry did tell him how lucky he was in gambling and how his luck seemed to have corrupted his view of life, ruining his ability to really want to work for a living. He told him about his career as a young law clerk and his time spent as a city marshal in Nevada City, California.

Then, he told of his women, how he had loved Pauline, and about her ill-fated delivery of their child while he was in prison. He recounted his involvement with the Vedders and how that had landed him in San Quentin. He told Friday that he had had one chance at love and redemption and had botched it badly because of his split-second decision as accuser, judge, and juror of another woman's husband, and that he felt he was bad luck to any woman with whom he became involved.

Just then, the third young woman entered the tepee and walked slowly to Henry. She held in her hand a small jar, which contained an ointment of some kind. She dipped her head to Friday as if to say, would you please interpret for me? Friday broke out into a hearty laugh, and she gave him a beseeching look, as if to say, please, don't embarrass me.

Friday turned to Henry and explained, "White Flower wants to know if it would be good with you if she tried some healing ointment on your wound. She and the other two women you saw are daughters of our medicine man, Great-with-the-Earth. He just died after surviving five wives at the great age of ninety-two."

"These three young women are the offspring of his latest wife. They are one of the reasons we are here, the Utes stole them from us when we left for the southern lands this spring. We came back to rescue them and some horses that they also took. The young man who wants Yellow Flower, the second oldest, will fight our Ute captive tonight for her hand in marriage and for the right for our people to come back here next spring to hunt as we move back to Dakota Territory, our sacred hunting grounds for centuries."

Henry nodded his head to the young woman. She leaned close to him and gently rubbed the ointment into his scar, which immediately stopped itching. Henry inclined his head to White Flower. "Thank you." She nodded, looking steadily into his eyes without seeming too bold, smiled slightly, and left.

"Beautiful. Right, Henry?"

Henry grinned, "Quite."

Friday gave Henry a knowing wink and said, "Continue, now, with your life's story, soldier."

"Yes, indeed, White Flower is lovely and kind but I have sworn off women. I am a bad omen."

Friday interrupted Henry, "She wants you. That is evident."

"But I won't spawn a child with her; it would probably die or turn out badly for her. I don't think I could live life knowing a part of me was out here living with you in these dangerous times for you and your people. She needs to give up her idea of a white child because it will only bring her trouble."

Friday only said, "We'll see. Now go on, Henry Plummer."

Henry began telling Friday of his killings, not only did he kill Vedder, but also two more men. "All in self-defense," he asserted, "but still, I have caused three men to die. In my book, that makes me a bad man."

Friday turned and looked piercingly into Henry's eyes. "And now you want to go kill more? You're a difficult man to understand, Henry Plummer. Why don't you just go home to Maine and work as a lawyer? You could do some good for mankind without killing one more person."

Henry shrugged his shoulders. "That is my plan, but first I need to avenge the wrongs done to my women. I know I won't be satisfied until I do that."

Friday sat silent for a bit and then began his story. "Let me tell you my story. I have had a fortunate life until now. I have had the best of both the white and red man's way of life. When I was still Black Spot, my people broke camp and left me one day as my friend and I played out in the prairie. At first, we thought it a lark, an adventure, thinking that someone would come back for us. But, no one did. Our mothers did not miss us until it was too late to come back.

"I had my bow and arrow and at first we had no hunger. But after a few days, we missed our other food as well as our mothers, families, and warm, safe tepees. We built a makeshift shelter, but when a terrific thunderstorm went through the prairie, we found it very insufficient. It blew away with the first gust of wind. We found a pile of rocky boulders where we could burrow down and at least escape the bolts of lightning. That was when we met Thomas Fitzpatrick, a trapper and mountain man finding refuge from the storm also, as well as from some evil Crow warriors who had followed him south hoping to kill him.

"He was the first white man we had ever seen close up and my friend, Raven Chaser, would not stop crying. Thomas was kind to us and we felt comforted. After the storm passed, we crawled out from the boulders and willingly followed Thomas. We told him the best we could, at seven years old, where we thought our people had gone. We spent the next three weeks trying to find them but it soon became evident that we were two lost orphans. Thomas needed to return to St. Louis for business, and he took us with him.

"I liked St. Louis, a big city with much to see and eat. Thomas introduced us to many wonderful, different foods and even took us shopping for white boys' clothing. I loved the zoo and seeing all the different animals that I never imagined existed. I constantly asked Thomas to explain this, and to identify that, and why something was the way it was and not something else. I kept picking up his books in our hotel room and trying to read the words that so enticingly danced across the pages. I sat and scribbled after I watched him write letters to his family back east."

"September came and I hadn't noticed the passing of time, but Raven Chaser had. He began crying for his mother, and for the prairie. One day Thomas told us that he would be going back to our summer hunting ground, and then on to the mountains to trap for the winter, and he asked us if we wanted to go along and look for our people or if we would want to go to boarding school in St. Louis. My curiosity got the best of me and I decided to stay in St. Louis. Raven Chaser went with Thomas. They never did find our people, and Raven Chaser became lost that winter and I never did see him again."

"For eight years, I stayed in St. Louis during the school months enjoying a world that had opened up to me. Thomas would come each spring and take me back to the prairie until September came again. We never saw one sign of my people until the eighth summer. By then, even though I am as dark as a Native could be, I no longer felt like an Indian. I forgot who I was until that day when we came across Arapaho camped near the place where we always began our summer trek. Thomas stopped to talk to their leaders and I began mingling with the children, who sadly, seemed so different to me. Before I knew what was happening, this woman had me in her arms crying out my old name, 'Oh! Black Spot! My Black Spot!'"

"I didn't recognize my old name since Thomas had called me Friday from that first day, a Friday, when he found me and my friend. I had always disliked the name Black Spot because it didn't mean much. A black spot could be anything, so when Thomas renamed me Friday, I accepted it gladly. I also didn't know my own mother; the only thing I remembered was her smell. She liked to rub on her skin the yellow flowers from the tumble mustard, which gave her a sweet smell. I remembered that, and when she begged me to stay with my people, I agreed, stating that if by fall when school began again and I felt unhappy with my people, I would go back to St. Louis with Thomas.

"Thomas and my people made a plan as to where to meet in late August, and I stayed behind while Thomas moved on. At first it was difficult for me. I felt out of place and awkward with my people and my family. My father had died and my mother was with a different man and had had two more children with him. I had a half-sister and a half-brother. My little sister loved me, but my brother made things tough for me, which has made me the warrior I am today. I couldn't blame him for his distrust and jealousy. I learned quickly how to keep quiet and not to speak out against the mean tricks and things he did to me.

"My people had many more horses than I remembered them having, and that's what kept me with them come fall. I, now fourteen, was expected to learn to ride, and ride I did. I soon became the best horseman of all the boys and better than some men. The horses seemed to respond better to me and my quiet ways. Often, I would just go be with them that first summer when the other boys still showed resentment.

"Thomas met us in August, and I told him that I had decided to stay with my people, at least for a while. I begged him to not forget me and if he could bring me books each year, I would be very grateful. He promised to meet me each June close to where my people had their spring camp. We met every year until '54 when he died suddenly that fall. I still miss him, and the books he would bring me." Friday stopped to wipe tears from his eyes.

"But, I have a good wife, and she never complains when she has to pack up the books I have kept over the years. I do wish my two sons could be educated like I was, but that seems impossible now. But, my friend, that is enough of my story for now. I will tell you the rest after the battle. We must go now and watch."

Henry balked. "Battle? What battle?"

Friday responded by holding his hand out to Henry to help him stand. "Like I told you, Henry Plummer, we can't afford to even kill our own Indian enemies so our warrior, Black Coal, will fight the Ute warrior, Black Hawk, who stole his woman, her two sisters, and a dozen horses. They will fight, hard and deadly, but not to the death. Whoever wins keeps the horses and chooses where they want to hunt next spring. The women will stay with us because that is only right. Did you know the Ute people are slave traders themselves, and they are also polygamous? Makes me wonder why they can't get along better with the Mormons since they are of the same ilk as far as women are concerned. You'd think the Utes would be tired of stealing and then defending themselves from the Mormons. But, they continue to steal their horses, livestock, and even food and are in constant battle with the sect."

Henry followed Friday out into the night taking the places left to them within the ring of warriors surrounding two men who stood regarding one another with hatred so extreme, Henry could feel the heat of it. Black Coal appeared to be as dark as Friday but not nearly as good-looking. He, too, had a big ugly scar running over his forehead which no hat could ever hide. His nose ran long, dividing his high cheek-boned face in two, ending beak-like just over his narrow lips. He stood much taller than his opponent but seemed narrower in the chest and hips. His long black hair hung in a thick heavy braid to the middle of his back.

Black Hawk stood defiantly almost a head shorter than Black Coal. His chest was immense and hard muscled. His entire body seemed to ripple with strong muscles, thickly laid on his arms, back, and buttocks, with sinewy ones running down his legs. His hair had been clipped short, even with his chin, which stood out prominently as if as defiant as it owner. Other than his hideous chin, Black Hawk seemed almost a pretty man with wide-set eyes, a Roman nose, and beautiful, full lips. Henry knew that Yellow Flower had lain with both men and wondered if she wouldn't have preferred to remain with Black Hawk, the handsomer of the two.

Friday introduced Henry to his Northern Cheyenne friend and ally, Little Wolf and his son, Two Moons. Henry nodded to them, and Friday then made an announcement in a language Henry couldn't understand but knew it was to begin the battle between the two men. They both stiffened and raised their arms and began circling. Henry could see that each man had a massive knife tucked into his leather loin cloth.

The men continued to circle one another until Henry thought he would become dizzy watching them. Then, they began a sort of wrestling match. Twisting each other's arms when they could, tripping one another, throwing each other around as if they were sacks of grain. It looked more like a tumbling act Henry had watched at the circus when he was young.

They began a new tactic, punching one another, aiming at either the head or the belly. Black Hawk seemed to have the upper hand in this, sucker-punching Coal one after another. Coal grabbed Hawk's hair and suddenly pulled his head back with it and punched him in the nose. Henry knew it had been broken; he could hear the bones crack and saw that blood foamed out of each nostril. This infuriated Hawk, who now went for Coal's right eye, digging in with his thumb until blood began pouring out.

Suddenly, Black Coal pounced nearer to Black Hawk and sliced into Hawk's right arm. Hawk had his knife out and luckily, it looked as if he were left-handed since his right arm now bled profusely. Henry hadn't even noticed when and how they had gotten their knives out; they were so quick. Hawk made a low growling sound in his throat and lunged at Coal, slicing his left leg. They circled repeatedly, going around the warrior-made arena. Each time one would strike out at the other, they would jump aside, just in time.

Henry couldn't believe the bloodletting when Coal made progress with his knife stabs. Hawk now had a wound in his left side, both his legs, and a slice across his cheek bone. Henry could hardly stand it, the length of the battle, the blood, the disfigurement of such a handsome man; Hawk now had a broken nose, which would never be the same, and his cheek would bear the scar forever. Friday must have sensed Henry's dismay because he leaned close and said, "Don't worry, soldier, it's almost over."

Suddenly, Coal had Hawk laid out on the ground, threatening his jugular with his knife. Hawk attempted to grasp Coal's knife-armed wrist but could not over-power him. He kicked his legs in frustration and screamed out in pain as Coal cut off his right ear. Coal stood up and backed off. Hawk struggled to his feet and turned and walked to where the horses stood. He slowly mounted and rode off in defeat.

Henry didn't know he had been holding his breath until he let it out and gulped in more air. Friday called for Yellow Flower to come attend to her man, and each of the warriors slowly stood up and began to drift off with their blankets to sleep close to the fire, which young Two Moons now stoked with more wood. Friday turned to Little Wolf and invited him to come and share the pipe. He looked at Henry and asked if he was ready to hear the rest of his story.

Henry followed the men into the warm, cozy tepee wishing he could just curl up somewhere and sleep. The two Natives puffed on the pipe but Henry refused to indulge. "My lungs keep me from smoking."

Friday laughed. "Oh, have a puff; this sweet grass is good smoked, too. It doesn't burn the lungs and throat like that tobacco you white men smoke."

Henry, curious, reached for the pipe and took a puff. No, it didn't feel bad at all. But later he refused the proffered pipe when it was passed to him. He sat quietly as Friday and Little Wolf discussed where they would hunt tomorrow. Soon, Little Wolf stood to leave, wishing Henry well with the rest of his travels with Friday acting as interpreter. Henry nodded his head and said, "Good luck, to you, too."

Friday put the pipe aside and said, "Before I finish my story I need to ask you, what you think of our way of dealing with our Native enemies?"

Henry just shook his head. "I don't really know. Makes me think of our men who insist on boxing for money. It's the new thing that men now do for entertainment and for betting. I, personally, do not approve of boxing, two men beating each other up and being paid for it. But, at least this battle tonight did seem to settle things. I doubt that Black Hawk will ever steal a woman or a horse again." Friday snorted. "You'd be surprised. Those Utes thrive on stealing. I don't understand their ways at all. But speaking of stealing, let me finish my story. I and Little Wolf and some of our men are here for another purpose other than to take back our women and horses. This last February the Arapaho along with the Northern Cheyenne, Little Wolf's people, signed a treaty with the United States government at Fort Wise in the territory of Kansas. We agreed to give up our ancient hunting grounds north of here, which are still full of game and buffalo.

"In giving up this land, we agreed to move south into Indian Territory with the government promising us money, houses, tools, equipment for farming, livestock, and even our own mills for cutting timber and grinding grain. The government promised a reasonable portion of rights to the timber and water in our new lands. Each family was to become individual owners of forty-acre pieces of farmland. Acreage was to be set aside for the establishment and the support of schools where we could educate our children. We were to be paid $15,000 per year for each tribe for fifteen years. We agreed that moneys could be taken out of this promised money, totaling $450,000, to defray the costs of breaking up the land, fencing it, building houses, schools, and storage houses, and to provide the food items necessary to keep us going until we could raise our own." Friday shook his head, sad.

"We agreed to all this in good faith. We took our people, our families, to this place assigned to us. We arrived at Fort Washita in April and found that the Secretary of the Interior had not yet sent the check to fulfill these promises. On May 1, the fort was abandoned by

U.S. troops and the next day, Confederate troops from Texas moved in and took over. No one has helped us. We have found that the game is scarce, as is water, and there are no buffalo. Water rights, humph," Friday snorted. "There is no water to have rights over or timber. It is an awful place and my people are starving as are the Cheyenne.

"We are here, Henry, to hunt, to bring back enough food to get us through the winter, and next March we will return to our former lands where the game and buffalo are plenty. The United States government has not kept its promises so why should we? What do you think of that, Henry Plummer?"

Henry sighed, "I think it is a travesty and it makes me wonder if there were no civil war now, what would have happened."

Friday frowned, "I don't see the other Indian nations in any better circumstances than we are. I don't think the U.S. government has ever kept a treaty with any Indian Nation. I wanted to do this Henry, my people wished to do so, to become as the words of the treaty say, 'settled in the habits of industry and enterprise among ourselves.' We wanted to learn to become independent and to raise our own food. We are not stupid. We know that our old way of hunting and gathering can no longer be, can't sustain us even though our numbers diminish continuously. So, what do you think of it all, Henry Plummer?"

"I am very sad for you."

"It makes me feel much sorrow for my people and for the other nations. All I can think to do is to fight back when the time comes. We've tried meeting with the people in Washington, and we've signed treaties. I can't think of what else to do. So, Henry Plummer, on a lighter, happier note, would you consider fulfilling White Flower's wish to have a little half-white child. She motioned to me earlier that tonight would be a good time."

Henry shook his head back and forth in wonder, "Why would she want that? I don't understand."

Friday chuckled, "Well, for one, you are a handsome man. You have a presence; people know immediately that you are a thinker, and that you are kind. Sometimes, for whatever reason, it does help to have a child around with white blood in them; perhaps it proves we aren't so barbaric, that we can propagate with whites. I don't really know."

Henry thought a moment. "Wouldn't that ruin her for a proper marriage within the tribe?"

"No, not at all. It would make her more desirable, especially since fifteen of my warriors have seen you, watched you, and know what kind of man you are."

Henry remained silent, thinking. Here he was being offered a beautiful, young woman to make love to without any attachments. He'd paid for sex with less knowledge or respect for the woman. But, what if she did become pregnant. He would have a child out there in the wilderness, facing whatever fate that was in store for these people. Henry imagined a son of his fighting to near death as he had witnessed that night and shuddered.

"Well, soldier, you think about it. Meanwhile, let's have another puff on the pipe."

Henry smoked with Friday and suddenly felt quite tired and almost weak. It sure had relaxed, him whatever they inhaled, and he had to pee.

"I'm going out for a pee and a dip in the river. I'll need to think about this."

Friday chuckled and tossed him a blanket. "I'll see you in the morning, Henry Plummer."

Henry stumbled down to the riverbank, peed into the bushes, and then removed his clothing, carefully hanging it from the branches of what Friday had called cottonwood trees. He slowly waded into the water and shivering, plunged his entire body into the frigid June stream. It felt good after the heat inside the tepee and the warmth that had flooded his body when thinking about making love to White Flower. She was very lovely and refined, no comparison between young Emily and this young woman of the wilderness.

Henry slowly walked out of the water and onto the river bank, snatching up the blanket and wrapping it around his wet, chilled body. It was the rough, scratchy wool that he recognized as government issued. He felt embarrassed for his country's shoddy, dishonest treatment of these people who, in his view, had owned this land for centuries before the white man. But, he had no idea how to rectify this situation for his friend or his people. Henry sighed and walked back to the tepee, wishing that he still had his own private campfire.

White Flower waited for him inside, looking so tempting that Henry put all doubt out of his mind, succumbing to his own fertile thoughts. Friday was nowhere to be seen, and after Henry sat down beside this night's bed partner, he turned to White Flower and gently picked up her hand and softly kissed each knuckle, signaling that he would make love with her.

Henry woke early the next morning. He slowly and gingerly extricated his body from White Flower. She had wrapped her long, lovely limbs around his hips and waist. Henry felt great regret on removing himself from such a warm, pleasurable place. He tenderly swept away a tress of hair from her cheek and stooped to kiss it, whispering, "Thank you, sweet angel of the prairie."

Henry pulled on his trousers, shirt, and jacket, donned his big, black hat and just as he leaned over to exit the tepee, he heard White Flower say, "Thank you, Henry Plummer."

Henry walked to where the horses were tethered, careful not to step in the streaks of blood and gore, which lay in what had been the arena for last night's battle. He saw Black Hawk's ear lying there in the grass and dirt and fought to keep from losing his stomach. He checked to see if everything was in its proper place in his saddle bags and finding his stash of money, counted some out.

Little Wolf stepped out of a tepee, and Henry walked to him and handed him the wad of good, federally issued money. They shook hands and nodded to one another. Henry mounted Avenger and started out for the trail. A few minutes later he heard Friday yelling, "Henry Plummer! You dog! I wasn't asking for money!" Henry only lifted his hat, waved it in the air, and galloped off. Henry had left $400 and hoped it would at least keep the starvation-wolf away from Friday's people until they could return to their hunting grounds.

Henry made good progress after that and didn't see anyone until he stopped at Fort Bridger. It was a fine fort, newly rebuilt after being burned a few years earlier. It had much to offer in news, supplies, and advice. Henry refurbished his food goods and greedily listened to news of the war. The Confederates had named Richmond, Virginia, their capital. Arkansas, Tennessee, and North Carolina had seceded from the Union, and U.S. troops now occupied Baltimore and had seized Alexandria, Virginia. There had been other 'engagements' at numerous places in Virginia.

Henry had encountered a small wagon train at Fort Bridger, but when he arrived at Independence Rock he saw his first real wagon train composed of mostly German and Scandinavian immigrants who had just recently entered the States, and who had organized to leave for Oregon as soon as the weather had permitted. They had traveled for a long time and were jubilant to have reached Independence Rock by June 25.

Trappers had named the huge granite outcrop Independence Rock because they met there every Fourth of July to trade and celebrate. Now, a prominent point on the Emigrant Trail, it took on a new meaning. Settlers moving west to Utah, California, or Oregon knew that if they reached the rock by Independence Day, they would more than likely reach their destinations before snowfall.

Henry joined the many people that either carved or painted their names on the face of the rock. That night the wagon train held a big celebration with food, drink, and dancing. Henry found these warm, humorous, and hardy people quite entertaining as well as generous with their food and drink and regretted parting with them.

July 14, Henry reached Fort Laramie. Happy to be there, he felt like celebrating. He had run out of coffee, tea, and sugar since he had met many wagon trains, one after another. He had traded nearly all these things for some amazing home-cooked meals and had met so many interesting people; he felt he couldn't have done better had he traveled all of Europe. He had seen just about every nationality from Europe and the Scandinavian countries. The foods he had tasted were just as varied and delicious.

Henry met up with a bizarre army officer at the store as he made his purchases. The man had lost one ear, a piece of his nose, and three fingers—all in saloon fights. He told Henry he figured for all the barroom battles he had engaged in, he may just as well join the U.S. army. He quickly rose in the ranks, he told Henry, just because he didn't have any sense to be frightened during a fray and had taken many risks. Ross Kearney invited Henry to a party in the officer's quarters in the huge, ostentatious looking white house.

Soldiers nicknamed it Old Bedlam since so many celebrations there had ended up in craziness. Henry enjoyed the event immensely and came away thinking that all these people traveling, all these men serving in the army, anyone in general, in these times, seemed to think one had to live life to the fullest because who knew what tomorrow would bring.

Henry continued to follow the Platte River Road into Nebraska Territory. The first landmark he saw there was the famous Chimney Rock, which was a huge outcrop of rock with a high, narrow piece of rock reaching high into the sky from the exact center of the mound. Henry chuckled when remembering that the natives called this phenomenon, Elk Penis.

Henry stopped at Fort Kearny where he resupplied his food bag, and shortly after leaving, he turned off onto what had been named, Independence Road. He followed this trail down into Kansas. First, he stopped at the Rock Creek Station, another outpost on this cutoff trail, where he spent the night, renting a room just so he could sleep in a bed again. By September 20, Henry reached St. Mary's Mission, which appeared to be more of a town than a mission and straddled the Fort Leavenworth Road sitting next to the Kansas River.

Henry booked passage on a steamboat that made weekly runs to Kansas City. Henry checked into a new hotel and enjoyed his first hot bath in months. He had a gigantic steak along with mashed potatoes and gravy, some good wine, and apple pie for dessert. After that he went up to his room, fell into bed, and slept until one o'clock the next afternoon.

Henry ate a hearty breakfast in the hotel's dining room and then found a barber shop. After that he visited a local saloon, telling himself that he needed to do so since his barber had been a quiet man and hadn't offered any information. The saloon had patrons of many sorts and pursuits, hosting what appeared to be farmers, soldiers, politicians, ruffians, criminals, and men already running from the war. Talk was loud and plentiful, and all Henry needed to do was to sit quietly and listen to the many conversations flowing all around him.

The most interesting news came from talk about what people seemed to consider the most important and bloodiest battle fought so far, which had occurred on July 21 near Manassas, Virginia. They called it Bull Run after a tributary creek to the Potomac River. Union Brigadier General McDowell had been coerced by public opinion into attempting to march on the confederate capital of Richmond in hopes of putting a quick end to the rebellion. He encountered General Beauregard and his Confederate troops, who proved to be just as green.

But the Confederates had received reinforcements from troops led by Joseph Johnston and Thomas Jackson, causing the Union troops to retreat without orders to Washington. The battle proved to be devastating on both sides, and the nation now understood their civil war could be long and bloody. Some deserting Confederates sat in a corner amongst themselves, and Henry could hear them toasting and drinking to one of the Confederate leaders they now called Stonewall Jackson. One of the men stood up, declaring loudly, "Here's to Thomas J. Jackson, who, stood like a stone wall with his well-disciplined troops."

Henry wondered why they weren't there, alongside Stonewall, then, if they thought him so wonderful, and he lowered his head, shaking it as he downed his drink and snorted in disgust, Friday-style.

"Give this young man another drink, would ya son? He looks as if he needs to relax a little."

Henry turned to his neighbor, "Why would you say that? I'm not too happed up about anything, just hate to hear braggarts that really have nothing to brag about, you know?"

Henry liked the older man the moment they began conversing. Henry explained to Joe, Joe Jacobs was his name, that he had just gotten off the Emigrant Trail to "do some long-awaited business" in Kansas.

Joe just laughed, and asked, "Now, what would that be, young man. You really don't seem too business-like."

Henry smiled and said, "Well, let's just say that I needed to come here and am now trying to get the lay of the land and to find out what's happening here, especially where and with whom all the proslavery and antislavery sentiments lie. If you would indulge me in some information, I would be grateful, and, then, perhaps I'll trust you enough to tell you what my business is."

Joe looked Henry over, long and hard. He finally spoke. "Well, son, how long have you been out of the range of news?"

Henry smiled, "I left Salt Lake City months ago. I read my last newspaper there the morning I left. I just hope that not all the battles so far had the same outcome for the Union as Manassas."

Joe laughed, "I take it, then, that you're a Union man?"

"Yes," answered Henry. "And, if you don't want a thing to do with me now, I will understand, sir."

"No, son, don't you worry, it seems we're of the same mind. I'll try to help you out with whatever you need to know."

Henry nodded. He took a long drink and then asked, "So, Bull Run, the Manassas Battle, that's the war news as of now?"

"Yes, don't mean a thing, really. Bloody as hell for both sides. A terrible initiation for them all, I would say."

"What's going on around here? Is there still much border strife between the Kansans and the Missourians?"

Joe leaned back and slapped his leg hard. "Well, now, that's an entirely different story. Lot's shenanigans going on between the slavers and antis; it's all-out civil war, as I see it. The Kansans and Missourians have been watching each other real close to see how each would react at the outbreak of war. In June, Unionist Brigadier General Nathaniel Lyon drove Governor Jackson from the Missouri state capital at Jefferson City. Jackson then called for 50,000 Missourians to come help with the resistance.

"They ended up with a formal Missouri State Guard commanded by a Major General Sterling Price. Our Kansas governor, Charles Robinson, saw Jackson's proclamation as a declaration of war. He called for Kansas to take the offensive, and Jayhawkers led by James Montgomery and Charles Jennison answered his call, although, both men have caused considerable strife and mayhem long before this. People around here wonder whether Jennison acts out of hatred of slavery or because of his love of plunder.

"This summer's been hot and crazy on Jennison's part. On June 19, he raised a sizeable 'army' and has been harassing Missourians ever since. In July, Jennison killed a number of secesh in Morristown, Missouri, and in August, he looted stores in Harrisonville.

"This late August, 1,200 troops gathered and organized the Kansas Brigade led by Senator James Lane, an extremist, and in my view, one of the most crazed Kansas anti-slavers. Following the state line, looting, burning, murdering, and even raping all along the border, Jennison and Lane have kept Missourians terrorized.

"Just yesterday, Lane and his bunch sacked Osceolo, Missouri, ransacking the entire town, hardly anything left of it, we hear. They robbed the bank, sacked and destroyed stores and homes, looted the courthouse, and set fire to the whole town. Heard the men got so drunk they couldn't even ride outa that place, had to ride out in wagons and such. Now, I can see fighting for what's right, but acting like asses, I'm ashamed for them. And, murdering and raping, that's downright criminal. Supposedly, they executed nine men yesterday."

Henry sat quiet for a minute and then ordered a drink for them. He rubbed his scar, thinking. "Tell me, please, what makes these men tick. Why are they so violent? Couldn't they just protect the Kansas border without being so mercenary? You can't tell me that all Missourians are confederate minded. Are they?"

Joe shook his head, "Many of them aren't until these Kansans git through with them. I've heard tell that many of these men, these poor farmers, after being burned out and robbed, go join up with the Confederate army. Don't blame them."

Joe sat stroking his chin. "Well, Henry, first I think I should tell you that initially, Missourians started this hateful border war. Beginning in the 1850s, they messed with people here, you know, after the Kansas-Nebraska Act, which did away with the Missouri Compromise. We were supposed to rely on popular sovereignty to decide whether Kansas would be admitted as a free or slave state. Makes them nervous, I guess, to think that if Kansas becomes a free state, their slaves could easily escape to Kansas and could never be captured and returned.

"So, when these anti-slavers moved into Kansas, Missourians became agitated, the Bushwhackers organized, and began raiding our border. They've got strong leaders, these Bushwhackers, men who keep them under control such as William Quantrill, Bloody Bill Anderson, and Jeff Thompson. They live out in the bush and come into our Kansas towns to do their vicious robbing, plundering, arson, and killing. Out in our countryside, they use ambush tactics to capture men, their horses, wagons, you name it.

"In May, the Missouri government organized the Missouri State Guard and appointed General Sterling Price as their commander. Price comes with a fine reputation. He fought in the Mexican-American War, with success and honor. He served as Governor of Missouri from '53-'57, and before that he made a successful life for himself as a lawyer and a planter. Price and his men have been appointed expressly to protect their border and to keep Kansans from organizing any further to raid and harass their people.

"Charles Jennison studied medicine and practiced in Wisconsin and then later in Minnesota. But I've never seen a doctor so bloodthirsty, opposite of what he's been trained and sworn to do, if you ask me. He moved here to Osawatomie in '57 and quickly became a loyal follower of John Brown as a radical believer in a free-state Kansas. Soon, he had organized a group of men and began raiding in Missouri.

"He loves plundering and sometimes has so many horses, cattle, and hogs along with wagons, carriages, saddles, bridles, furniture, silver, china, jewelry, he has to hold a public auction to get rid of it all and turn it into cash. We know that he has executed at least two pro-slave men by hanging.

"Senator Jim Lane has organized the Kansas Brigade, which he has led into many border frays and has also engaged in the most vicious guerrilla fighting. His actions at Osceola yesterday are a fine example of how he operates. Between Lane and Jennison, much of Missouri's moveable wealth has been transferred to Kansas, and they have also helped turn many a Missourian into a Confederate. So, there you have it, Henry. I do know that Jennison has been told he could muster men as the Seventh Regiment Kansas Volunteer Cavalry."

Henry ordered another drink for them both, twirling the glass he had just emptied. He shook his head, not knowing what to think about Joe's revelations. He had imagined his participation in the fight as more disciplined and honorable. He wasn't quite sure what he had expected, but surely not this violent destruction of homes and people, let alone the looting. Nothing that Joe described sounded noble or upright. He wanted to feel good about his acts of revenge, like he was making things better, somehow. Henry finished his drink and bid Joe good night saying he needed to walk and get some fresh air.

"When does Jennison plan on mustering the men for the Seventh?"

"He's got until November 1 at Fort Leavenworth."

"Thanks, Joe. See that you take care of yourself. Nice talking to you." Henry shook his hand and left.

CHAPTER 11

NOVEMBER 1861— MAY 1862

Henry still wished to join a Kansas anti-slavery organization and decided that becoming a member of the volunteer regiment would be the best way to carry out his plan. He and his horse, Avenger, boarded the steamboat and went as far as Kansas City, where Henry bought supplies and then started down the trail to Fort Leavenworth. Both Henry and Avenger enjoyed being out on the trail again, and Henry wondered what to expect of barrack-life, hoping they wouldn't spend too much time at the fort.

When Henry arrived at the fort, he couldn't believe the number of men milling around. He asked a group of them where he could find the commissioner's office, and they pointed to a small, square building situated close to the gate. There were numerous large buildings built high, almost looking like churches with attractive towers. Henry discovered later that these served as lookouts, so no matter what building you were in, you had easy access to viewing the surrounding area.

Henry tied Avenger to the rail in front of the commissioner's office and entered. Several men stood in a line ahead of Henry. He signed up as a volunteer for the Seventh Regiment Cavalry but for the shortest time possible, twelve months. He swore the oath promising to protect his fellow soldiers, the United States of America, and to obey his commanding officers. The clerk gave Henry instructions as to where to take his horse, where to pick up his rifle and ammunition, and where to go to arrange for his lodging.

Henry found the fort to be quite extensive and complex with many buildings: the commissary and storage buildings; the Quartermaster's office among the many barracks; the chapel, which overlooked a large, hilly, and wooded cemetery; the three-storied general's house of red brick with large windows and a screened porch; the artillery and its barracks; the arsenal, with rows of cannons and wagons; the mess hall; the officer's saloon and eatery; and finally the stables overlooking a large pasture. As Henry settled Avenger in his pasture, he was amazed by the number of horses.

Henry hated barrack living the minute he moved in, and though neat and well-organized, he could smell the mingling odors of dozens of men wafting through stale air. The latrine smelled worse, and though the groups of men talking kept their voices low, the constant hum made Henry feel anxious.

When Henry followed them to the evening meal at the mess hall, he experienced his first moment of pleasure, smelling the appetizing scent of roast beef and gravy. But, that too left him feeling disappointed when he discovered that the delicious aroma gave false testimony to the taste of the food. Sleeping in the barracks was as bad as Henry had imagined; the snores, men talking in their sleep, teeth grinding, scratching, and the awful smell of farts along with those resounding noises all kept Henry from a deep and restful slumber.

He woke up the next morning and asked another early riser where a man could bathe. The man told him that if he were up to it, he could ask permission and stroll down to the river; otherwise the pumps outside the latrines would be his best bet. Henry walked to the gate, where the officer gave him permission but warned him to not be too long because they would be bugling to roust the men and begin serving breakfast.

Henry took his time walking down the steep hill to the Missouri River. Not too far away, he could see where it converged with the smaller Kansas River. A light mist rose off both streams, fighting to survive in the sun's fresh, hot blaze. Henry soon encountered a well-worn path among the willows and took off his clothes when he reached a section of the bank where the river curved in, making a natural bathing hole. He quickly waded in until the water covered his private parts, and as he lathered soap and scrubbed away, the sluggish, weighed-down feeling from a sleepless night soon dissipated.

Henry felt hungry, thinking that there would be no way for the cooks to ruin something as simple as breakfast. As he began his trek up the hill and he looked up, the fort appeared majestic sitting on the bluff overlooking the Missouri. The tall buildings within the walls stood out because of their towers, making Henry think of European castles. The immensity of the area inside the walls allowed the original designers to retain many of the trees and bushes that naturally grew there. As Henry walked back in through the gate, he thought the place pretty.

Breakfast, consisting of sausages, biscuits, and gravy, didn't taste bad, and it finally assuaged the empty, hollow feeling in his belly. Henry listened closely to the talk around him. The hall soon became a din with the hundreds of men speaking at once. It sounded as if he had just made it in time since today would be the day the men would be assigned to the eight different companies of the Seventh Kansas.

Just as they finished breakfast, the men were quieted and told to go to the center of the marching grounds to hear their final orders and with whom they would fall in with as each company roster was called. Close to a thousand men walked out into the wide, open field. They were told to get in line at one of the five tables directly in front of them.

Henry entered a line and soon stood before the gentleman at the table.

"Name?"

"Henry Plummer."

The man ran his finger down a list of names and said, "You'll be in Company J under the command of Lieutenant-Colonel Daniel R. Anthony." He pointed in the general direction where a group of men already stood. Henry walked toward them and when he reached them, he looked them over. They appeared to be decent. Henry began looking at groups around them and saw that there was one group that looked as if they belonged someplace much like San Quentin. Henry returned his attention to his own group, glad that most of them seemed gentlemen and sounded, for the most part, well educated.

After the men had been divided up, they were told to have a seat on the grass and that they would be addressed by several the company leaders. First, John Brown Jr. spoke to them. He stood a tall, handsome man with surprisingly kind eyes, considering his recent imprisonment and bad treatment by the Confederates at the prison where he had been held. He had a full beard and moustache and appeared quite intelligent. He would command Company K.

Marshall Cleveland spoke to them next and announced that he would lead Company H. He had short black hair, a trimmed moustache and beard, a long thin nose, and eyes that looked out into the world piercingly. He seemed to have acquired every tough, criminal-minded, ex-convict, and ruffian type of man into his company. Henry had heard that he was a former convict himself and felt relief in knowing that he had been placed with a much more refined group of men.

Next, Henry's company's leader, Colonel Daniel R. Anthony, addressed the assembly, and Henry thought his the most lunatic approach to things, hearing him state that above all else, the regiment should, whenever conceivable, free as many slaves as possible and encourage an insurrection on their part. The man had a high, large forehead and short, curly hair. He had a well-trimmed beard and was handsome. He spoke of his involvement in the Underground Railroad in Leavenworth. At least he had high ideals and standards and was not afraid to do something about them. He also sheepishly told the crowd that his sister was the famous, Susan B. Anthony and that they had both been raised to embrace social issues to which they should devote their lives.

Next, James H. Lane addressed them, and Henry realized there was no end to fiery, obsessive, and irrational people ready to fight against slavery. The unbridled hatred he saw in each of these charismatic leaders unnerved him, and he wondered if he was up to "mustering" with such individuals. A vision of Pauline and the tears she had shed when he went to remove her black stocking floated before his mind's eye, and he knew, he damned well knew that, yes, he did belong here.

"Doc" Jennison, commander of the entire regiment, gave the last rallying speech. He appeared to be just as radical as the others, urging everyone to remember what Quantrill and the Bushwhackers had done to Kansas in the 1850s.

"We will ransack, loot, and burn every pro-slaver's home and belongings just as he and his men have done to us. We will free every slave and put them into our service and ensure that every Confederate-minded man we meet will be crushed or killed by our hands. We will make sure that the mention of our new Seventh Volunteer Calvary makes every pro-slavery person's heart quake." With that said he swept off his coon-fur hat and bowed to the assembly of men.

Henry thought, of all these leaders that spoke, Jennison seemed the most insincere and the least commanding. His dress seemed affected, like the rest of him. He wore layer after layer of outlandish clothing over trousers that gathered around his knees, meeting buckskin, full-calved boots. His peered wildly out of his skull, and Henry felt sorry for anyone who had ever been victim to his healing, finding it difficult to believe Jennison had ever been doctor enough to be called "Doc." They were all expected to address him as Doc Jennison.

Jennison finished his talk with the reminder that he personally thought of the regiment as the Independent Mounted Kansas Jayhawkers. "The regular army will be taking care of the eastern section of Missouri, and we will be handling these border towns and farms. We will march out day after tomorrow. We have lots to do, so get some rest, make sure you have collected all your rations and bedding for we'll be doing all our eating and sleeping out on the trail. Bring as much warm clothing and blankets as possible because the old-timers predict a cold and wet winter. But we won't stop for weather; we won't stop for anything.

"Our objective, men, is to protect the Union supply trains in Jackson County against those god-damn Bushwhackers, who can't seem to keep their hands off our supplies, and, most of all, to put down Confederate-minded people, and to get those rebels to pledge their allegiance once again to the Union. We'll be following a scorched-earth policy; after we loot, we burn everything. That's it men, practice your marksmanship and become familiar with your new rifles. If we come across a Confederate unit, find cover, trees, buildings, or whatever, to stay alive while shooting the bloody hell out of them. We'll be breaking your companies up into squadrons now."

They started out early the next morning with Company H riding ahead of the rest of the column so far that at times Henry couldn't see them. Their first stop was in Leavenworth where the men entered the saloons and sacked them one by one. Henry could only watch, amazed at their behavior. He couldn't believe the waste of time and that they were stealing from Kansans. By the time they left town, most of the men were sloppy drunk.

That night at their first camp, hardly a man ate an evening meal. Henry and a few other sober men gathered firewood and got the campfires burning. They cooked their meal, joined the others for a drink or two, and then made their beds. Sleeping was the easiest part of the day because by the time they were ready to retire, many of the drinkers had passed out and all was quiet and peaceful.

Sullen men greeted the next day, making coffee and breakfast at their campfires, attempting to erase the effects of the previous day's debauchery. Company H went on ahead as before, and soon Henry could see burning homes and fields. Cleveland's men were doing what they did best, looting and burning. They left piles of plunder near the road for the men bringing up the rear with empty wagons to fill for an auction. Jennison stayed behind to finish his work in organizing the regiment and would join them later.

Henry's company came under fire when they reached the Little Blue River. His company had come across some Missouri irregulars who were just getting up for the day. They managed to drive the Missourians from their camp, a high price to pay to chase off only a handful and steal their horses. But, rabid Anthony, Henry's pet name for him, called it a victory. Henry also wondered what in the hell happened to Company H, why hadn't they joined in the fray?

They kept moving south, slowly, stopping occasionally to burn some wealthy farmer's home and what crops they could find in the fields or stored away. Many owners and their families had fled to either Europe or New York for the winter, so these forays onto their land, plundering household items, stealing livestock, horses, and their Negroes didn't bother Henry much. He didn't care for the burning and was already sick and tired of its stench. He smelled it when he rode, when he ate, and when he slept, and when he looked out into the landscape all he could see was an ugly, gray haze hanging over the land.

Henry also disliked the way the Negroes that his company had so proudly freed were being treated. Many of the squadrons took advantage of them, putting them to work as cooks, collecting firewood, setting up camp, taking care of the horses, and then decamping every morning. The former slaves had been given horses, mules, and wagons for transportation as well as food, and those men who could ride and shoot well were incorporated into the forces. But it was mostly the attitude these men held toward these rescued people that bothered Henry, and he came to believe that most of the men were in this for personal gain or just for the excitement and the excuse to kill, loot, burn, and bully people.

Then, there were the rabids such as his commander, Lieutenant-Colonel Anthony, John Brown Jr. and his entire company of fanatical abolitionists, Doc Jennison, and the regular army general, James H. Lane who looked out at the world through the exact same piercing, wild eyes, crazed with uncompromised hatred for all Missourians whether they were rebel or not. Missouri had seceded from the Union on October 28 and would be admitted into the Confederacy late November. That was enough excuse for the radicals.

The few men seen as the column passed all claimed to be Union supporters, but that did not stop the raiders from taking all that was of value off their persons and sometimes shooting them execution style.

November 17 Anthony had his men loot and burn Pleasant Hill killing eleven guerrillas in the process and recapturing a wagon train, which the Lieutenant claimed as Union property. The next day they went on to Independence and though not destroying the town, did much damage to buildings and homes, plundering again until they had all the empty wagons filled with furniture, valuables, and food stuffs. The day after this noble venture, Companies H and J began the march back to Fort Leavenworth with their heavy loads of goods, droves of livestock, horses, and hundreds of Negroes.

November 30 companies H and J were ordered to West Point, Missouri, to counter a thrust by Price. He never appeared, but the two companies made good by looting and burning the town bringing home 150 mules, 40 horses, and 129 Negroes. The freed slaves received 60 horses and mules, some oxen, and wagons full of furniture and household goods. Some of the newly freed men were armed and given a speech to stir them up against the rebels.

December 13 the Kansans burned out Papinsville and the next day, Butler. Then they were satisfied to go back to Fort Leavenworth for Christmas. Jennison held an auction to get rid of the plunder and turn it into cash. Company J and K had been chosen to help with the event. Henry couldn't believe the number of things sold that Kansans claimed to be theirs in the first place. "Oh! That's my mother's china, been in the family for generations!"

"This silver has been in my family for years."

It seemed to Henry that the Kansans and Missourians, besides hatred, found themselves passing personal items back and forth across the border.

On Christmas day many of the men received passes to go into town. Henry felt low-spirited and maudlin because out on the marauding trail, he had been thinking a lot about his life and how he had no one, no family or home to go to as did many of the men. He rarely communicated with his family in Maine.

He didn't know what else to do with his time but to spend it in a saloon. Luckily, Henry walked into one that had faro tables, and he settled down to do some gambling. It had been a long time since he had last done so, but he did well and worried about what to do with his money.

Henry kept his money on his person always, and his mind kept wandering to a forbidden place. He detested this new life he had chosen and couldn't help but think desertion. He had not yet been ordered to do something that clashed with his moral values. He hadn't been forced to shoot anyone, and he hadn't been asked to set fire. But, he knew the time would come, and then what would he do?

He laughed when he thought of all the non-Kansans and non-Missourians who had percolated into this border war. Henry knew for sure that most of these men did not have the same mission as did he, attempting to make things right and fight the battle against slavery. No, most of these raiding and plundering men bragged continuously how they were here for the sport. Henry referred to them in his mind as the Mercenaries.

The Jayhawkers began a new raiding campaign with a vengeance the morning of New Year's Day. They rode out "cleaning up" what they had missed before as they had traveled south, choosing smaller, poorer places. It broke Henry's heart to see these people burnt out of their homes that he knew had cost them much to build. Henry worried about where they would go now, these homeless people, all of whom had declared allegiance to the United States. Henry knew by their faces and the indignant fervor in their voices that they spoke honestly.

Henry also felt fury and shame whenever a younger man appeared; they found an excuse to shoot him, right there on the spot making themselves both judge and executioner. He would watch the horror turn into grief on a young woman's face, who would gather her children around her trying to shield their eyes from their father's violent end. This is no way to fight a war, he thought, but then remembered the many shocking stories of the war in the east. It seemed the entire country had been tainted by a wave of ugly hate and violence, infesting the nation with a disease that made people act vicious and deranged.

By the time they reached Pleasant Hill, their object of punishment that day, columns of smoke rose up into the frigid air behind them. Henry could look back and see exactly where the road ran by the plumes of smoke. He observed how the regiment never strayed far from the main road. Why was that? Too lazy? Would they go further into the land and woods once they had destroyed everything along the byway? Henry's mind wandered again to that forbidden place, thinking of leaving the craziness, abandoning his post, and getting as far away from the madness as possible.

They moved onto Morristown for their afternoon's delight. Morristown had not yet been targeted and there was much to do there. A few richer-looking places stood out among the many humble abodes. Anthony ordered them to attack the well-to-do places first and had his closest in command enter the homes and shoo out whoever was within, while he sat out on his horse, looking bored. Henry couldn't believe the nonchalance with which his commander viewed this awful mission. Most times the house would be empty, and Henry would breathe a sigh of relief.

At their last chosen target, an elderly couple living with an aged son whose mind wasn't right came slowly and but proudly out their front door leading him by the hand. Henry could see his dementia immediately by looking at his eyes, which wandered around in their sockets as if lost not knowing on what to focus. Their son seemed to sense danger and began to circle around his parents, refusing to stand still and simply hold his mother's hand. He began a strange moaning lament that Henry could not understand.

Anthony ordered his favorite henchmen to fire the house, and the woman began crying and screaming out, "No! Please! The fire will scare him crazy! Please!" As the flames burst out and windows shattered, the poor afflicted man went wild. His parents attempted to hold him but were much too weak to keep him within their grasp. His circling around like a raging animal in pain became more intense as he now loudly barked out jumbled words in his hoarse hardly-ever-used voice. Anthony suddenly lifted his arm and shot him. The poor soul died instantly, and there was stunned silence.

Anthony leveled his gaze and gun on the couple and ordered, "Now git, before I shoot you." At that moment, a gunshot rang out and the lieutenant grabbed at his right arm, which held his weapon.

The elderly man lay dead with a revolver lying beside him. His woman grieved over him weeping and cursing. Without warning, she picked up the revolver, sat down between her husband and son, grabbed her husband's lifeless hand, and shot herself in the head.

The men went about their business, silent and shocked. Anthony ordered Henry and three other men to bury them as he nursed his nicked arm. Henry looked at his commander as if he was as daft as the man he had just shot.

"Sir, what if they have relatives that would prefer to do it themselves, proper in a church with a sermon, some words spoke over the grave in the church yard?"

"Just get on with it, son, before I shoot you for being insubordinate!"

"But, sir, it isn't right," Henry returned in an as even-and-reasonable tone as possible.

Anthony gave him a deadly look and yelled, "Just shut up and do it. Their family can dig them up if they want. I don't need to leave these bodies behind, unburied. I won't have it. Won't risk the consequences."

Well, thought Henry as he performed the unpleasant task, at least Anthony has some sense of right and wrong to the point he wants to cover up his wrongdoing. The rest of the men were ordered to leave this place alone as far as plundering was concerned, another sign that Anthony's conscience stung him. Henry felt glad for his officer's sorry state of mind and couldn't help but decide that, yes, he more than disliked the intense man; he hated him.

The next day they moved on to Rose Hill the next day which was a picturesque little burg full of several elegant homes. Anthony seemed to have slept off his remorse because he ordered just about every home looted and fired, and then went about decimating the countryside with renewed vigor and purpose. Doc Jennison's company caught up with them and soon the area became so smoky one could hardly see more than twenty yards ahead. They burned down more than forty-five houses.

He ordered more than the usual amount of men shot as they swept through the town and countryside. Little did they know that Rose Hill was a little settlement full of pacifists, and that is why there were many younger, healthy men still around. A man kept trying to explain the situation but to no avail. Anthony wanted him shot and gestured the order to Henry, but Henry pretended not to understand. Fortunately for Henry, the rider next to him understood the order was for him and summarily shot the unfortunate man.

As they moved further south out of town, Henry saw, to his dismay, more well-to-do homesteads ahead with crops still in the fields. Anthony rode up to Henry and ordered him to burn the crops.

"Can you at least find the balls to do that, Plummer?"

Henry nodded, concerned that Anthony now knew his name and that meant he was on his list and not a good one. As Henry rode off to round up men to help him, he attempted to recall the image of Pauline being thrown in front of the moving wagon, of men, Bushwhackers, pushing and pulling her out of the hotel, swearing and cursing at her. But, he could not recapture the hatred, the vengeful spirit that had lain in his heart and mind so long.

He figured his conscience was telling him that he had accomplished what he had set out to do, and that this destruction and annihilation of the enemy had gone too far. Besides, Kansas would be admitted into the Union as a free state January 29. The origination of the border war between Kansas and Missouri was now moot. These bullies should go fight in the real war and test the manhood they seemed so proud of and fight real men instead of attacking defenseless old men, women, children, and pacifists.

Henry finished his unsavory task and galloped down the road to the next farmstead. The house looked newly built and had two swings hanging between wooden posts along with a homemade slide carved out of wood that had been sanded smooth and varnished to a high gloss. Children, Henry thought, there are children living in this house, and he swallowed hard as he approached the mayhem that surrounded the house and yard.

"What's going on here?" he asked as he noticed several men lying about either dead or dying.

A man from Company H explained to Henry that a handsome woman had come out of the house to greet them, and her looks had given some men the urge to rape her before the rest of the regiment arrived. She began shooting at them, once their intent became obvious to her. She had taken them by surprise not only with her outburst but by shooting three men, dead, with incredible accuracy. In the confusion that ensued, she escaped into the woods.

Just then Anthony rode up and after listening as the man retold his explanation for the turmoil around them, he looked at Henry with a challenge in his eye, and ordered him off into the woods to retrieve her and bring her back. Henry rode off, reluctant at first, and then he had an epiphany. He could ride out and find her, save her, and save himself from this hysteria. Henry took off on Avenger. He pushed him hard and the horse took off doing honor to the racing blood in his veins.

They entered the woods and were forced to slow down because of the verdant forest. Henry finally stopped and listened, not knowing which way to go. He was rewarded with the sounds of sobbing and got off his horse, moving in that direction as stealthily as he could among the immense piles of deadwood and undergrowth. Then, he could see her and saw that she looked near to collapsing. He tied Avenger to a sturdy branch and inched his way toward her and when he was close enough, grabbed at her, finding it a struggle to subdue her.

"Listen," he said, as her pinioned her arms behind her. "I'm on your side. I'm am sick and tired of this awful, deadly marauding and want out. Just calm down and we'll ride as far away from this as possible, through these woods. They're too damn lazy to follow us for long. Don't worry." She stilled, digesting his words and then began to struggle again.

Henry tried a new tactic. "Please, I'm sincere. God send me to hell if I'm not."

"Swear it on a loved one's life."

Henry laughed bitterly. "I'm sorry but the love of my life died having our baby. I'm here only to avenge what the Bushwhackers did to her years ago and now I've had enough. There is no sense to this border strife. It's done. These men I came with are the worst sort, and I can't be a part of them any longer. Is there someplace safe where I can take you, to relatives, friends, or someone else? Do you have a husband?"

She nodded but said, choking on her words, "Yes, but he is dead. I just received word three weeks ago."

Henry could feel her body heaving with grief and sobs. He slowly let go of her arms and pulled her around to face him, wrapping his arms about her. She laid her head on his shoulder and cried until she began hiccupping. Henry moved away from her, gently pushing her mass of rich, black hair from her face, tucking it behind her ears.

He put his hands on her shoulders and then held up her chin with one hand, looking her in the eye, saying, "We need to move on or else they may catch up with us. Will you ride with me?"

She nodded and said, "There's a cabin about ten miles from here. Will that be far enough, you think?"

Henry walked back to get his horse. They rode in silence with her giving directions to a path she knew, the only break in the quiet between them. When they reached the cabin, Henry helped her down from Avenger's back.

"I'll go find some firewood and put the horse out back." He handed her his saddle bag containing his rations. "Here's some food to get us through the night. Perhaps I can find some game while gathering wood." She nodded and walked into the cabin.

By the time Henry returned she had opened the cabin and was sweeping debris out the door. Henry carried in the wood he had gathered and tumbled it into a box sitting next to the fireplace. He looked around the cabin and saw that it was well furnished. A full-sized bed sat in one corner and on the opposite wall stood a chiffarobe. On the other side of the cabin a table sat in the corner and a small wood stove across from that. Shelves above the stove held cooking utensils, pots and pans, and a collection of dishes, glassware, and cups.

Henry went out and gathered more wood. This time he set the wood into the fireplace so it could be easily fired. He came in with one more armload and then took his rifle out to hunt for something for dinner. Even though they were both in dire straits, hiding out from crazed and fanatical Jayhawkers, Henry felt happy and at peace just being out in a heavily wooded area hunting again. It made him think of home, which brought his mind around to what he was going to do now. Where could he go? He had become a deserter, and they were usually shot on sight if recognized by any military person or the home guard that specialized in hunting down those who deserted.

Then he remembered the number of Confederate men he had met on the trail who were all heading to Washington Territory, which covered an immense area in the far northwest corner of the United States. They expected to not only escape capture, but also to become rich with all the gold mining rumored to be so viable out there. Henry shook his head; he would much prefer to go to Salt Lake City where there was law and order, but that would probably be too risky since it seemed to be the hub of civilization in the great northwest. He could easily come across someone from his past who would recognize him, jeopardizing his safety and well being.

Henry returned to the cabin with two rabbits but told the woman they would need to wait until much later to start a fire or to cook any dinner. He was quite sure they were safely out of range and far enough away from any search parties. He explained to her that Jennison's men preferred to make camp early so they could enjoy the pleasures of eating and drinking to the fullest, and they never camped but a mile or two from the main byway.

Henry went out to skin the rabbits and make them ready for roasting. He had unpacked his saddle bag and laid out what food he had and was pleased that there was a pump inside the cabin so water wouldn't be a problem. Darkness had descended by the time they got everything situated for the night. Two large, stuffed chairs sat in front of the fireplace and they each sank into one. The woman had shaken and aired out quilts earlier. Henry covered her with one, saying, "This will have to do until later."

Without any activity on which to keep her mind, the woman must have started thinking about her predicament because she began to shiver and shake until Henry could hear her teeth rattling. He stood up, picked up his other saddle bag, and rummaged around in it until he found his bottle of whiskey. He poured them each a cup and handed her one. "Here, this should help. Drink it slow."

He settled into the chair again, arranging his quilt, sipping on his drink and trying to think of something to get her mind off her troubles. "I guess it's about time we introduced ourselves. I'm Henry Plummer, born in Maine, but been all over the West for the last eleven years."

She took several sips from her cup before saying, "I'm Bess Cohen. My parents named me Elisheva which is Hebrew for Elizabeth and it means 'my God is abundance.' My parents lived their lives in a very traditional Jewish way, but when I married just after they both died, I took on the name Bess. I always thought Elisheva quite a name to live with because everywhere I went my name became a conversation piece. Now I'm just Bess, and people think about me instead of my name when meeting me."

"It suits you."

"Thank you. I have always liked Elizabeth as a name. I think of Queen Elizabeth and try to be as strong a person as she."

Henry smiled a bit grim, "Yes, the Elizabeth I once knew was a tough, strong-minded woman and by your performance today, I'd say you live up to that name quite well. Shooting three men, fatally, at once, that would be quite a feat for any man. Where did you learn to shoot so well?"

"My husband, Aaron, taught me when we first married. He wanted me to be able to defend myself when we moved out to Kansas from New York City. We would practice with targets often until the children were born, and then when the war came about, Aaron had me practicing again with both a rifle and a pistol." She stifled a sob at the mention of her husband and bit her lip.

Henry sat quiet for awhile out of respect for her grief and then couldn't help himself, "So you have children? Where are they?"

"They're with my in-laws who moved here recently to be near us. They live in Little Richmond. Twins, Michael and Mary. They will be two next week, so I need to get to them as soon as it is safe. I have no idea what to do now. But, I had to defend myself, those awful men wanted to …"

"Yes, I know. They're nothing but a bunch of bullying n'er-do-wells. I should have never volunteered for such a radical and rough-minded regiment. The entire time I was with them, I couldn't approve of what they did or how they did it—too much senseless blood-letting and destruction of property. I know your Bushwhackers behaved in the exact same way but, still."

Bess sat up, straight. "What do you mean by your Bushwhackers? We're Union people, not confederate. My husband died for the Union cause."

Henry apologized and said, "Yes, one of the mistakes Anthony made was to think of every Missourian as a rebel, and if he took the time to ask who they stood with, he'd never believe them anyway. How long have your children been with their grandparents?"

"I took them there a week ago. We made a plan that I would come here; this is our cabin, and I was to wait for them here if the raiders ever came to our farm. Even though Little Richmond is yet another fifteen miles away, we knew they would hear about any raid happening on the western border. News travels fast and that's how we knew they were getting closer, coming further south."

They sat in silence for a while, and then Henry suggested they light the fire and roast their supper. Henry insisted on sleeping on the floor when it came time for bed but Bess refused to allow it.

"You saved me today and have been nothing but a gentleman. If you don't use that other half of the bed, then I will sleep on the floor, also."

Since the cabin hadn't warmed up that much, they both went to bed with most of their clothes on so Henry felt comfortable with the arrangement that first night. When he woke up the next morning it was quite chilly. He stacked wood into the stove and quietly put on the rest of his clothing.

Bess still slept as he crept out of the cabin into the cold, clear dawn. There had not yet been a snowstorm this far south and the trees still held many of their colorful autumn leaves. Henry enjoyed the beauty of the woods as he hunted. He had no luck with four-legged meat so he went down to the stream that flowed below the cabin and caught some fish, glad that he carried line, a few hooks, and some dried meat for the job.

By the time he returned to the cabin, Bess had coffee boiling and had made pancakes with Henry's supply of flour, dried milk, sugar, and a bit of baking powder she found on the shelf. They had their first laugh together over the sorry-looking, finished product; the missing egg made all the difference in Johnny cakes. But, she had found a jar of wild strawberry preserves, which made them much more palatable and covered their homeliness.

After breakfast, Henry attempted to change his appearance as much as he could. He shaved his face completely bare of hair and had Bess cut his shoulder-length hair. She looked at him critically and decided they needed to change the color. She told him of some berries in these woods that people used as red dye and clutching the shawl she found in the chiffarobe around her, she left to go find some.

After the berry makeover, Henry looked different enough for him to sneak into Little Richmond for supplies and news a few days later. Bess had decided she needed to let more time pass before contacting her in-laws and hoped that they would come on their own. They would know more of what was happening, after all.

Bess decided to bathe and filled the big tub they had found out back with heated water in which she delightfully soaked her sore, aching body. She hadn't slept well due to her subconscious effort to avoid touching Henry while in bed. She had just stood up leaning over to pick up a towel when Henry walked in. He'd returned earlier than expected.

"Oh! I'm so sorry."

She blushed when Henry knocked on the door later and she let him in. Henry avoided her eyes and went about listing off the things he had bought in town as he unpacked his bags. "I didn't hear anything about any raiders being around Little Richmond. There's been a small skirmish in Kentucky, Arizona has been confirmed as a Confederate territory, and the USS Lexington has bombarded Fort Henry in Tennessee. I bought more sugar, flour, powdered milk, eggs, a chicken, butter, some sausages and dried beef, and potatoes. That should get us by until we can leave. Here, I bought this for you. I'm sure you'll become tired of your dress after a few days. A sweet lady helped me determine what size to buy."

"I'm sure you'd have a better idea what size I am now that you've seen me naked," she said as she undid the ties around the package.

Two pretty dresses fell out of their wrap along with undergarments that made her blush again. She held one dress up and said, "Oh, this should fit, thank you, Henry. You have fine taste. She examined the other garment and liked that one, also. Now, get out of here so I can change and when I come back, I'll wash some clothes in my bath water."

Henry felt satisfied to please a woman again. He thought of Bess as a strong and yet delicate person. The vision of her round buttocks, long shapely legs, and the one breast that he caught a glimpse of made him feel like a man again. The indecency he had been a part of in the past months as a Jayhawker had made him numb and he felt as if he were becoming alive again with normal urges and feelings. But he thrust his passions and his attraction for Bess aside; he couldn't become attached to another woman who he would eventually be forced to leave.

They fell into a comfortable routine with Henry leaving in morning while she did her toiletries, dressing, and fixed her part of breakfast. She would leave whenever he wanted to change his clothes. They always had something hanging over the stove and beside the fireplace to dry. Bess cleaned, baked, or cooked constantly; there was not much else to do. The cabin sparkled from her sweeping and polishing. In the afternoon they would take a walk together while Henry hunted for the evening meal. There were a few books in the cabin, and they had read each one twice by the time two weeks had passed.

One morning they lay in bed talking and made the decision to go into town together so Bess could see her children and make plans with her in-laws. Henry got up and noticed how chilled the cabin was and looked out the window to check on the weather. Snow came down slowly and must have been doing so for a while because it covered the ground. Henry stoked the fireplace and hurried outside to get his hunting done. By the time he came back, a strong wind had come up and it was difficult to see. The gentle snowfall had turned into a raging blizzard.

They were forced to abandon their plans and were cabin-bound except for using the john out back. Each time Henry went out, he had to clear a path to it with the shovel that had luckily been left at the cabin. He appreciated his tall leather boots as did Bess, who also used them each time she made her trek out to the little house.

Desire for Bess plagued Henry. But he didn't believe that just because a woman's husband was dead that she was a free woman. No, fresh widows were not fair game and still belonged to their husbands. By the time the snow and wind stilled, they had both begun to go a little mad. Henry had brought two newspapers from town and after reading them to death, they began using them in the john. Soon, they ran out of things to read and began playing charades, which became old soon enough. Henry could not stop thinking of more carnal ways to pass the time and every so often, when he caught a glimpse of Bess' face, he could sense she thought the same by her blushes.

On the fourth day, the sun shone bright and hot, enough to start thawing the snow and they decided to go into town as soon as things dried up a bit. Henry began going out in the morning for his usual routine of hunting and washing up in the stream. Since Bess needed to get out of the cabin or go crazy, he had her put on enough stockings so she could wear his boots and get some fresh air.

The morning they decided to attempt a trip into town, they woke to the sound of horses neighing. They quickly dressed and Henry, grabbing his rifle, stepped out with trepidation. An older couple sat in a buggy with two small children looking at Henry with startled eyes as he stepped away from the door. He saw that they had brought a horse for Bess for the ride home. He turned and yelled, "Bess, your family is here."

She came out buttoning her bodice and in bare feet ran calling to them, "Michael, Mary, I've missed you so."

Her father-in-law lifted each child down to her and came around to help his wife down. Bess carried each child on her hip and Henry stepped up to her taking the boy and said, "Let's get them into the cabin." He set the boy down and began stoking the fire. By then everyone had entered the cabin and when he turned, the older man stood glaring at him, demanding an explanation as to why he was there.

Bess hurriedly explained things while hugging her children giving them kisses all over their faces. Though still hostile, the in-laws seemed to accept Bess's story; it jived with all they had heard. They also announced that the governor, disgusted with the violence and destruction by Jennison's regiment, had ordered them to Humboldt, Kansas, where they were told to wait until further orders. It was rumored that they would be sent back to Fort Leavenworth in March, where they would stay until May and after that, they would be given orders to protect the Emigrant Trail. Henry felt relieved.

Bess nearly swooned when they told her that her house and buildings had been untouched and that her three hired men had escaped unscathed. A small group of Quantrill's men had come along and shot the devil out of the Jayhawkers, who had turned and fled north again. Now, they had been sent in disgrace to Humboldt, and all of Kansas was under martial law, with the regulars controlling things.

It all sounded like good news to Henry except that he wouldn't be able to leave the region too easily even with the regular army in control. As Bess and her mother packed her things, he spoke with her father-in-law about possibly renting the cabin for six more weeks. He agreed, happy that Bess would be free of him and the problems that Henry's being with her, though innocent enough, could cause. Henry waved good-bye to them all and had made his farewells with Bess in a gentlemanly manner. He walked back into the cabin both relieved and yet saddened. He would miss her greatly, and loneliness dragged at his heart.

He sat down to read one of the tired old books, which wasn't going too well considering his mood and the indecision concerning his leaving the area without being seen or caught. Where should he go? Then, he heard someone pounding on the door.

"Who is it?" he called out cautiously.

"It's me, Bess."

"Bess!"

Bess gripped him by the shoulders the minute he opened the door, shaking him excitedly, pleading, "Please, stay with us until you leave. David and Mary plan to leave as soon as they get us settled. The men will be gone for another month, until they can start working the land. Please, come be with us. I need you; a man, I mean, to be there for me and the children. Just wait until tomorrow and we'll be waiting at home for you." And, with that she ran to her horse and galloped off.

Henry packed up and left the cabin the next day. He stayed with Bess for a scant three weeks. He slept upstairs in the children's bed while

Bess and her children slept in hers. All went well except for one night when Henry woke to find Bess nestling up to him, waking him from a deep sleep. She had been crying, and as Henry attempted to comfort her, she asked him if he would make love to her.

"It's been so long since a man has held me, made love to me, I don't know when I'll be loved again. Please?"

Henry refused, explaining to her his beliefs about newly widowed women. "You are a beautiful, young woman and will soon have so many men interested in you; you'll have a new husband in no time. Besides, you've barely been a widow, and I must leave. I am a deserter and have no other choice but to go far, far from here. I need to lose myself where Union law isn't yet established. I love you, as a friend, and I want you as a woman, but I can never have you. Do you understand? I must go whether I want to or not, and right now I surely don't. Let's not start something we can't ever have."

Bess stepped out of the bed and shed her flannel nightgown. The moon shining in the window glanced off her smooth white skin and glowed just enough for her nipples, standing at attention, to show their rosy color. Henry groaned and shucked off his drawers underneath the sheets and rose up to meet her as she slithered back into his warm bed.

Henry prepared for his departure the next morning. He would be leaving a week earlier than planned, but after last night, he needed to go. He had not only fallen for Bess but for the children, also. He had read to them, pushed them on their swings, helped bathe and dress them, and they had begun to call him Uncle Henry. He left the next day with a leaden heart. Just as he left the lane going into the yard, a young man, swarthy, dark haired and mustached, came tearing down the lane on his horse barely acknowledging Henry, giving him a quick, automatic wave as he raced past him.

His looks made Henry think of Bess' little boy and he stopped, got off Avenger, and stood watching as Bess flew out her door and into the arms of the stranger. Stranger? No, thought Henry, as he watched the children do the same. Her husband, Aaron, had come back. He was happy for Bess and her family, but his heart ached with loneliness.

Henry realized, then, that he had sentenced himself to banishment in the wilderness where women like Bess, Spooky, Consuelo, and especially his Pauline most likely did not exist. He leaned his head toward Avenger's neck, resting it there, weeping quietly. He was a damn lonely loser and had killed three men out of anger, no better than those blasted vigilantes in the Lode. Who was he to sentence them to death?

But then that black dog reared up again and told him they all deserved what they got. And, you didn't mean to kill them, really. Did you? Henry shoved the black bastard away, shut up you! He slowly shook his head from side-to-side, damn it all to hell, he could change. He could do it. Emotion caught hard in his throat and he inadvertently let out a strangled groan as he renewed his vow to stay out of trouble, no more gambling or saloons. He felt forlorn and abandoned as he mounted Avenger and signaled the beast to move out.

CHAPTER 11

MAY 1862—
NOVEMBER 1862

Henry followed the California-Oregon Trail until he reached the Snake River Crossing where the Montana Trail intersected with the Snake River, and from there he followed the river up through Idaho, which lay inside the Washington Territory and then to Lewiston. He had been lucky in that he didn't see anyone who recognized him.

He did have the misfortune to catch cold when traveling over the Teton Range in the far western Dakota Territory. The winter that had been slow in arriving had taken its time in leaving, and Henry had been forced to travel through snowy, icy, mountain passes the entire time he traveled through the Teton Range. When Henry arrived on the first of May at the Luna House hotel in Lewiston, he, fevered and delirious, signed the guest registry with his own name.

He stumbled up to his room where he fitfully slept through a three-day fever, feeling as if he could cough his lungs out at times. By the time he reached the point of deadly dehydration, one of his neighboring hotel guests had alerted the clerk, who sent for a doctor.

Henry woke up to pounding on his door.

"Mr. Plummer, this is Dr. Grosberg, I've been sent to you by the hotel management. May I come in?"

Henry struggled out of bed and opened the door barely able to stand. "Oh, my," was all the doctor could say as he tucked himself under Henry's arm and helped him back to bed. "You are one sick puppy, my lad."

The doctor worked with Henry for some time to get his fever to break, and finally after it did, Henry declared he was hungry. He hadn't eaten in over a week. The doctor had some broth brought up to the room, and Henry began his slow recovery. He spent six weeks in his room, sequestered, hardly able to be up and about for more than an hour at a time. The doctor checked on him daily, making sure Henry had enough laudanum to remain sleepily docile and food that soothed his throat and sustained his body.

Henry became skeletal and looked with dismay at his shriveled muscles and sometimes bloody handkerchiefs. His childhood curse had come back to haunt him. Henry saw no one except for Dr. Joseph Grosberg, whom Henry came to call Doctor Joe, and the chamber maids loved to talk and flirt with him as they did their work. Several of them began bringing him delicious, but hearty, home-cooked dishes, and Henry began to gain weight. He asked Doc to bring him something that he could use to lift so his muscles could regain their strength. By the end of June, Henry could leave his room long enough to walk around town just a bit.

Henry could see that Lewiston, for a mining camp that had sprung up less than a year ago, had a lot to offer. It was now a boom town, the gateway to the gold mines that had also been non-existent just two years ago. Placer gold lay in such rich abundance that more and more mining camps developed weekly, and the traffic in and out of Lewiston increased along with them. Thousands of miners flooded these discoveries bringing with them such needs as food, shelter, legal aid for claims and disputes, doctors, women, saloons, and gambling. The town had almost a dozen doctors and lawyers, drug stores, six hotels, a dozen gambling joints, and two dozen saloons, along with an equal number of bordellos.

Henry made full use of the gambling joints as he recovered; he needed to replenish his nest egg since the hotel and doctor bills had taken their toll as well as his generosity with Friday and Bess. Soon he accumulated enough money and health to make him start thinking about the future. He liked Lewiston but for the lack of good, decent women. The sweet, special women with whom he had spent time and came to love, had spoiled him and he no longer wanted anything to do with prostitutes.

Mining and all that came with it didn't interest Henry, and he certainly didn't feel up to the competition for claims out in the gold fields. After his experiences in Kansas and Missouri, Henry had no desire to enter any contentious situation; he had had enough of those. Henry kept to himself, no longer trusting others and loving his anonymity. And yet, his loneliness bit into him.

Henry tired easily and went to bed early every evening. One night he woke to pounding on his door and when he opened it, he wished he hadn't. There stood two men from his past who he most definitely wanted to stay in that long-ago time. William Ridgley and Charles Reeves, two former inmates from San Quentin, had come to fetch him for partying. They had been paging through the hotel registry and saw his name, and coerced Henry's room number out of the hotel clerk. Henry told them that he had been very ill and that he needed his sleep. They continued to hang at the door attempting to persuade him to join them.

Henry's strange bout of detachment suddenly faded, and he told them to wait for him in the lobby while he dressed. They took him outside of town about three miles where a traveling saloon, complete with music and girls, had put up its tent. It was late August with the night air soft and warm, making Henry happy to be out and about even if it was with two ex-cons. The place crawled with miners from nearby mines, and there was much talk of the war and everyone's differing sentiments began to poison the earlier drunken camaraderie.

Pat Ford, the owner of this mobile establishment, began chasing men out before things became too heated, but to no avail. The entire company of men soon fought one another with fists and broken bottles. Henry tried to escape with a few other wise ones, but a man came swinging at him with a broken bottle, slicing his arm. Henry simply turned his back on him and continued to make his way out of the tent, but his attacker followed him out into the night and reached for his gun. Henry automatically reached for his and shot him dead. Henry felt sick, and frightened. God, if only he had stayed safe and content in his hotel bed!

He found Avenger and rode off at a gallop for Lewiston, thinking of the number of men he had killed in his life. He hated himself and these god-forsaken territories where guns were the law. He had to get out of here and fast. He'd go north and catch the steamer at Fort Benton heading for St. Louis.

He stabled his horse when he reached town and crept up to his room. He sat in stunned horror. At dawn, pounding made his door all but come off its hinges. He opened it and there stood Chuck Reeves, bleeding and still drunk. "We gotta go Henry. Someone saw you shoot Pat Ford and they're coming after you."

"I didn't shoot Ford! Someone attacked me and it wasn't Ford, but I got away before anything else happened!"

"Nah, there's more than one witness, seys you killed Ford."

Henry shook his head in denial knowing that he did kill someone, but it wasn't Ford. It's useless, he thought, as he gathered his things together. "Where's Ridgley?"

"He's shot up bad, had to leave him."

"Oh! Christ!"

They were met by a large group of agitated men out in the street as they left the hotel. "There he is, the man I saw riding away just after Ford was shot!" They grabbed Henry by the arms and pulled them behind him, binding them. Then, suddenly, some man exclaimed, "Nah, that's not him. I seen the one who shot Ford, he had long, blonde hair and wore a bandana. That ain't him," he said, pointing at Henry.

The mob stood around arguing, with Henry denying his involvement in Ford's death the entire time. They decided to let Henry go just as another bunch of men rode into town with their own prisoner, hands bound behind his back.

"Got him! Ketched the one that shot up poor old Ford. Yup, watched him fill Ford with gunshot! Let's string him up! We need these guys like Ford. Can't be shootin' them up or we's won't have any place to go drinkin' or dancin' with the girlies."

The crowd left Henry and Charles standing, so anxious they were for a lynching. Charles undid Henry's hands, and Henry, even though he knew better, followed the swarm of bloodthirsty men out to the edge of town where they had found the perfect hanging tree. Henry's yelling hurt his throat and chest terribly, and when he lost his voice completely and fell into a coughing fit, he asked Charles for the bottle of whiskey he knew he carried. The warmth of the liquor gave him his voice back and settled his cough and he began shouting again until he had their attention. "Say, men, wouldn't you all feel better in the morning if you just turned him over to the law tonight and let a judge and jury handle this proper? It ain't right to …"

"You jist shut yer mouth, son. Didn't you jist get let off the hook? Don't you know when to quit when the quitten's good? Now, jist git and let us be goin' about our business."

Henry persisted, "That's why I'm suggesting you just turn him into the lawmen. I was innocent, and you almost hanged me. Let the law decide. Lynching and mobbing are just as unlawful and murderous. I studied law, and it's considered unconstitutional for citizens to take the law into their own hands. Vigilanting is plain unlawful. It isn't right. Who knows how many of you will be on the jury and decide his fate anyhow? If any of you believe in God and his mercy, think about how he'll judge you, come Judgment Day if you hang an innocent man."

Henry's knees nearly buckled when he heard the grumbling assent and saw the men mounting their horses, leading the accused man back in to the jail. He and Charles walked slowly back into town with Charles making the comment, "You are one crazy, mixed-up man, Henry Plummer."

"Ain't that the truth," Henry answered.

Charles Reeves became attached to Henry as if he were an extra right arm. He never left Henry alone, and Henry soon yearned for his former loneliness. Chuck drove him mad with his continuous talk and his begging to go up into Dakota Territory were gold had just been discovered.

"We can be some of the first ones there and won't have to fight for our claims. Just think, Henry!"

Henry laughed, unwillingly and said, "I am thinking, and I don't know what my thoughts are, except that I'd like to heal up a little better before hitting the trail again."

Come September, Henry felt well enough to leave Lewiston, and they crossed Idaho heading east to Montana, another section of the Washington Territory. They stopped at a small settlement named, Hellgate, and while there met two brothers, James and Granville Stuart, who planned on leaving in a couple days for the Deer Lodge Valley, where they lived at a place called Gold Creek. Yes, they told Henry and Charles, there had been gold there, but it had quickly panned out to nothing, and the miners had moved on to a place called Grasshopper Creek.

"Gold dust is said to be just hanging in the sage brush, there," offered James. "But, of course, that's just an exaggeration. But, there's plenty of placer gold there for sure."

The Stuarts invited Henry and Chuck to trail with them as far as Gold Creek and since Henry still felt a little ill, they invited them to stay as long as he needed. The warm Indian summer weather along with the fact that he could sleep inside again, helped Henry heal quickly and they were able to leave within a couple of weeks.

Henry determined to leave the west forever. Before they had left Lewiston, Henry decided he needed a meaningful place where he could do some soulful thinking. He had gone to the edge of town where tents of different religious affiliations stood. He thought about the irony of how fast and easily men could build carnal establishments and that only much later, Godly ones were erected.

He sat in the back of the Catholic tent and watched people, mostly women, light their candles and kneel to pray. Their loving devotion and faith seeped into Henry's heart, and he felt at peace. The serenity had encouraged him to search his soul and to ask forgiveness for the wild and violent life he had lived, while he wondered what had happened to his free will and determinism.

He wanted, desperately, to shape his own life as much as possible from now on, and to escape the haphazard way in which he had lived thus far. By the time they were ready to leave Gold Creek, Henry had decided, once and for all, to go back to Maine, study the law, take the exam, and become a lawyer. When they left Gold Creek and the Stuart brothers, he told Charles his plans and bid him farewell, turning his horse north to follow the trail to Fort Benton.

Henry reached Fort Benton and discovered that the last steamer for St. Louis had left two weeks before. The fort offered no work and didn't have much to entertain a man. Henry saw it as an impossible habitat in which to spend the winter. It seemed small, only a few acres, with one adobe building mixed in with four wooden structures and home to only a handful of Indians, several horses and dogs, and fewer white men.

Henry had decided to trail down to Bannack when a man came to the fort seeking help in protecting his family and their little mission out in Blackfeet and Sioux country near the Sun River. He had already secured one man as help, and Henry groaned when he saw him. John Farnsworth, whom Henry had personally escorted to San Quentin, had also been hired. He slapped himself on his thigh, pissed that his past wouldn't stop dogging him. This convict now went by the name of Jack Cleveland, but he was still the same, leering at Henry as the young, schoolteacher-turned-missionary introduced them to one another.

Henry hoped he wouldn't have any problem with "Jack" as the young man described their new positions. "I and my family have been here all summer attempting to work with the Blackfeet Indians, teaching them everything about white culture, including, most importantly, farming. We have had little effect but plan to try it for one more year. They have moved on for the winter, but the Sioux, being pushed out of Minnesota, have threatened to raid Sun Valley Farm, and I need a couple good men for protection. It is only me, my wife, Martha Jane, our two children, Mary and Harvey, and my sister-in-law, Electa Bryan, out there along with a young nineteen-year-old named Joseph Swift and an Indian named Iron. We need help not only with the Indian raids, but also with putting up an adequate store of firewood and getting the land ready for crops next spring. There are also many repairs necessary for the houses to be winter-ready. The heavy rains earlier ruined our crops, but I have great hopes for next season."

The weather remained summery as the three men made the two-day trip to Sun River. The cottonwoods and the willows along the river were just turning after the first hard frost, and the sun shone down brightly, making Henry feel optimistic. James Vail, Henry's new boss, appeared to be a decent, but tragically idealistic, young man. Henry liked him and respected his high moral standards and sense of urgency in helping the Natives, who he realized, after his encounter with Friday, faced nothing but a hopeless future. Henry wished there had been more James Vails born instead of the many greedy men determined to eliminate the pesky problem presented by the Natives by simply wiping them out of existence.

Good food and gratefulness awaited them when they reached Sun River Farm. Henry immediately liked and trusted Martha and felt a bit pleased and amused at the glow of admiration fifteen-year-old Mary exhibited when introduced to him, and he enjoyed the energy and excitement of ten-year-old Harvey. Henry didn't know what to think of young Joseph. Iron reminded Henry of a Friday without an intellect. He appeared thoughtful, but still struggled with the language difference and only knew what education the Vails had imposed on him over the summer.

They had just sat down to the inviting meal that Martha had set out when they heard screams from outside. Henry exited the cabin first and ran to where he heard the shrieks of hysteria. He raced into a garden where a young woman held a shovel, twirling around in angst, screeching "Snake! Snake! Oh, dear God, help me!" Henry reached her first, gathering her in his arms and carrying her out of the garden.

He attempted to set her down but she wouldn't have that. She clung to him so tightly, he could feel her breasts pressing into his chest, the heaving of frantic breathes in and out of her bosom, the tiny waist, and lovely feeling buttocks, and when he looked into her deep-blue eyes he was lost. He stood there like a simpleton taking her in, and she stared back just as enamored.

They both came to when James came to them with a pitchfork full of the chopped up remains of the rattlesnake that had caused the ruckus. He laughed and said, "Well, Electa, I don't know why you're such a disaster, the poor snake had no chance at your vindictive hand." They all had a good laugh as they walked back into the house while everyone, talking at once, told stories of the dreaded invasion of the rattlesnakes all summer, along with the annoying pestering of persistent mosquitoes.

The soft, warm Indian summer still hanging over Sun River Valley made Henry's developing relationship with Electa easy. They walked together along the banks of the river, spending every daylight minute available to them until Electa had to go in help with supper. Henry told her everything about his past, holding nothing back; he sincerely wanted to begin an honest and decent life and knew he needed to be forthright with this young woman.

He told her of his three killings. "I really didn't mean to kill them. I just reacted and then they were dead. Each one of them, I swear, planned on killing me first. But I just can't forgive myself for ending their lives. When I get in one of those haunting humors, I realize that perhaps I could have avoided murdering them if I had done things different." Henry stopped short and asked, "Have you ever read anything about determinism or free will? I really can't figure those ideas out, try as I might."

Electa shook her head. "Determinism, no, but I do know about free will from the Bible. My father, you see, was a Methodist minister. I've read the Bible faithfully for years. All I know is that from what I've read in the Bible, God gives us the strength and knowledge to make the right choices if we believe in him. To me it's simple. You think about what you should do and determine your next move. Is that determinism?" she asked, looking up at Henry.

Henry shrugged. "Maybe. But it isn't just that simple. In my case I didn't have time to think." Then, he abruptly stopped walking, thinking, yes, you son-a-bitch, you could have stood a moment thinking things through. His sudden standstill caused Electa had to catch hard onto his arm to keep from falling. The warmth of him as she all but tumbled into his arms gave her a huge jolt deep inside of her. She had never felt desire like this before and hurriedly excused herself, running to the cabin to help with the evening meal.

During supper Henry could feel the tension between them and wondered what he had done wrong. You shouldn't have told her the truth, idiot, whispered the black hound. Henry shook his head, attempting to chase off the beast.

"Is something wrong, Henry?" Martha queried, always worrying about pleasing people with her homey food.

Henry looked up from his plate, amazed that she could read his mind and blushed. "No, everything is fine."

Martha smiled. "Good. You've worked so hard all day reroofing; I want to at least please you with a tasty, satisfying meal.

Henry blushed again, realizing she felt only concern in repaying him for his work for which he was hardly paid much in return. "No Martha, you just caught me daydreaming and thinking about something else. Your cornbread is the best I've ever tasted and the baked ham is something I haven't had in years. Delicious. All of it."

Henry hung around playing chess with Harvey while waiting for Electa to finish with her after-supper chores. As soon as she finished, he asked the young boy if they could leave off where they were and end the match the next evening. He hurried to catch up with Electa as she went out to feed the chickens their nightly meal.

"Electa. Have I done something wrong? Did I offend you with my confessions?" Henry grabbed at her arm and pulled her to him urgently, "Have you given up on me already? You think I'm no-good now, don't you?"

Electa looked up at him in surprise, pulling her arm from his grasp. "No! It's nothing like that. I … I … don't know what to think or feel about you. I just need some time to sort it all out."

Henry tagged along behind her as she fed the chickens. "Please, please don't think the worst of me. I do have a conscience. It nags me all the time. I call her my saintly person. And, when the devil comes calling, I think of him as a big, black, ugly hound, nothing but a dog. For some reason, that helps me …"

Electa's back was to him, but her peals of laughter interrupted his verbal admission that he had named his two opposing inner voices. She leaned over, clutching as her stomach, not able to contain her amusement, chortling even more when Henry, dumfounded, asked her what was so damn funny. She could only shake her head. When she looked up at him, tears flowed freely down her cheeks, making Henry chuckle, also.

"What's so funny?" he asked again.

Electa wiped at her tears and composed herself. "Henry. I think you are the dearest, funniest man I have ever met. You are a cause for merriment. First you tell me about killing three men, and then, you tell me you've named your struggling conscience two different names."

Henry interrupted her, telling her defensively, "I told you something I've never told anyone and you laugh at me. What's so strange about me naming them? Tell me. I'd like to know!"

Electa, calm and dignified once again just shook her head. "Henry, I adore you for the honest sharing of your deepest thoughts. I don't think you are an intentional murderer and I respect you for having such a battle between good and evil within yourself. My father always said that a man with a conscience was a good man, on his way to sainthood. But, a man that showed no remorse for anything he did wrong walked the path to hell. He worried much more about those people who lived without self-reproach than he did the contrite."

Henry looked down into her big blue eyes that fascinated him and drew her tenderly toward him. Before she could stop him, he kissed her sweetly on the lips. She responded, making Henry feel his desire and he pulled back a bit so she wouldn't feel it. But she wrenched her body away from him, anyway, running from him a bit and then stopping, slowly turning, and proclaiming in a loud whisper, "That! What just happened is why I need time apart from you. You scare me. What your body makes mine feel, frightens me. I've never felt this way. I've lived a protected life and have never had a beau. Please don't touch me like that again until I say so."

They continued their evening walks near the river but on a more formal basis. Electa told Henry of her life, idyllic and slow before her mother died, and that when her father remarried she had served as a source of envy for her stepmother. She decided to leave with James and his family to help with the children and to teach the Indians at his missionary, hoping to make some sort of difference for the natives. Henry loved her for that and decided she would be the perfect, rehabilitating force in his life.

Henry decided he needed to do things right with Electa and became the perfect gentleman in his courtship of her. One day, when the work had slowed down, Henry asked Martha if he could use her kitchen to fix a picnic supper for Electa and him. She looked at him sideways, evaluating his prowess as a cook. "Have you cooked much, Henry?"

He laughed sheepishly, blushing. "No, but I think if you could spare some of that delightful bread you make, I could make some sandwiches and I do know how to bake potatoes," he offered hesitantly.

Martha laughed and said, "Let me help you, Henry. I'll teach you a few things. Go make your invitation to Electa, she could use a night off, and I'll meet you in the kitchen after our noon dinner."

They met in the kitchen with Martha insisting they make fried chicken, for everyone. Henry would pack some just for Electa and him into his picnic basket. They butchered and fried two hens that had quit laying and made a potato salad loaded with eggs since the hens still able to produce had gone crazy with the cooler weather and all. They went out into the garden, picking the last of the tomatoes, slicing them into a delicious dish topped with a little salt, vinegar, and sugar. Martha bragged some about her tomato crop as well as their knowledge in making the apple cider vinegar that would come in handy all through the winter months.

Henry went down to the river for a bath and but for his nervousness, enjoyed the water. It still ran cold in this country, even during the summer months and early fall, but was bearable and only helped to clear his head and steady his thoughts. He worried about how he would approach Electa with his marriage proposal. By the time he had finished, he still didn't know exactly what he would say; hoping the moment would declare itself naturally, and he would know how to ask her.

It was a perfect evening as they, together, laid out one of Martha's quilts. The cottonwood trees had turned golden and had not yet fallen but gave off an earthy smell of life that intoxicated their senses. The air was sweet, just warm enough for a last picnic, while a gentle, hardly noticeable breeze rustled the trees, making them give up a scent that smelled of fresh wood and an almost piney scent. Henry picked up a leaf that had floated gently onto their quilt, feeling its still waxy and flexible texture. He held it to his nose, smelling the clean, but yet musky smell of it. It made him think of old men, still living and vibrant, and yet giving off the smell of decay that clings to those with not much longer on this earth.

The thought of death compelled him to fulfill his mission of the evening, and Electa, noticing his deep thoughtful state, asked if he was alright.

Henry smiled. "I am so fine with you at my side. I have a question for you."

Electa stilled his tongue by leaning down and kissing him, taking his breath away and causing all decent and meaningful thoughts from his mind. When she finished, she sat apart from him, sitting up straight, and reaching inside her shawl, she brought out a bottle of wine. Henry couldn't believe his eyes. Wine? From the Methodist preacher's daughter?

Electa blushed and sheepishly admitted that the wine had not been her idea but Martha's. "Martha told me that every young couple with feelings for one another should have a little wine at their picnics." She giggled, and said, "But, she did warn me that since I have never had any, besides during communion at church, I should be cautious with it."

She poured them wine and Henry had enough presence of thought to make a toast. "To you, Electa, I hope you fulfill all your hopes and desires and do the good deeds that you wish to perform while on this earth."

She responded with, "To you Henry, I hope you can chase that demon dog out of your mind, once and for all, and find peace and happiness in this life."

They clinked Martha's good wine glasses together and sat drinking, silently mesmerized by one another. Henry took in her beauty: her wonderful blue eyes, so innocent and shining; her dark tresses falling from a small bun at the crown of her head; the curve of her cheeks as they met her long, elegant neck; and, lastly, her breasts as her chest moved up and down with breaths that came faster and shorter as her aroused sensuality took over her.

She drank him in, along with her wine: his intense gray eyes, smoldering and hot with desire; his soft sun streaked hair peeking out of the hat he never took off; his handlebar moustache, marking him a grown man; and his wide set shoulders hovering over a muscular chest, heaving with desire.

They came together with Henry pulling them down to lay side-by-side on the quilt. He cradled her head in his right arm as he brought his lips down to hers. They kissed passionately until she reared up and away from him, demanding, "Henry, tell me what it is like to have sex. I don't have any idea what it will be like, my mother died so young, my stepmother was so distant, and Martha shies away from it when I ask her about it."

Henry leaned back on his elbow, looking intently into her eyes dewy with passion. "You really want to know? Let me show you. I promise we won't be making love but you'll get a good sense of what it is like."

He leaned into her, kissing her deeply while guiding her back down onto their soft accommodation. "First we'll kiss for a while and then I'll kiss my way to your bosom."

They kissed long and deep and Henry felt delight when she opened her mouth more and began making forays into his mouth with her tongue. Soon he found himself making his way to her breasts with feathery kisses up and down her throat, neck, and décolleté. He wrapped his arms around her delicate waist, lifting her up and bringing her close enough to him until he could softly place his lips on one of her hardened nipples.

She gasped and then stilled, waiting. He looked into her eyes and asked, "May I?" as he slowly unbuttoned the bodice of her dress. When he moved to do the same with her petticoat, she stopped him, but he found contentment in suckling her through the fabric of her underclothes. She gasped and let her head fall back, allowing him better access to her bosoms. Henry continued to pay tribute to each of her breasts, giving them each a turn going back and forth between them. Electa became soft and lax, intent on enjoying the pleasure he offered her.

Henry slowly reached down and lifting her dress and petticoat found his way to her sexual core. By then she was beyond resisting and let him move his fingers, teasing her and making her moan. He felt wetness through her under draws and slowly began seducing that part of her with his fingers. He was very hard by now and had to concentrate to control his emotions and desire. He continued tantalizing her desires through her breasts.

Eventually Electa cried out and Henry knew he had pleased her. It took all he could muster to pull away. He took one of her hands as she lay limp in his arms and brought to the core of his sexuality. "Feel this?" he said, between pants. "This is what I would make love to you with and it would even feel better."

When Electa came to her senses, she pulled herself together, silently buttoning her bodice and after giving Henry a quick kiss on the mouth, stood up to leave, saying, "I would love to stay, Henry, but I must go before I lose myself in this and make a big mistake."

Henry quickly stood and gathered her into his arms without too much resistance on her part. He kissed her and asked, "Is it a big mistake to love someone? Because I think I love you, Electa Bryan."

She had slipped out of his arms and started walking away. But when he declared his love for her, she stopped short, turned, and came closer.

"Really Henry? You think you love me, well, I think the same. That I love you, I mean."

Henry came nearer and got down on his right knee, picking up Electa's hand and kissing it. "Will you do the honor of marrying me, Electa Bryan?"

She looked down at him and said in a severe tone, "Well, Mr. Plummer, after seducing me as you just did, I think it would be very appropriate to do that very thing. I accept your proposal but you will need to talk to James, do it proper. Both he and my sister are very protective of me, and have taken care of me for a long time, and I respect their opinion. I cannot do such a thing without their consent."

She wrapped her arms around Henry's neck and kissed him. "Now that we've come to an agreement, I'm starved. Let's eat," she said matter-of-factly and bustled to the picnic basket and began unpacking its fare.

They ate ravenously while she chattered on and on, happy and excited. Henry remained silent basking in her joy.

The next morning when Henry approached James, he couldn't get a word out about his proposal to Electa. James, worried about what he had to say, took over the conversation, telling Henry he needed to let him and Jack go. He was short on money as it was and felt that the winter rations he had set aside would not be enough to feed them all. If the winter was extremely hard; they wouldn't be able to hunt much game either.

Henry understood and held his tongue about marrying Electa until Jack knew they were being let go. Henry hoped Jack would leave first and go anywhere but to the gold fields in Bannack where he planned to stay and work for the winter. Jack's resentment of Henry had grown as he watched him and Electa. He hadn't even had a chance with the comely wench and continuously sneered at Henry, "You're my meat, Plummer, just watch out."

Henry waited a week for Jack to sort things out, but he seemed to have no idea where to go or what to do. Each night when the two men retired to their cabin, he would sit there and complain about the Vails and their stupid mission and lack of planning. The Indians had moved on so were no longer a danger. Henry fully understood the situation and held no resentment toward James and Martha, at all, only wishing them the best.

Henry waited a week until he approached James about Electa. Meanwhile, they had been chaste with one another, and Electa seemed satisfied to be engaged to Henry and not much in a hurry to marry him. When he told her his plans, she happily agreed with the idea of waiting until spring, especially since they would have to wait for the Methodist minister, Reverend Harry Baines to return to Fort Benton.

Henry made sure both James and Martha were together when he presented them with his proposal to marry Electa and his plans for the winter. After all, Martha as Electa's sister had just as much say in the matter as James. He and Electa had it all planned out, she would appear in a short while, making sure Henry had some time alone with her benefactors. Henry felt quite nervous as he knocked on the door because Electa suddenly seemed so apprehensive and unsure about the outcome of his request.

Henry took his hat off, the respectful thing to do, as he stepped into their cabin. He bowed slightly before Martha to ensure a lock hair fell over his scar. He cleared his throat and began.

"James and Martha, I have come to ask for Electa's hand in marriage. I sincerely love and respect her, as I do you, and would take very good care of her for the rest of her life. I know things are uncertain now, but by spring, I should have a better notion of what I am going to do with my life and how to support the woman I love. I plan to spend the winter in Bannack mining gold and will return in the spring for Electa when we will marry. We want to be married by a minister and I understand that Reverend Baines will return to Fort Benton come spring. He, god willing, will marry us."

James sat silent, long enough to make Henry even more uneasy. Henry could see that he hadn't been aware, at all, of his and Electa's courtship. Martha, on the other hand, clapped her hands in genuine joy and consent, inwardly feeling she had played the role of matchmaker. She liked Henry despite that they did not really know him or his past, but his deportment around them had been polite and his efforts to please them with his work, sincere. That was enough for her.

But James had other notions about the situation. He liked Henry, as well, but hadn't connected with him as his woman had, obviously. His mind, so full of worry about the Indians, money, food and supplies, and what the winter held in store for them flooded his mind to the point that he didn't observe or conceive what was going on around him. He loved Electa like a brother and instantly decided that he did not know Henry enough to allow him to marry her.

James cleared his throat, looking intently into Henry's solemn gray eyes, hoping to see some sort of affirmation. Because he couldn't quite see what he expected, he said, "Fine. Sounds good enough, but I won't give my consent until spring when you return. I want you to spend a month with us again then before I make my decision. We don't really know you, and I think it necessary to check into your past, if possible, and to have Reverend Baines weigh in on your character, so to speak. I respect his judgment of people and …"

Just then Electa burst through the door. She stopped short when she saw concern and disapproval in James' face, disappointment in Henry's, and puzzlement in her sister's. The atmosphere of the room became awkwardly still as a stagnant pond, and the tension there almost crackled; it was so evident.

Henry coughed the first sign of his lungs acting up and he thought, damn, damned those things, don't give out on me now. He nodded in agreement and turned to Electa saying, "I'll let them tell you the conditions and terms of our engagement. I will be back in the spring when we, hopefully, will marry. I must go now, pack my things, and head down Mullen Road to Bannack. I can't waste any time since I want to be well set when that happens."

He turned to James and offered his hand. "Sir, thank you for hearing me out, and I promise not to disappoint. Thank you, Martha, for the great food, the cooking lessons, and for supporting me." He stopped and kissed Electa on the forehead, asking her to wait for him outside while he packed his things, and turned to leave.

"Henry," James spoke out. "Please understand, I must do what I feel is best for Electa. Give us, her, six months to sort this all out and make sure it is meant to be. I know I'm not that cognizant about what goes on around me, but I do have a perceptive sixth sense about things, and it is telling me we need time."

Henry donned his hat, nodded, and said, "Fine, James, I'll try to understand."

Henry strode angrily to his cabin, furious. It shocked him that he hadn't had his way completely. He was so accustomed to talking his way through things. He did understand how James thought, and why.

Yes, he had only been with them for a little more than six weeks, and, yes, they didn't know him well. But, what better prospects did Electa have out in this wilderness? He felt insulted and belittled by James' cautionary attitude toward him. The black dog reared up to have his say, Yeah, would he want her marrying someone like Jack Cleveland? Oh, shut up, you stupid beast, Henry yelled in his mind.

Henry shook as he packed his bag, shaking his head in dismay. Well, I'll just have to prove to them that I am good enough for their precious Electa. Then, his saint stepped in and pointed out, don't take it out on her. It's not her fault. She loves you. For now, asserted the black dog. Henry sighed and went out to say his goodbyes to his intended.

Electa stood with the sunlight glancing off her shiny black hair. She looked so lovely; it broke Henry's heart to think of leaving her. She looked so sad and forlorn he decided he had better buck up and act like a man about this. He shoved his anger aside and put his bag down, enfolding her into his arms and kissing the top of her head. Her hair, warmed by the sun, smelled heavenly and he inwardly groaned. God, he did not want to leave her.

His throat caught as he began to speak. "Electa, I'll be back the first of May, or as soon as the ice goes out and the Reverend can return on the steamboat. I would love to take you with me now, but I can't guarantee what life would be like in Bannack for you. It's a new and most likely very rough mining camp, and I just couldn't risk taking you there. Besides, I know you want to do things right. So, I'll leave with the promise to return, come spring."

She clung to him so, that he had to pry her fingers loose from around his neck so he could look down into her eyes and proclaimed, "Electa, I love you. I will return. Wait for me?"

She only nodded. Her eyes brimmed with tears. They kissed deeply, and Henry mounted his horse. He rode off, looking back every so often until he could no longer see her.

CHAPTER 12

NOVEMBER 1862— APRIL 1863

Henry arrived in Bannack the first of November after a one hundred eighty-mile trek through a kaleidoscope of scenery, beautiful, colorful fall foliage contrasting with faded grasses and sagebrush. As he neared the settlement, he could see that the surrounding landscape held nothing but spent, brown and yellow vegetation, the largest of which were now leafless willows along Grasshopper Creek with a few scrawny cottonwoods mixed in among them. Jack Cleveland had started out with him against Henry's wishes but Henry had been able to get ahead of him after one of Cleveland's nights of heavy drinking, heading out early one misty dawn while the other man still slept.

Henry took in the muddy, one-sided street as he came slowly into town, hoping that come spring, things would appear more welcoming and desirable. The street had been built up only on the one side with rough-cut log cabins faced with wooden-planked store fronts, some painted and some not, all looking washed out and sun faded, like they had been there for years. Different shades of gray and brown dominated the scene.

Henry stopped in front of a building that had been white washed, a saloon called the Elkhorn. He tied his horse to the railing and walked inside were he discovered the owner of the establishment was an acquaintance of his from San Quentin. Henry had taken care of him when he had been sick with pneumonia. They knew each other well and had been on friendly terms. Henry felt gratitude for the man when he treated him as if he had never seen him before.

Henry ordered a whiskey and asked Cyrus where a man could stay for the night and if there was any permanent sort of housing to be purchased. Just as Cyrus began answering Henry's inquiries, Jack Cleveland walked in, shouting, "Plummer, you asshole, I've still got your meat, you son-a-bitch! Leaving me on the trail like that. You're on my list, and I've still… *got*… your meat."

Henry rolled his eyes at Cyrus as Cleveland, already drunk, ranted and raved at him making Henry the center of attention of the dozen other customers.

Henry finished his drink and walked down the street to Hotel Meade, the one building with color and class, built out of solid red brick. He moved his things into his room and went down to the small dining room for supper. After supper he found shelter for Avenger in one of the two stables in the tiny town. Henry returned to his room eager for a night's sleep in comfort. The mattress, he discovered, left a lot to be wished for, but it was a bed and he was indoors. Soon he slept.

The next day he purchased a house in the section they called Yankee Flats—Henry's first move toward establishing himself as a respectable, middle-class man. He soon recognized the class distinctions in this growing mining camp. The Yankee Flats held mostly northerners, many from Minnesota, who all held the Union close to their hearts and looked down upon the other section of town full of the more transient, and what they called secesh whiskey rowdies.

Paroled Confederates and deserters had inundated Bannack, coming only for the easy gold pickings along the creek. They would accumulate gold dust enough to pay the rent, eat, and then would spend the rest on drinking and gambling. They would go back to mining when they had spent the last of it. They bragged to Henry that sometimes all they had to do was to pull up the sagebrush along the creek bed, shake the roots into their pans, and they could capture a sizeable amount of dust. The rest of the gold lay shallow, just underneath the water line of the creek, yielding large quantities of the precious metal when dug into and panned.

Henry found all this to be true, apart from the sagebrush roots, and soon he had established several viable claims for himself, which he worked faithfully and steadily. Like Carson City, the burg had no banking facilities. Every time Henry stepped into the Elkhorn, there sat Cleveland, leering threateningly at him. Henry didn't doubt that the man would rob him if given the opportunity.

Henry's small house, cabin, like all the rest of them, had only a hard, dirt floor. He kept his pick and shovels in his house when not using them and devised a solution to his dilemma. He dug up a section of his bedroom floor where he stashed his bags of gold pebbles and dust. He then would stomp down the disturbed dirt, glazing the surface with water, until it looked as hard and polished as the rest of the floor. He ordered a large chiffarobe from Salt Lake, and when that arrived, he placed it over his buried nest egg.

Henry couldn't stay away from gambling; he had joyfully observed that the Elkhorn had its own faro table and he frequented it often. He reserved his winnings for his everyday living expenses. His gambling was the one exception to his plan for respectability as well as his occasional drinking. He vowed that once Electa arrived, he would stop doing both, but until then, life would have been lonely and boring without these vices.

He soon had as many friends from the secesh camp as he did in Yankee Flats and hoped that having his feet planted in both sections wouldn't become a problem. He kept a quiet, gentlemanly reserve about him always, earning respect from both sides. Everyone admired the unreadable, composed face he kept while gambling. The only person who could break him out of this veneer of self control was Jack Cleveland who was forever attempting to start a fight with him.

One day after a long, grueling effort at his claims, Henry stepped into the Elkhorn for a drink and a bit of food and found a man at Cleveland's feet, licking his boots. Henry looked at Cyrus and asked, "What's going on here?"

"Nothing unusual," responded his friend, "That man's always bullying someone. Either makes them slick around on his boots, or he makes them slither around on the floor like 'the god- damned slimy snakes that they are,' to quote him."

Henry turned to look at the embarrassing scene and asked, "This happens, always?"

"Yes, daily, everyone hates him, the big, fat bully. I'm surprised someone's not killed him by now, the devil. And, where he gits the money, I don't know. I haven't heard anyone tell of a day's work by that mistake of a man. Never. Where does he git his gold dust when he never works on a claim?"

Henry knew. He always kept a bit of dust sitting around in his house. He had made a habit of leaving little offerings of dust in his house for the petty robbers who continuously haunted the village. A day did not pass that someone had been robbed of their hard-earned pay dirt. Men hanging around town would be wanting one day and then the next, suddenly, would be flush, buying rounds of drink for everyone.

There was no law in Bannack but for a man who was trusted enough by the townspeople to be accepted as their "self-appointed sheriff"—Hank Crawford. But, he never did anything to investigate these petty robberies or to capture and interrogate well-known culprits, some of whom even bragged about their thieveries. He only stepped in when there was a questionable outcome in the many gunfights in the saloons or out in the street, causing at least one man's demise. In this town all men carried guns, which appeared to be the actual law.

Henry had seen Jack Cleveland lurking around his cabin plenty of times and had even awakened to find him in his home. Henry would come to with gun in his hand, and Cleveland would be out the door in a flash. Henry felt nothing but contempt for this man for whom he made these little piles of gold dust available, hoping to keep him happy and his mouth shut. Henry did not need a man, even of Jack's ilk, spouting off about his questionable past.

In January, a fierce snowstorm blew into Bannack, announcing winter's late arrival. A man named George Edwards went out soon after the storm abated to check on his cattle, and when he never returned, the townsmen went looking for him only to find him dead, shot through the head. Later that week, Jack Cleveland, who had been recently bumming from everyone, bought drinks by the dozens for all who would accept them. After drinking himself into a stupor one evening, fellow patrons of the Elkhorn searched his pockets and found a sizeable amount of gold dust in a bag hanging around his excessive waist. Even though everyone agreed it most likely belonged to the poor dead man, nothing was done.

Henry recognized the suspicious and incriminating opinions many people held for one another, including him. All he could do, he reasoned, was to continue showing his best behavior. But one afternoon when he walked into the Elkhorn and was confronted by Jack Cleveland, he lost his mien of gentlemanly conduct. The man was on the fight and when his blurred, drunken vision produced Henry, he went wild with insults and the usual, "Ah, there's Plummer; he's my meat."

Henry went up to the bar and ordered a drink, trying to ignore the misery Cleveland had begun inflicting on an innocent man. Suddenly, Henry couldn't tolerate this any longer and walked to Cleveland's table. "That's enough; everyone knows you're nothing but a drunk and a bummer when you haven't been stealing. You need to shut your mouth and leave this poor man alone."

The man hurriedly left and Henry turned to go back to his drink. Cleveland stood up and said, "Mind your own business, Plummer. You're still my meat."

Henry turned around, incensed, and said, "You son-of-a-bitch, I'm tired of your shit, so just shut up!"

Cleveland reached for his gun but Henry was quicker and shot him in the belly. Cleveland fell to the floor, pleading "You wouldn't shoot me when I'm down?"

"No." Henry said in a soft, stern voice. "Stand up."

After Cleveland stood wavering, Henry fired at him again, twice, once in the chest and once in the head. Henry stood still for a moment and then other patrons helped him to the door warning him, "You better leave, get out of Bannack!" Henry wandered home, chastising himself for losing his temper, and he waited for whatever law there was to descend upon him.

Henry paced up and down the length of his cabin until the hard dirt floor had a three-inch trench worn in the middle. Henry berated himself verbally and out loud, since hearing his own voice made it even more real. "Can't believe you did this, Henry Plummer!" said his saint.

"Well, the son-a-bitch deserved it!" fired back his black hound.

"Why do you always go for your gun?" berated the saint.

"Guns are faster and cleaner. Why get your hands all busted up in brawl, stupid? You did the smart thing," spoke out the black demon.

This was the first time he had ever really killed someone in anger. He ran his hands through his hair in anxious frustration.

"Why hadn't you at least let the man lie there wounded? Perhaps he would have turned tail and left town after healing," asserted his saint.

"He was a human vulture, always picking on people, stupid. He needed to be snuffed out, deserved it."

Henry pushed the black bastard out of his mind and concentrated on what his saint had to say. But, before he listened he thought hadn't Cleveland been only a little more than a mass of carrion? The man had been a stagnant piece of flesh living off the misery of others, drinking himself into a state of hateful, rotten, not-quite-dead humanity.

"What would your mother think?" queried his saint.

Henry could imagine her, there in the barroom, standing next to him and reaching out gently, with tears in her eyes, beseeching him, staying his arm with the soft, tender touch of her hand. "Don't, please don't, Henry. You know it's not right. Now put your gun down and let him live, dear."

Henry remembered the time he shot every kind of bird that ate on a poor, dead, little deer. He had hated them, and when he went home for more powder and shot, he had to ask his mother for it. She had looked at him in concerned shock. "Why Henry, I just saw Grandfather give you some yesterday. What happened to it all?"

Henry told her his story. "I shot a bunch of crows, dozens actually, and buzzards and vultures, too. Oh, Mother! They were all gathered around this little deer, eating its eyes out, its mouth, its belly, everything!

And, they were all so ugly and mean. Fighting one another and squawking like hell the entire time."

"Henry, don't you use language like that."

Henry hung his head. "But Mother, it was so awful, terrible. I just had to kill them all. And, then when they were all dead, more came, just as noisy and mean acting."

Nabby reached out, with tears in her eyes, and gathered Henry into her arms. "Henry, dear, animals don't, can't bury their dead. Something must take care of their dead bodies. Nature created these vultures to eat this carrion flesh, otherwise there would be dead animals fouling up the Earth for long periods of time. If you think it's upsetting to you, to see these poor dead creatures, what do you think it must be like for God's creatures. Think of what the mother deer would feel if she had to wander by her dead baby for months before it rotted away entirely."

Nabby let Henry go for a moment and then reached out, gently holding him by his arms directly in front of her. She took one hand and captured his chin and held it, still looking him in the eyes. "I think, Henry, you have learned your lesson well, one that you will always remember. You can't erase or kill evil or evil-seeming things in the world. There is a reason for everything and it is not for us to understand everything. Only our Heavenly Father can do that, as well as purge the world of evil. In life, you will always come across evil men, the vultures of the world, people who feed off others, treating them as if they were no more than carrion. Just remember, there will be times you cannot make right out of wrong. You will have to look the other way and carry on with your own living. Don't ever forget your favorite motto you always talk about, live and let live. Sometimes evil has its place in the world just like the carrion-eating animals and birds."

Henry wished, like hell, that he had thought of that before shooting Cleveland.

He remained in his cabin for three days, condemning himself until Hank Crawford came and told him there would be no charges against him; he had done Bannack a favor in ridding the town of the bullying, thieving monster. But, when he began walking through Bannack he knew what a difference his actions had made. People still showed respect but with a tinge of fear, dipping their heads to acknowledge him while crossing the street. Even in Cyrus' saloon, some men would get up and leave when he entered, and Henry realized his actions had most definitely tainted his reputation.

The Stuart brothers moved to Bannack two weeks later to establish a butcher shop. Henry helped them find viable claims and showed them how mining was done on the banks of Grasshopper Creek. After that, he would find himself counseling others on the subject, helping them to find their own claims to work.

A small band of Shoshone natives lived in the hills above Bannack and having an amiable relationship with the people of the town, began intermarrying with the white settlers. Granville Stuart married a Shoshone woman named Aubony with whom he had instantly fallen in love. She was quite sweet in nature and was a wonderful cook.

Charles Reeves also took a Shoshone wife but only for housekeeping and sex. One night she ran screaming from their cabin, refusing to return to him because he had become abusive. Charles and two other men stormed up to the Indian camp, shooting through tepee walls killing several men. The band of Shoshone packed up and left that same evening.

A miner's style trial was held with the entire mining camp weighing in, voting, as to what to do for punishment. They decided to handle Henry's killing of Cleveland also and addressed his case first. They, without much fuss, acquitted Henry. After the prosecuting representative and the defense made their cases concerning the other three men, they took a vote. All three men, it was decided, would be banished from Bannack. A few weeks later because of the cold weather, the banishments were rescinded, and the three men walked the streets of Bannack as if nothing had happened.

Hank Crawford, assuming his duty as sheriff, confiscated not only Reeve's and the other two men's guns but also Henry's and sold them to pay for trial expenses. This angered Henry since he had been acquitted, and he protested, indignant. Others stepped in and set up a miner's court, which ordered Crawford to recover the guns and return them to the four men.

Crawford, humiliated, began a feud with Henry accusing him of wanting to kill him, letting everyone know that he feared for his life. Henry called nonsense on that and said, "I have no intention to do him any harm."

But, further damage had been done to Henry's reputation, and he felt the brunt of it. Two merchants advertised their fear of Henry and his temper, along with Crawford. Henry attempted to reassure one of them as they met on the street. "Why, Mr. Dance, do you always pull out your big Bowie knife when we meet and begin whittling?"

"Because, Mr. Plummer, I never intend for you to take the advantage of me."

Henry, concerned, said "Mr. Dance, why would I ever want to do you harm? You have never threatened me."

The older man just shook his head and walked on. After that Henry began hearing rumors that Crawford was "out to get him first" making Henry cautious and fearful as he walked the streets. He avoided the self-appointed sheriff always and began carrying his rifle.

One morning Henry stood in the middle of Main Street visiting with a man sitting on his wagon. Henry had his foot on one of the spokes of the front wheel with his rifle lying across his leg with his back to the sidewalk. Crawford stepped out of a store and fired at Henry. The ball entered Henry's elbow and traveled through his arm, lodging in his wrist. Henry turned to Crawford and said, "Fire away!"

Crawford shot again, missed, and then ran. After that the town's people ostracized Crawford, and fearing for his life, he left for Fort Benton.

Dr. Jerome Glick, a very capable surgeon, insisted the arm be amputated but Henry would have none of that, "I'd rather be dead than to be missing my right arm; I need it to survive in these lawless parts." Dr. Glick operated, under the threat of death from Henry's friends if Henry died. He slowly removed all the bone fragments but was not able to remove the ball in Henry's wrist, leaving Henry a painful reminder of Crawford's attack.

After living through the surgery, Henry had to fight off a deadly fever after which he began a slow recovery. As soon as he was able, he began target practicing at the edge of town to develop his gunman's skills on his left side. Soon, he felt ready and able to protect himself, proud that he could train his subordinate half to be as strong as the dominate once had been.

In March, Idaho Territory had been carved out of Washington Territory, including the sections called Idaho, Montana, and Wyoming. Not one penny had been granted for government, nor had these parts been given any civil or criminal codes, leaving them lawless. Bannack continued growing as did criminal acts in the town. Many more petty thefts occurred; no one's nest egg was safe. One afternoon, two gamblers had a shoot-out in the Elkhorn, killing one another and an innocent bystander, and, that same night, a drunken rowdy shot an unarmed Indian.

In May, the town decided it needed leadership and protection, and held an election. They voted in Walter Dance as mayor and Henry as sheriff. Henry's altercation with Crawford and his defiant call for him to "fire away," along with his hard-fought attempt to recover physically, had convinced the town's people that he would make a good sheriff. Henry's friend George Chrisman offered him a corner of his store where Henry could set up his office. Henry moved a desk and chair in to his 'office,' put a badge on, and felt he was now officially the sheriff. But, he wanted more; he hoped that someday he would be marshal again.

Two days later Henry rented a small wagon and team of horses to take him to Fort Benton to marry and bring home Electa. He hurriedly appointed D.H. Dillingham as his chief deputy and three men—unfortunately of the tough, rowdy crowd—Ned Ray, Buck Stinson, and Jack Gallagher as deputies, which made people nervous and wonder about Henry's sense of judgment. Henry recognized that he still had a disadvantage, physically, and chose these men for his own protection as well as the people who elected him.

Everyone hoped that Henry would stay long enough to establish some sort of order, but he had a wife to collect, and he left them May 6 under four deputies who had no experience in the business of keeping the law. Gold was discovered in Alder Gulch at the end of the month causing a stampede of hundreds of miners to a place they eventually christened Virginia City.

People became wealthy overnight in this new gold country that out produced, by a hundred-fold, the gold dust and nuggets that had been harvested on Grasshopper Creek. No one thought to establish a bank, but most likely, that would have been robbed, also. The robberies along the trails in and out of these fresh, new establishments, especially between Bannack and Virginia City, increased along with the new wealth.

Holdups along the trails made people nervous when heading out on these isolated journeys. Many men, especially those making runs to Salt Lake with huge amounts of gold to deposit, left at night and as secretly as possible to avoid ambush. Men fought over claims, as always, and lawlessness still plagued these small but growing mining districts.

By June, Dillingham, still acting as sheriff, suspected his fellow deputies of attacking wagon trains and travelers on the trails and decided to go after them. He shared this with Edwin Purple, the town gossip, who announced this to as many fellow citizens in Bannack as possible.

Any man or group of men who made frequent trips along the trails became suspect regarding the many holdups. There also were a number of stage stops that everyone used to break up their journeys, ranches, where they could find food and drink, a warm place to sleep, and fresh horses. The men operating these also became suspect, all being considered toughs and rowdies.

The most infamous and tainted ranch, the Rattlesnake, lay a short distance from Bannack to the east. Two men of questionable character ran the Rattlesnake along with their cook, Erastus "Red" Yeager. After that there was Stone's Ranch, Demsey's Cottonwood Ranch, Cold Spring Ranch, Pete Daley's Robber's Roost Ranch, and Laurin's Ranch. Each of these places were quite desolate but necessary to the stage routes.

Anyone considered on the edge of respectable citizenry who owned and ran an establishment where travel plans could easily be heard came under suspicion. People viewed Cyrus Skinner, owner of the Elkhorn and his friend Buck Stinson who ran a part-time barber shop in one corner of Skinner's bar as prime suspects. There was also guilt by association. Everyone suspected anyone with a colored past or anyone who kept company with these secesh whiskey rowdies.

After the substitute sheriff's suspicions became well known, Buck Stinson and two comrades ran up to Dillingham on the main street of Virginia City and shot him in front of many witnesses. Dillingham, suffering from wounds in his leg and chest, bled to death immediately.

Miners from all over the area rushed into town, and a miner's trial was held with hundreds of men involved. Jack Gallagher arrested the three men for their assassination of a fellow deputy and law officer. One man was immediately declared innocent because he had been heard to yell at Dillingham, "Don't shoot, don't shoot!" The other two men were sentenced to hang. But after much of the crowd dispersed, the remaining men called for a new vote. The ayes and nays issued forth seemed equal and mayhem ensued. In the end, Deputy Gallagher rode up and announced, "They're cleared. Let them go!" Such was the justice dealt out by a miners' court.

Henry returned on July 2 with Electa, to a town just as sullen and quiet as Henry's new wife. July 4 wasn't celebrated due to the strife of the civil war. No one dared exhibit their emotions or speak their views in such an impassioned atmosphere where everyone believed that possibly, organized crime had sprouted in the region. Henry's absence and the increased frequency of robberies had prompted some to think of taking the law into their own hands.

CHAPTER 13

JUNE 1863— JANUARY 1864

Henry arrived at the Sun River Farm on June 2 anxious to marry Electa. He rode up to the Vail cabin, anxious to see her and stood at the door for some time before someone answered it. Martha finally opened it and just stared at Henry, hostile and wary, not saying a word.

"Martha. How are you? You're looking fine. Where's Electa? I'm can't wait to see her and tell her all about Bannack. I've done well this winter, Martha, with the gold mining but now I have been elected sheriff. I do hope she'll … approve …" Henry stood looking at Martha, dumbfounded. "What's wrong? Its Electa isn't it? Is she ill? Oh God! Please tell me she's here and doing fine!"

He couldn't help but remember two other times when he stood at someone's door and received bad news about his loved one. His face had turned ashen and he looked as if he would faint away. He clutched at his chest because his heart beat so hard and rapid. His stomach roiled, and he felt as if he would be sick and prayed he wouldn't vomit.

Henry's concern warmed Martha some, and she answered him politely, "Oh yes! Electa's okay, but you will need to speak with her. Come in. Let me go get her."

Henry stood at the door, worrying. God, Martha had made everything sound so over-with. Will need to speak to her? What did that mean? The will need to speak to her made it seem as if there was one final detail to handle and then, what, all was in the past and over with? What the hell? Will need to speak with him until what?

Electa came into the kitchen and stood silently assessing Henry. "We heard you had been shot. Are you okay?" she queried in a cold, bland voice.

Henry regained his composure somewhat when he saw her standing before him obviously in good health, but the tone of her voice and the way she looked at him made his heart race again. He nervously took off his hat, shaking his head to let a lock of hair hide his scar.

He stammered a little when he answered her. "Y … yes. Yes, I'm fine. My arm is a bit mangled and scarred now, and when the weather changes I have some stiffness and pain. But other than that, I'm fine. How are you?"

"I'm okay," she said, looking at Henry so intently he felt as if she were searching for something but couldn't quite find it. He stepped closer to her, and she stepped back, holding out her hand to signal him to stop. Now he knew something was terribly wrong. He remained silent, not knowing what to say next. The silence grew long, and their unease thickly hung in the air. Electa sighed, and it came out almost a sob. She nervously fingered the lace on the bodice of her dress, and Henry noticed she had become much thinner than he remembered.

"Are you really okay? What's wrong? Have you been ill; you're so thin."

Henry, uneasy, reached up and scratched at his scar, which tended to declare itself, prickling whenever he felt uncomfortable and upset. He ran his hands around and around the brim of his hat.

Henry swallowed hard and asked, "Electa, please tell me what is wrong? Why have you lost so much weight? Have you been ill?"

Electa looked into his eyes while hers misted. "Just heartsick, Henry. When we heard that you had two different shootouts in Bannack, killing one of the men, James decided that I shouldn't be marrying a man of your temperament and demeanor. I told James and Martha about your past because I don't believe in keeping secrets, especially from them, and James said that you had had just too many altercations with people. Why? Why, Henry, did you kill again? How could you? I understood that you wanted to change. You know, you really shouldn't even carry a gun."

Henry closed his eyes and prayed a silent entreaty, Please, dear God, don't have me lose another woman that I care for so much. Please.

Henry cleared the lump out of his throat that had crawled up from his aching chest and said, "Well, Electa, I can't hardly leave my guns at home since the towns people of Bannack just voted me in as sheriff. They seem to approve of me, and I'll have you know both men intended to kill me first, like always. Crawford did shoot first, and Jack Cleveland drew first. Besides, everyone knew Cleveland for a thief and a murderer. He killed a rancher one morning and stole gold dust off his dead body. Crawford told you all this, I'm sure, with his own words all dressed up to make me look as bad as possible. He was the one who turned tail and ran."

Electa nodded. "So, what about Cleveland, who made you God to decide if a man should live or die, Henry?"

Henry, to lighten things said, "That's what my saintly side always asks me."

"Not funny Henry. It's certainly nothing to laugh about, and obviously your good side always seems to lose out to your black devil. I can't be married to a man like you. At first when James forbade me to marry you, I couldn't stop crying and mourning. I quit eating. But in time I began to see the wisdom of his decision and began to heal. I am not quite over you, Henry Plummer, but know this—I no longer wish to be your wife." Electa's voice caught and she began to weep soundlessly but beseeching Henry in a small voice to just go away, forever.

Henry strode quickly to her and enveloped her with his arms. He pulled her close, and she rested her head against his chest while he caressed her hair. Soon he began landing soft, gentle kisses on the top of her head, saying, "Ssshhh, don't cry. We'll work it out."

Soon they were kissing, deeply, and Henry moaned from his pent-up sexual desires. He lowered his arms and pulled Electa tightly to him and when she felt his desire, she weakly whimpered, "Ohhh."

Martha had gone out to fetch James and when James stepped into the cabin, the normally complacent man went crazy with frustrated anger. He, too, had suffered from the decision to forbid Electa's marrying Henry. His entire family had because they had all been taken in by Henry and each in their own way had become quite enamored with him.

"What in the hell is going on here. Electa, what are you doing?"

"Father watch your language," was all Martha could say while thinking of the many times Electa had damned Henry and swore to never fall for his charms ever again. She had even declared hatred for the man when she had been at her very worse in trying to forget him. Martha had held her close, comforting her night after night, during that time. Nighttime had been the most painful for Electa.

The two lovers reluctantly parted, panting and blushing. Electa remained silent while Henry began making his case to James.

"James, sir, I understand how and why you feel the way you do after hearing reports from that crazy Crawford. I had no problem with the man, but he just became hell bent, because of his resentment of me, to kill me. And, Jack, you know how he was and what he was like; he pulled his gun on me first. He also proved to be a thief and murderer—all of Bannack would attest to that. He should have been tried, convicted, and hanged."

James cleared his throat, which was hoarse from yelling at Henry. Henry's words had softened him a bit but he still had to finish telling his point-of-view on Henry's actions and the consequences.

"Electa told us about your past and the men you killed in shootouts. We can't have a man like that in our family. You will only cause us much grief, especially Electa. I don't want that to happen. Can't you ever stop and think in these situations. Do something else, such as, since you're very strong for someone of your stature, giving them a taste of your fists? I believe that if that would happen, they would all run, just as Cleveland had done this winter. He came to Fort Benton, buying a ticket for the first steamer out, which just left the other day, by the way."

Henry's face lit up. "Has Reverend Baines arrived yet?"

"Henry, you will not be marrying, Electa. Get that into your head."

Electa burst into tears and ran from the room with Martha close behind. She had dreaded this day. Now she would have to begin her work all over again in rehabilitating Electa, making her promises, repeatedly, that there were many fish in the sea and that she would find a good man to marry just like she had with James.

The two men remained standing in the kitchen their eyes deadlocked; each man trying to put into words their own argument. Henry finally drew a long, shaky breath.

"James, I know things look bad, and you do need to realize that I do not like killing and have tried, desperately, to stay out of those situations because when I do end someone's life, it eats at me. But, that damn Cleveland followed me and made life miserable for all of Bannack, not just for me, and Crawford, I don't know what got into him. He became angry because the miner's court held to judge another shooting, decided he should give me back my gun that he had confiscated. The people of Bannack now trust and respect me so that they just voted me in as sheriff."

James shook his head and exclaimed, "My God! Henry, do you think being sheriff in Bannack is going to make your life or Electa's, any better, safer, or less guilt ridden should she marry you? Now you will not be allowed to marry my sister-in-law!"

"I'll have you know that I love her and ..."

"Just give it up, Henry. Leave. Now. Just get away from us. Leave!"

Henry stood his ground, shaking his head.

James walked briskly to the shotgun hanging over the kitchen window, lifted it off its hooks, and leveled it at Henry. "Don't think I won't shoot you, Henry Plummer. Now leave. Be the gentleman that you are and leave us. This has not been easy for any of us, Henry; we all like you. But I'll not put Electa's wellbeing and happiness in jeopardy. Now, go. Please."

Henry sighed and walked out to his horse. James followed.

"Can I at least see Electa once more before I go?"

"No. I don't think that would be wise, Henry."

Henry mounted Avenger and headed toward Fort Benton where he would pick up the Mullen Road south and west to Bannack. His heart, throat, and chest felt as if he had consumed a meal of bullets swallowed whole. He rode into Fort Benton and purchased some supplies for the trip home, buying entire sacks of flour, corn meal, sugar and coffee, salted pork, and some whiskey since provisions were always short in the gold fields. He tied Avenger to the back of the wagon, which he had left at the fort along with the pair of horses he had rented, and left.

He felt dispirited and heartsick, occasionally, shaking his head at his bad luck. He just couldn't seem to keep a woman, he thought, no, never, always something in the way or some misfortune. He thought and thought. How could he have lost the chance to marry a good woman, and one that promised to be as passionate and loving as Pauline had been, bless her heart. Henry felt guilty when remembering his Pauline, but he was a living man, vibrant and young enough to want all the benefits of sharing a bed with a wife and of fathering children.

Suddenly, he thought, No, God damned it! I'll not take no for an answer, and he slowly turned his wagon and team around, making his way back to Fort Benton, trying to come up with some argument that would make James, everyone, change their mind. He took the trail heading back to Sun River Farm. With the memory of Electa's willing and warm kisses giving him the courage and confidence he needed. Yes, she does love me. I love her, and we'll marry.

Henry had come close enough to the farm to see them all working out in the meadow. James was plowing up a stretch of land, for wheat or oats, Henry thought, and the women and children looked as if they were spreading grass seed on the other end. Iron, their Indian man, was busy felling a few smaller cottonwood trees on the edge of James' field. Joseph busily worked on the new well they hoped would be better than the old one dug several years ago.

The weather couldn't have been more perfect, not to cold or hot and surprisingly with no wind. The sky hovered over all, a clear, almost indigo, blue with only a few clouds scuttling to the north. Henry pulled up in front of the main cabin and unhitched the horses from the wagon, making sure to tie them securely to trees under which they could graze. He untied Avenger from the back of the wagon, still wondering what move to make next.

He decided to ride out to the meadow where the women worked. He knew he could steal Electa away and work on her first, since she still loved him and all. Perhaps once James saw how in love they were, and how earnest he was, he would change his mind. Henry looked up at the beautiful sky and feeling the warm sun felt suddenly peaceful and thinking things would work out as he wished.

He looked out into the horizon to the east and thought, when I finish my time as sheriff of Bannack, Electa and I will head back east and begin a new wonderful life in civilization where I won't need to carry a gun any longer. They'd go to Maine, well out of the reaches of the Civil War, since Henry felt sick of fighting. He looked again to the east and became alarmed when he saw a huge dust cloud rapidly approaching the farm. Damn! Could it be the Indians he had been hired last fall to fight returning?

Henry dug into Avenger's side, urging him into a gallop. He raced across the meadow to the east, flying past Electa, Martha, and the children, ignoring their stares of wonder. He slowed down when he got to the ridge overhanging the Sun River. When he came nearly to the top of a red rocked butte, he jumped off Avenger, tied him to a tree, half stooping and half crawling the final few yards to the peak. He bellycrawled the rest of the distance and watched as the cloud of dust drew near. Yes, it consisted of about three dozen Indian warriors, of what band or nation he wasn't sure.

Henry made his way back down and took off on Avenger at a gallop. When he neared the women and children he yelled, "Indians, about three dozen or so coming this way with guns, rifles. Run! Run like hell to the cabin and arm yourselves!"

Henry didn't stop to see if they heeded his warning but galloped to James and then Iron, yelling the same alarm. They all gathered at the house and waited with hearts in their throats and beating rapidly.

No one spoke a word while each man took on a woman or child, checking their weapons to make sure they worked fine and had been loaded correctly. Martha prayed silently. She prayed for their safety and for some way out of this danger. She also entreated her maker for the preservation of her windows. They had just finished putting in the last piece of glass they had ordered from St. Louis last fall. She had looked forward to the delivery of that almost as much as the arrival of Reverend Baines. They had also been able to stock up on provisions in Fort Benton upon the arrival of the steam boat *Emilie*. They had just enough to get them through the summer.

She began giggling at the ludicrous petition she had made to her Lord. Everyone turned and stared at her, and James harshly whispered, "Ssshhh." Martha could not stop laughing and the effort of holding it in made her laugh even more, and tears rolled down her cheeks. James only shook his head.

Henry, of course, crouched next to Electa, and they communicated with eye contact. Hers seemed to say, thank you, while Henry's held a constant entreaty of, please, give me one more chance. Henry thought, it's so good to be a part of a family again, even if it is only to fight off the Indians. He loved that belonging feeling as he looked around at everyone. Martha crouched next to James and each one of them had a child by their side. Iron and Joseph had each taken up a station on the other side of each child, and Henry sat stooped next to Joseph.

Everyone understood that James, Henry, and Iron would, if necessary, each break out a window and fire the first rounds of defensive shots. When they needed to reload, Martha, Joseph, and Harvey would take over the stations at the windows. They had organized this system last fall when Henry and Jack first came home with James, when they anticipated Indian raids. But Henry knew they had never expected more than a dozen attackers since the Indians camped in the area typically were small, containing not more than ten or so warriors.

Now they faced the probability of fight off more than three dozen men, and Henry worried about the outcome. James must have been in the same mindset because he hoarsely whispered, "Let's all join hands while I say a prayer."

They held hands with scared-out-of-your-wits sweaty palms as James petitioned God in a normal voice as if his whispers wouldn't be loud enough, and despite the tension, Henry smiled, thinking of how they all had been whispering and staying as silent as possible as if that would make any difference.

"Dear Lord, please deliver us from this danger that we may live another day to serve you. Send your Holy Spirit down upon these natives, allowing us to strike a peaceful bargain with them that will show them the Grace that you extend to all souls living on this Earth."

The Indians slowed as they approached the farm, and it felt like forever until they reached the cabin. James whispered, as if it really mattered, that, "They look to be part of the Dakota tribe, actually a mix of Anishinabe and Dakota. I can tell by the way they dress their hair. They're sort of a lost tribe right now. They don't want to be assigned to a reservation anywhere, especially not in the Dakota Territory."

James crab walked to a kitchen drawer and pulled out a bleached white flour sack made into a kitchen towel. "I'm going out and talk to them."

Martha gasped and beseeching him with her eyes, finally saying, "Oh, James, please be careful."

James slowly opened the door, holding both hands up with the towel clasped tightly in one hand. He stood there waving it back and forth. The warriors had lined up, circling the house two horses deep. It looked as if Henry's estimation had been nearly correct. The leader spoke some broken English until he realized that James knew enough of their talk, making it possible for them to communicate in that language.

As Henry watched the exchange, he could tell the discussion was fraught with tension. He could see James shaking his head back and forth, and the Indian curling his lips as he spoke out what looked to be a threat. James shook his head once more and held out his hands in supplication. Henry slowly stood and backed away from the window, creeping toward the door and pulling a white handkerchief out of his pocket. Electa gasped when she realized what he was doing. He motioned Ssshhh, opened the door, and slowly walked toward James until he stood next to him.

"What do they want?" He asked in a soft voice.

"Food. And we don't have much to share since I'm just about out of money. We just laid in supplies enough to last us the summer. I can't give them much of anything right now."

"Tell them the wagon over there," Henry motioned with his head, "is loaded with flour, sugar, pork, beans, whiskey, and coffee. They can have it all." Henry thought for a moment, and then said, "But if they won't drink the coffee or whiskey; ask them to leave it."

James gave him a strange, sideways look and repeated Henry's message to the warriors, who quickly gather up the provisions from Henry's wagon, excitedly talking the entire time. They then galloped off across the meadow and were soon out of sight.

James walked back to the cabin, collapsing onto the bench beside the door, shaking his head. "I don't know what I would have done, Henry, without you here. Thank you."

Martha came out and kneeled before James, hugging him to her and laying her head in his lap, weeping tears of relief. James reached down patting her shoulders with shaking hands. "There, there, Martha. We're safe now again, dear."

Electa slowly moved toward Henry, and he gathered her up into his arms. The children came out with Harvey standing before his parents, declaring, "Well, I don't know why you had me practice shooting targets all winter if we never get to fight those Indians."

James shook his head sternly. "Son, we are not here to shoot Indians, we're a mission. We are here to teach them white man's ways, and to feed them when we can. If we teach them how to farm and raise gardens, crops, and livestock, then they won't be hungry. I've explained this to you before. We white people, first the trappers, then the buffalo hunters, and now miners, and always the farmers, have ruined their traditional way of life. We owe them some form of help since little by little we are taking their land away from them. I only wish to put a little bit of right back into all this wrong."

James turned to Henry and said, "Well, Henry, you might just as well stay for dinner, and we'll talk after."

Henry and Electa married on June 20. Electa wore her finest dress which was a simple, homespun brown dress. They left immediately after the ceremony and a simple meal, heading south and west for Bannack. Henry planned to wait until he carried Electa over the threshold of his humble house to consummate their marriage and enjoy their wedding night. When they arrived at Bannack, Henry stopped at his little office where the town's people stormed Henry with news of the latest lawlessness during his absence and questioned his choice of deputies.

Henry felt overwhelmed and embarrassed at his constituent's revelations and assessment of his judgment but decided to concentrate on them the next day. He had better things to do this evening. He nervously headed down the street that led to his cabin, praying that Electa would approve of it.

He had added a large room to the back of his cabin, turning it into a bedroom with two smaller rooms attached, hoping that someday they could use one as a nursery for any baby that would come along, and the other a bedroom for when the child was older. He hoped that would happen soon since he was approaching the ripe age of thirty-three. Most men by this age would have been married, settled down, and had fathered several children by now. Then he became sad thinking of Pauline and their baby son lying in a grave far away. And, then, he thought of Spooky and little Henry and decided, that, yes, they should have a child.

He had laid down a rough wooden floor and installed two glass paned windows, which allowed the evening sun to shine in, making the room seem golden and warm. Each tiny bedroom had one small window. He ordered a bright colored rag rug and an equally cheery log cabin quilt from Salt Lake City. He hoped Electa would enjoy sewing curtains for the rooms and had sent for white muslin fabric. He also sent for three dresses for her and hoped he had ordered the right size.

Electa seemed pleased with all his efforts, and he promised her she could order more furnishings from Salt Lake little by little. She raised her eyebrows at that and queried him with, "But Henry, I thought you promised James we would go east after you finished your year as sheriff?"

"Well, yes, Electa. But I want you to be happy and comfortable in the meantime."

She nodded, okay, and began hanging her few clothes in the oak chiffarobe. When she returned to the front room, Henry had a fire going in the fireplace and three wrapped boxes lying on the kitchen table for her, which she delightedly tore into with joy. It had been a long time since she had been presented with so many gifts. She ran into the bedroom and tried on a blue dress made of soft lawn material, trimmed abundantly with lace. The bodice just came to the top of her cleavage, and Henry, turned on by her lovely décolleté, moved toward her.

Electa welcomed him with open arms saying, "Do what you did to me when we picnicked Henry, before we …"

Henry laughed and finished her sentence. "Make love?"

Electa pleased Henry very much, despite her lack of experience. She's a natural, smiled Henry as he watched her sleeping a peaceful baby's sleep after. Her dress lay on the floor in a tumble, and he stooped to pick it up, hanging it with her other dresses. He then went into the kitchen, quietly closing the door before he began to cook them a beef stew. After he had that started, he finished unloading the wagon and returned it and the two horses to the stable.

Joe, the owner, supplied Henry with more information about events he had missed while gone fetching Electa. "Yes, lots of people moving out of Bannack to try their luck in Alder Gulch. It's a town over there already, became one in just six weeks. Not everyone's movin' though. Did you see that spanking new building as you entered town? Set up by this fellow, Nick Wall. Man's got money even though he's just another one of those confederate parolees. He was a major in Missouri's Militia that mustered at Camp Jackson. They planned on going after the Kansas Jayhawkers, hoping to wipe them all off the face of the Earth, making sure Missouri stayed secessionist and entered the Union as a slave state."

Joe stopped to spit out his chew, took a deep breath and continued. "But a Union captain put a quick end to them, surrounding the fort in May of '61. Wall was a prisoner of war held at the St. Louis arsenal before being released on parole along with many others. The feds gave them a choice; either stay in St. Louis or go to the western territories, but don't even think of joining up again to fight in the war.

He stayed in St. Louis, working as a steamboat captain, and that's when he fell in love with this country, coming up the Missouri to Fort Benton. He's of a mind that these parts will soon become separate territories and then states, makin' his eyeballs swim with dollar signs, thinking of all the money to be made when that happens.

"Started a store at Gold Creek when they were diggin' over there. He's the one that made gold discoveries in this here region possible. You know, Tom, Tom Cover, he was only able to find gold here at Grasshopper Creek, because Nick gave him, just handed out all these provisions to him, free, mind you, sos Tom could wander around lookin' for gold. Tom was down on his luck, starvin' and penniless; and, for some reason this Nick Wall guy just looked him over and gave him whatever he wanted."

Joe stuffed another chew in his mouth and when he had it all soft and wet, began talking again. "Yup. Tom put a claim in Wall's name, and soon Nick was over here. Went in on the Bannack Ditch with a partner and makin' lots of money now. He's not here now. He goes back and forth, from here to St. Louis where his family lives. But, his store is quite nice, carries everything from horseshoe nails to women's underclothes. Has lots of foodstuff, too."

Henry went home to find a beautiful woman, with cheeks still flushed from lovemaking and sleep in his kitchen eating a bowl of stew with gusto.

"Delicious, Henry. I'm so hungry suddenly. Don't know why. Getting over the nervousness, I guess."

Henry just smiled and walked to her, kissing her on the top of her head, working his way down. Soon they were in bed again, and Henry discovered that his new wife had a huge appetite for another pleasure besides food.

Because of the increased crimes and killings, Henry eventually found that he did not have much spare time to devote to his domestic life, and

Electa realized she had become second on Henry's list of considerations. After many lonely hours, she became even more embittered.

Henry's problems ranged from the never-ending series of petty robberies along the trails to men fighting over claims and a strong, politically minded faction of newcomers that didn't respect him and his law-keeping skills. Samuel T. Hauser, a former railroad executive and highly politically ambitious man had just come to the area and disapproved of Henry. Henry's friend and new acquaintance, and equally ambitious young politician, Nathaniel P. Langford liked Henry and put his name forward to Hauser as a possible deputy marshal for the new territory.

Hauser dramatically warned him against Henry as a choice. "Plummer is a dangerous man with a past," he proclaimed. "Even though it well known that he's a Union supporter, he's still too Democrat for us to chance appointing him deputy marshal. The Republicans, who control most of territory politics, would never trust him, and that won't help us."

"But, you're a Democrat," Langford protested.

"Yes, but I know how to deal with both sides. And, I, like you, want to see Montana as a separate territory from Idaho, keeping much of Idaho's mineral-wealthy lands within its borders. It will be a continuous struggle until Montana can claim statehood, keeping the rich Idaho land."

Langford shook his head. "I know Plummer's going to take it hard, us not supporting him. He has been coveting the deputy marshal position for months. He's been a good friend to me and my family." He laughed, saying, "I found him helping my wife stretch calico over our walls after we put up more chinking. He gave us the cloth after he discovered he had ordered too much. We've had him for supper many times, and he repays us by tutoring our boy, Nick, in arithmetic and reading. Both our children love him because he comes to supper with some sweet for them. He's Uncle Henry to them."

Hauser only snorted and said, "He still has a dangerous, soiled past."

By now Bannack had reduced it numbers to a little over three hundred while Virginia City had increased to three thousand. Henry often found himself traveling to and from Bannack and Virginia City to perform his duties, leaving Electa alone. Conflicts in mining disputes continued to take up much of his time, and in August, he had to perform the execution of a man who had shot and killed his partner over the division of their holdings along Grasshopper Creek.

Henry had scaffolds built on the edge of town, hoping to prove his renewed faithfulness to the legal system and his ambition to be an effective lawman. The hanging bothered him for days and he questioned his choice in work. Days after the execution Henry remained contrite and confused, eating little, pacing up and down their front room night after night, and having problems making love to Electa. When he was able, he allowed himself to tell Electa about his doubts and fears. He hated the miners' courts, which were quite sketchy in the fairness and justice they dealt out but were the only form of that had some semblance to a court system in the territories.

He had rid himself of his deputies due to the cloud of suspicion still hanging over them from the Dillingham case but was still called upon often to give advice to miners and help assess their new holdings. People still treated him with respect, but Henry could feel their trust in his performance slipping away.

Electa sewed and sewed until her fingers carried calluses. Henry ordered more and more things for her from Salt Lake, especially more fabric for her stitching pleasure. But, she quickly became tired of that and felt increasingly bored each day, waiting for Henry to come and take her to Wall's mercantile shopping. She felt crazed at times. She read the books and magazines Henry sent for but those only seemed to make her more aware of her lonely existence and she became bitter, looking at life as mostly dreary in this little place.

The only sweetness she could count on was when Henry came home each evening. She could not go out alone since there were too many rowdies, drunk at any time of the day, hanging around town. She looked forward to Henry's arrival, his escorting her to Main Street for shopping or a supper out, and then coming home to make love. They repeated their honeymoon night day after day with Henry doing most of the cooking while she languished in bed after lovemaking.

What more could a woman ask? She knew he spoiled her and loved her dearly, and yet that stupid sheriff job kept him away from her too much, both in proximity and when he couldn't get a piece of trouble off his mind. She recognized his occasional absentmindedness when making love and that irked her woman's pride. When Henry suggested they try making a baby, she looked at him as if he had lost his mind.

She worried about him, also. What if he didn't return to her some evening and someone came to the door to announce his demise? What then? The thought scared her, frightened her to the point that if she played that scene out too much in her mind, she would become ill, sick in her stomach. No, she couldn't risk bearing a child for them until they left this hell hole and returned to civilization. Henry talked to her about the law constantly—the Constitution and people's rights and all. He will make a very find lawyer when they moved east, she thought.

She began a campaign to coerce Henry into leaving his position early. Who would really care? But, Henry assured her he would care and that he would lose all self respect if he deserted the people who had voted him in as their sheriff. She became frustrated with him and resentful of the towns people, who, to her, seemed nothing but a bunch of whiners and troublemakers, gossiping constantly about everyone and everything. She became quite cold when other people tried to engage her in conversation, especially women. She just couldn't connect with them. But they all had children and some had nicer houses to care for, and they seemed so complacent, making her even more distant from them.

Then, the headaches began. Sometimes she felt as if she couldn't even see straight. Things would blur, and stars would swim before her eyes. Her lovely sunlit bedroom became a curse, and she hung the new quilt she had just stitched together over the windows. Henry insisted the doctor look at her. When Dr. Glick told her the best cure for these migraines would to become pregnant, she burst into tears.

As the summer wore on, the weather turned hotter and hotter with no rain, only impotent thunderstorms that would only spit a few drops of moisture or bring scanty bursts of hail storms. Most of the time, the wind blew, sucking the moisture from every living thing. It would howl around the corners of their little house, sounding to Electa like an angry vengeful spirit that wouldn't quite haunting. The country around them became as dry and bleached as the buffalo bones that littered the plains and prairies, and Electa began to feel as dried up and lifeless as those bones.

Henry's troubles as sheriff became more complicated because people became increasingly jittery and full of stories—tales that Henry found difficult to investigate. The instigators of some of these alleged robberies out on the stagecoach runs never could agree on common facts. They each gave different accounts of the holdups as well as descriptions of the perpetrators. Henry began finding it difficult to satiate Electa's appetite in bed because he found it difficult to pull his mind away from these frustrations. And, when he felt the need, a migraine usually ruined hers.

One day Electa found herself on Main Street, coming out of the mercantile with her carpet bag full of items—things she couldn't fathom why she had purchased since she and Henry had decided to carefully watch their spending, saving money for their move east. Hers eyes, blinded by the sudden searing sunlight, made her stop and she stood out on the wooden walk in a daze, waiting for them to adjust to the brilliance. Henry, making his afternoon rounds around town, saw her and rushed to her side.

"What in God's name do you think you're doing, wandering around town unescorted?"

Electa only shook her head, not able to speak, so shocked she was by her own behavior as well as her memory lapse. She felt quite ill. Her head throbbed, stars circled around her, and she felt as if she would be sick at any moment. Henry got her home just in time, and she ran out to the outhouse behind the cabin where she lost everything she'd eaten in the last two days, completely emptying her digestive system.

After that, Electa had no appetite and by August, she had become a ghost of her former self. Her mind seemed to have wasted along with her body, and Henry worried. But try as he did, he never could find more time to be with her, and he would come home to find her either angry or in a complete dispirited funk. She begged him to allow her to go out alone during the day, and he, in return, firmly told her that it just wasn't safe to do so without him. The evenings he returned from a trip to Virginia City were the worst since she had to stay home for two days alone without Henry's company or escort out and about in the town.

Electa could not take this situation any longer and decided to go east, alone, before the weather turned cold. She knew how cold and wintery it could become even as early as October in this desolate country. She sensed that staying on through the winter would completely undo her, perhaps even kill her.

One evening Henry came home to find Electa packing. When Henry asked her what was going on, she announced firmly that, "I have decided that I cannot and will not live like this, Henry. I'm going crazy, maybe just stir-crazy but I can't bear it any longer. Any time someone knocks on the door, my heart stops, and I wonder, is this it, is this the moment someone will tell me you've been killed? And, each time I see that ugly scar on your forehead and that wreck of your arm, I am reminded of your sullied past and your dangerous present."

Henry knew that his disfigurements were abhorrent to Electa. Her reaction on their wedding night when he had taken off his hat and wedding suit made him realize how awful they must look. The poorly healed gash in his forehead and his arm were truly abominations. But, still, he knew Electa could look past them because if she hadn't, their lovemaking could not have been nearly so passionate. He promised her that they would leave next May on the very day his time as sheriff formally ended. He assured her that he didn't and wouldn't take any unnecessary risks any longer. He would be extremely safe.

She came back with, "I've heard the people talk in this town and how they think you're a leader of all these robbing, thieving men out on the trails and that you call yourselves, the Innocents or Plummer's Gang. How every time you ride a stage coach it is never ambushed, but when you don't, there surely is one. I heard that the day I lost my memory and ended up at the store. I think that's why I became so ill after."

Henry shook his head in confusion, amazed that his own wife wanted to believe the worst of him. "I'm not a leader of any gang. I have never stolen from anyone and I don't plan to. Besides, most of those robberies never even happened. I can count on one hand the ones that did, and most of those were botched by the stupidity of the men attempting them. I simply want to live out my time here as sheriff, sell my claims, and leave as soon as I can. I love you and want to have children with you, and I am certainly not a thief or a bandit."

"Well, Henry, you certainly don't help yourself by befriending those that are talked about and mentioned most every time there is a robbery. I heard it all that day at the store. They didn't realize I was there, and they talked and talked about you and the Gang. Plummer's Gang, they call it; because, they said you've befriended many of these toughs and claim that you drank and gambled with them."

Henry began pacing, shaking his head in denial. "That's in the past and doesn't make me a criminal. I became lonely and bored waiting to go fetch you and I just fell victim to my old habits. That's all. I've not had a drink since you arrived and haven't sat down to gamble. I have spoken with those men and not a one of them will admit to such doings. I can't arrest them; all I have is rumors and inconclusive evidence, none of which incriminates any of them."

"Well, they are friends and acquaintances of yours and that speaks volumes to suspicious minds. Just leave with me tomorrow, so you're safe from all this suspicion and guilt by association. I want to at least go east as far as my hometown in Iowa, like we talked about at Sun River. I hate it here, this place full of such awful people—drunks, rowdies, scalawags, and never-do-wells. I can't ever leave my home and socialize. There's not even a church here. And, if you won't go with me, I plan to leave alone and live alone. I may as well, since I'm mostly alone now."

"I can't leave. I have responsibilities. You know that!"

"Responsibilities! You're being ridiculous. There is no law here to lend the definition of responsibility to your so-called job as sheriff. Everyone knows that law doesn't exist here, and that you're not really keeping people safe, especially out there in those wide-open spaces. I want to go home and leave this wild and crazy place. I want to go somewhere, anywhere, where civilized people live, and men don't shoot at one another constantly—a place where men keep their guns at home."

"I just can't leave, yet. Besides, do you really think people are that much better—in civilized places, where law exists? I don't think it is all that pure in those places. People are people, and there is always the danger, the chance, that someone will harm you, one way or another."

Electa rose to finish her packing and queried, "Oh, Henry! Will you ever make up your mind? Why do you still want to serve these people who say such awful things about you? You have been hurt so many times, and yet you believe in people, their goodness while still knowing their foibles, their tendency to do wrong to others. I feel sorry for you and worry so about you."

Henry just stood there shaking his head back and forth. No, he thought, I'm thirty- two years old and can't come to a belief about anything except that when a man is hired, voted in to do a job, he must fulfill and complete his duties."

Electa, exasperated over Henry's quiet and foolish looking stance said, "Well, you can at least ride along my stagecoach tomorrow and remove yourself from this danger for a while, at least. Henry, I know, I'm sure they are all out to get you, and I do care for you enough to not want to be here when they do arrest you and do God knows what. Come with me. Please?"

"They are not going to arrest me; they have no grounds. Besides, I'm still the law here."

Francis Thompson, who knew about Henry and Electa's love for one another and sensed the passion between them, moved to Bannack to start a mercantile store and was a big supporter of Henry's. He thought of Henry as a fine man who conscientiously worked to do his best as sheriff. Henry had done much to help him do repairs on his building and to turn the back rooms into decent living quarters.

When he watched Henry buying Electa's ticket and loading several bags of her belongings onto the stage; he couldn't help himself and approached Electa. "Well, Electa, going somewhere?"

"She shaded her eyes and looking up at him, said, "Yes, I'm going back home to Iowa. Henry will join me later." No one was more surprised when Electa chose to leave Henry than Francis, and when Henry asked him to be his stand-in sheriff while he accompanied Electa as far as the Snake River Crossing, he reluctantly agreed while shaking his head repeatedly. He couldn't believe their separation, thinking of how in love they seemed.

He bid them both, goodbye, and pining Henry's badge onto his coat, walked thoughtfully down the street. Man, he just couldn't believe. The one social event held in Bannack that summer had been a street dance where he had enjoyed watching them dance together. Every so often he could see Henry smile at Electa, kiss her hand, and give her a look that promised more romance later. He had become a bit jealous and had secretly wished for the same luck as Henry in finding a good loving woman.

Henry's departure with Electa only served to expose him to more suspicion and speculation because not one robbery was held while he was gone, and, ironically on his return trip he traveled with the new chief justice of the Idaho Territory, the honorable Sidney Edgerton. The formidable man had been appointed by President Lincoln and Hannibal Hamblin, Henry's old mentor and Lincoln's vice-president, yet another irony. Edgerton, traveling with his family and despite being told by one of the drivers that the sheriff was a man with violent past, appeared to like and respect Henry.

Sidney did see Henry as a good man and loving husband. He watched Henry's farewell to his wife, which even made him choke up. He could see Henry's eyes glistening with emotion when he finally turned away from Electa and mounted his big beautiful stallion, and felt his sadness as they rode together along the trail.

Henry's complete devotion to her had been apparent as he parted from her in a very respectful and yet tender way. He'd held her hands, and Sidney could see him pleading with her, when she shook her head, he simply brought each hand up, kissing them tenderly. He gathered in his arms and kissed her softly on her head. Then, he handed her a key and filled her hands with good, Yankee money, giving her instructions as if he may not ever see her again.

The Edgerton family purchased a cabin in Yankee Flats where Sidney filled the walls with new chinking, built partitions between rooms, and crafted furniture with the help of his nephew, Wilbur Sanders, and Henry. He watched the miner's court system with interest but never became involved because, "I've not yet been sworn in." He caught gold fever and claimed and developed as many holdings as possible.

Edgerton became fast friends with Nathaniel Langford, Samuel Hauser, and other men full of ambitious ideas for this area now being coined, Montana; all agreeing that Montana should become its own territory including a sizeable chunk of mineral-rich Idaho. They also discussed the possibility of organizing a vigilance committee to address the area's lawless and dangerous atmosphere.

Edgerton's nephew, Wilbur Sanders and his family loved Henry. Upon their arrival, he helped to make things a little more welcoming for them in Bannack. Henry helped them make repairs on their board-sided home, which needed much improvement. He helped them paint the outside, and showed them how to cover the interior walls so the cold north and west winds would find some resistance when they came blowing. Henry greatly appreciated this friendship since Electa's departure had left him so lonely and lost.

Mattie Sanders, their teenage daughter, very much liked Henry and would sometimes follow him about town with her friends, flirting with him. The girls discovered they could earn a little candy money by washing out the miner's screenings each evening after they called it quits for the day. Henry would try to shoosh them home, claiming it wasn't safe to be on the main street with all the shootings and killings, but they would just laugh and tease Henry. Henry, remembering his problems in Nevada City because of lovely, blonde Lucy, shied away from his teenage admirers as much as possible.

They made the claim that, "We make it safer than even you do; no one lets loose with their guns when there are children around." Henry nodded, thinking, yes, that's true, men only gunned one another down when the streets were empty of the innocents. He would sigh, wishing the time would soon come when law and order weren't so out of reach.

James and Martha Vail moved their family to Bannack purchasing Henry's house onto which they built two lean-tos with separate entrances, one for Henry and the other for Francis Thompson. An extensive and lasting drought, leaving no green grass and dry cows, had forced them from Sun River. The new living arrangements proved comfortable and amiable for everyone, with Martha soon losing her animosity toward Henry. Henry did his best to help Martha make his former, loveless cabin into a home. James taught school and worked for Thompson part time, making him happy to amply provide for his family once more.

But, again, suspicion hovered over Henry when a trailside robbery occurred on October 26. Two hooded men on horses completely covered in blankets held up the Peabody & Caldwell stage coach when travelling from Virginia City to Bannack. The stage coach had left Virginia City on October 25, expecting to arrive in Bannack that evening, but because of a snow storm, its progress was slow and by the time they reached the Stinking Water Ranch, the fresh horses had gone off in all directions, and it took some time to recapture them and hitch them to the coach.

They stopped next at Demsey's ranch to pick up a miner, Bummer Dan McFadden, who had been rumored to be carrying a fair amount of gold dust. They reached the Rattlesnake Ranch by sundown and discovered that all the horses had been sent out. They spent the night there with the owners, Bill Bunton and Frank Parish, acting as generous, gracious hosts, pouring out much whiskey and serving hot, satisfying food prepared by Red Yeager.

The extra horses still could not be found the next morning, and the stage driver had to hitch up the horses from the day before. Bunton decided to ride along on top with the substitute driver, Billy Rumsey. Their progress, slow because of the weather, made them an easy target for a robbery, and everyone felt nervous, especially McFadden who constantly squirmed in his seat.

Suddenly two masked men rode up and demanded the stage coach to stop and ordered everyone out. They then told the driver, Rumsey, to disarm the passengers and to relieve them of all their money and gold dust. He took several small bags of gold dust from McFadden but the robbers weren't satisfied. "Search him again."

"You, McFadden, if you value your life, give it all up."

McFadden, reluctant, removed his jacket and undid a shoulder strap holding a large, leather bag full of the wanted treasure.

When the stage coach arrived in Bannack, the passengers each had their own version of events to tell. Most of them agreed, however, that Bill Bunton's behavior deemed scrutiny. He reacted to the highway men as if scared for his life yelling over and over "For God's sake, don't shoot!" so dramatically that they wondered why he wanted to appear such an innocent victim.

Days later, many people questioned why their sheriff had made no move to investigate the holdup, making him more suspect, and he had no idea how deeply he had come under suspicion. The only people who understood his complacency were the Vails because he told them one evening at supper how he would never go after someone simply because of rumors, and that he refused to arrest someone based on hearsay.

On Friday, November 13 Samuel Hauser planned to travel by stage from Virginia City to Bannack and from there go east to St. Louis, traveling with Mormon freighters as far as Salt Lake City. The news had spread that Hauser would be carrying over $14,000 dollars worth of gold dust on behalf of two local merchants, and once in St. Louis would pay off the debt they owed and bank the rest, along with a sizeable amount of his own earnings.

Henry reluctantly rode the stage to Virginia City on the twelfth to prevent another holdup. He thought he could do at least this much in the way of protecting men and their gold. He had no idea as to how to investigate the latest robbery or how to accumulate accurate information since everyone in Bannack held their own opinions as to who was suspect.

Henry could see the surprise on Hauser's face when he climbed into the coach. Their polite exchanges were short and uncomfortable. Henry knew Hauser didn't trust him, and he blamed Hauser for the recent cooling friendship with Thompson and Langford. After Hauser had become friendly with Edgerton, Henry could feel the judge's disintegrating opinion of him as well, and he still felt anger toward the robust, opinionated man who had thwarted his ambitions for the office of deputy marshal.

They arrived in Bannack without incident and went into the Goodrich Bar for drinks where Hauser suddenly announced his traveling plans and how much money he carried. He then thrust the bag at Henry, saying, "I want you, as sheriff, to keep this safe overnight." After which, Nathaniel Langford took the older man aside.

"Mr. Hauser, what in the hell are you thinking? My God, handing all that dust and nuggets over to Henry. He's become suspect you know. Everyone thinks he's organized all these robberies. He's friends with everyone, including the rowdies and toughs we all suspect responsible for these holdups."

"I'm aware of all those facts. What better way to test his integrity and intelligence. It will all come out eventually, you know. He'll slip up in time, you watch."

"Well, I do hope you know what you're doing."

Henry's over-hearing his former friend, Nathaniel Langford, raising a fit with Hauser made him feel hurt that his former friend put him in the same category as the other toughs and suspected highwaymen.

Henry being the charmer that he was, thought and thought of how he could warm some of Hauser's frosty feelings. He didn't need such an influential man's misconceived notions of him to ruin his position or life. He thought of the ugly weather ahead for the travelers and decided to present Hauser with a rich, red, woolen scarf that Electa had knit for him since looking at it always made him feel sad, lonely, and hurt.

The next day Henry handed over the gold dust and scarf to Hauser who accepted both. Little did Henry know that the man suspected Henry even more thinking that Henry wanted him to wear the brilliantly colored scarf so Henry's "gang" could easily pick him out of the other men and steal his gold.

Hauser then asked Henry to ride a way with them but Henry said he had to go out to Rattlesnake Ranch to check on his sick friend, Frank Parish and save his horses from the Indians. When Henry ran into Edgerton's nephew, Wilbur Sanders, he also told him he had to go check on Frank. Later, when Sanders shared this with Thompson and Edgerton, they encouraged him to go out to the ranch and see if that was where Henry had gone.

Sanders spent the night at the ranch where Parish did indeed struggle for his life with a doctor in attendance but Henry never did show up. Henry's former deputy, Jack Gallagher, also waited for Henry and became furious when Henry didn't come as expected.

Henry came to the ranch the next morning and when questioned, simply said he had gone out into the countryside to find the horses and had gotten stuck in the snow storm, and had spent the night in a makeshift shelter. As Henry left to attend to the horses, he couldn't stop shaking his head, damn it, people did suspect him and distrust him. He thought about leaving and his saint insisted, "No, Henry. You must stay. Prove yourself and serve your constituents. You'll be fine. Be a man, do what a sheriff should do, the decent and honorable thing. Don't desert them now when they are all so nervous and frightened. They need you."

Henry's black hound reared his head at that, barking, "Go to hell, saint. Henry, leave now, while the leavin's good. These people are all out to get you. They tell stories about you all the time. You're a leader of a bunch of no-goods and thieve, in their mind. Leave. Now." Sanders had watched Henry's continuous shaking of his head while he saddled his horse, and when Henry turned his face to him and he saw Henry's angry demeanor, he began to wonder about the purity of his friend. Perhaps he wasn't innocent.

Later, Hauser claimed he observed Henry and three other masked men hovering in the trees just outside his camp, far from Bannack, on the trail to Salt Lake, and a young boy claimed he saw Henry on that night. The youngster swore he had been frisked by him, during which he had recognized the red lining of Henry's coat. The man had been masked, so the boy had no means of identifying him other than the coat. The rumors surrounding Henry and his whereabouts continued with no one questioning how he could have been in three different places miles from one another, on one stormy night.

Henry continued to sense the talk about town was now mostly about him. He would walk into a saloon, and men would stop talking. He felt eyes upon him, watching constantly, and when he would turn to address the stares, they would look away. He began to feel a sort of numbness, perhaps immunity to the rumors and looks. He knew he was immaculate in every way—thought, action, and intent. But then one day, more trouble for Henry arrived in town by the name of Nick Wall.

Henry, remembering Joe's revelations about the man months ago, decided he needed to introduce himself to him and make sure there would be no misunderstanding or conflict between them simply because they had been on opposite sides during the border wars.

Henry stepped to him in the saloon one day, introduced himself, and offered to buy him a drink. Nick looked him up and down and retorted, "No thanks. I've heard about you and don't want a thing to do with you, Henry Plummer. Sides I don't cotton to drinking alcohol, or gambling, or hanging out with robbers and thieves like you do."

Henry felt a chill go up his spine and felt as if Jack Cleveland stood before him once more saying, "I've got your meat, Plummer."

Despite his foreboding about the man, Henry attempted to be civil. "Well, sir, whatever you drink, I'll buy you one."

Nick just looked at him hard and said, "Don't you get it, I don't consort with the likes of you."

Henry smiled and said, "You don't even know me."

Nick snorted. "I've heard enough to know who and what you are, and I can't believe that you haven't been at least, let go as sheriff. Unbelievable."

Henry took one more chance at reaching the presuming man. "Tell me, please, what have you heard that makes you judge me so?"

Wall looked at him, cynical, and said, "You know what you are. That's what counts isn't it? Just stay outa my way, and maybe you'll be fine. Meanwhile, I've got business, real business, to take care of unlike you who, as I understand it, only collects his paycheck and turns the other way so thieves can thrive in this gold country, living off other men's sweat and pay dirt."

Henry watched the man leave and turned to order his first drink in months.

Henry heard much about this bitter rival—how he planned to move his store to Virginia City where it could serve many more people, and how he constantly talked of the need for a vigilante organization to take care of all these robberies, holdups, and murders occurring daily in this region. Henry snorted when he heard such talk. Daily occurrences! His left nut. If something happened monthly, that would break all records. He was sick of all these groundless stories and rumors, and if that ass attempted to start up a vigilance group, he would hear of it and put a quick end to such foolishness.

Vigilantes were just as outside the law as robbers in his mind. They were unconstitutional and he would call upon Judge Edgerton to help him. But, he admitted to himself, this fall there had been a considerable increase in actual holdups, which for the most part had been botched and stupidly planned.

Just days after a lovely Thanksgiving Day spent with the Edgertons, the Sanders, and the Langfords, Henry and the Vails heard of the latest hold up on the trail between Virginia City and Bannack. Three masked, blanketed men stopped the stage at gunpoint. Despite their masks and blankets, the main victim who gave up $400 worth of gold dust to them, identified the men as George Ives, Whiskey Bill Graves, and Bob Zachary, two acquaintances of Henry's and a former deputy.

After Henry questioned the man about the robbery, someone pulled the victim aside and said, "Don't speak with him, he can't be trusted. Now, I fear for your life." So harsh was his opinion of Henry.

Henry got nowhere in his investigations, and once again people complained about his behavior, thinking the worst of Henry and his intentions. A week later, on December 3, a very botched attempt at holding up the Moody wagon train occurred, leaving both masked men shot up and running into the woods for their lives.

Two weeks after that, a young man was found dead just outside of town on a small ranch. Suspects had been apprehended and a miner's court would be held in Virginia City, away from Henry's jurisdiction. Vigilantism had been talked of by many, and one of Henry's questionable friends, Clubfoot George, rode out for Bannack to warn Henry of the arrests, the upcoming trial, and the possibility of vigilantes interfering.

When George arrived in Bannack, he could hardly speak. The ride had been cold and long, and he had so much to tell, he had trouble as to where to begin.

Henry sat with George in an isolated corner of the Elkhorn and ordered them a drink. It being three in the morning; there was no one in the bar but the owner, Cyrus Skinner, and a passed-out miner sprawled out in the opposite corner. "Just have your drink, catch your breath, and then we'll talk," Henry assured the poor, rattled man. Cyrus brought them their drinks and sat down with his own. The men remained quiet for a time and when Henry thought George had collected himself, he began questioning him.

"So, they arrested Ives for the murder of young Tiebolt, huh?"

"Yes."

"Why Ives? On what grounds?"

George snorted, "just 'cause he was around when Tiebolt came out to Franck's ranch to fetch two mules. He was there when the boy opened his pouch to make payment for 'em and Ives seein' a goodly amount of gold dust in that purse made the smart remark, 'Seems a shame to let that loot just go like that. Those two mules, too.' Then, Ives and Franck tossed a coin as to who would chase after the boy, and Ives won. He came back not too long after with the gold and the mules saying, 'Didn't seem right to shoot the kid in the back, so's I called to him so's I could shoot him right in the middle of his forehead.' And, now Franck has agreed to testify against Ives. I can't believe, Henry, how quickly Franck folded like a cheap carpet bag."

Henry shook his head, "Well, I can. I'll believe anything when comes to that bunch. Were Tex Crowell and Aleck Carter there, too?"

"Yes."

"How 'bout George Hilderman?"

"Him, too."

Henry puffed out a long deep breath, "Could've been any of those toughs," he said, shaking his head. "Could've been all of them! Wouldn't surprise me."

"They say he was in pretty bad shape, birds already eatin' on him. Shot through the left eye and dragged to where they hid him in the bushes, his neck was all rope-burned."

Henry stood up and began to pace. "I wish that damn Edgerton would start doing his job and set up a court system around here. Guess he just left for D.C. to go do some politicking, trying to talk them into making Montana its own territory, they say. So, now they'll have to resort to another worthless miner's trial, again. That right, George? That what they're planning?"

"Yup. Had a big ruckus about it before I left. Pulled up the wagons and all, settin' up the court 'room'. Voted to allow counsel on both sides, voted for two twelve-man juries to advise the crowd as to how to vote on the final decision. Appointed Don Byam as presiding judge and declared Long John Franck as main witness for the prosecution. Hired Wilbur Sanders as prosecutin' attorney. Ives went and hired four lawyers from Virginia City. They's gonna start the trial early tomorrow morning."

"This is not good. Don't like the sounds of it," Henry said as he plopped down in his chair, weary and alarmed. He took his hat off and began rubbing on his scar and running his hand through his hair. "No way to stop it. Guess no one thinks I've got jurisdiction over there. Wouldn't trust me enough if I did. This is bad, boys, another kangaroo court won't sit well with those self-righteous fellows who are brewing up a Vigilance Committee. If they let Ives off, these men will go bat-crazy. They're gonna get all rabid and foamed up about everything that's been going on. These last few holdups have got them steamed. Let's just hope they can hold a decent enough trial to please everyone. Otherwise, we're in deep shit, innocent or not."

Cyrus finally spoke up, "Well, Henry, you could go after some of these men people are sure been doing the robbing. Startin' with the Bummer Dan McFadden job go after Bill Bunton and Frank Parish.

Then for the Leroy Southmayd deal, bring in Buck Stinson and Ned Ray, Graves, and Zachary. Run in Dutch John Wagner and Steve Marshland for the Moody Wagon Train debacle. I know you've hung out with these guys, drank with 'em, gambled with 'em, but Henry, if you want to survive, you've got to do something to make people feel safe, so's they know you're doin' your job."

Henry shook his head, "Can't do any of that. There's no proof; it's all hearsay and conjecture and, for sure, wishful thinking on many people's part—a way to get rid of these Confederate sympathizers, whiskey rowdies. Besides it could be anyone doing these robberies, some quiet-and-to-themselves miners, even."

Cyrus objected at once. "Henry Plummer! You know damn well those men named are responsible, who else but them? They're just that way, got no conscience or any sense. They just wanna rob people of their hard work and profits. Too lazy to do otherwise. Why do you care so much if you end up prosecutin' the wrong man for the wrong job? You can't always do what's 'xactly right, and, you know any one of those asses would turn on you, and finger you, if need be. You gotta git tough, Plummer, or else you'll just end up like them, eventually, at the end of a noose. You know people think you're their leader, 'cause nobody thinks they's smart enough to do any of this on their own. And, you know what? They're right. Put all theys heads together and you still ain't got one natural, thinking brain."

Cyrus ended his tirade with, "I'm going to lock up and go to bed and hope to hell Jake over there doesn't wake up before me. I'm tired, especially of all this crap. Henry, you gotta act and do it now to save yourself. You know everyone's got you raked in with all these damn thieving fools." Shaking his head and staggering off, he said, "Good night, you two. I'll keep my ears open to all the news that comes in from Virginia City, Henry, and keep you posted. See you in the morning."

Cyrus had more news by noon the next day. He'd heard that thousands of men assembled around the makeshift court with many of them taking up roosts on the roof tops. It was a muddy mess over there because it had started to thaw. Men walked in a foot of mud. They had been forced to keep a bon fire going, though, because there still was such a chill to the air.

Cyrus shook his head and continued, "They hired Charles Bagg, a funny looking little old lawyer to help Sanders out 'cause Sander's as nervous as a cat, afraid of reprisals for prosecutin' a known tough. Everyone's sidin' with Ives, saying they got no real case or evidence agin him. But, some men are bringin' up all the other rotten things he's done. He's just sittin' there, as good-looking as always, and actin' like the gentlemen he ain't. They've hired fifty armed men who're makin' a ring around the crowd sos things don't git outa hand. This bein' Sunday, they's going to quit early and begin agin Monday morning. But, Henry, this is the worse part, there's big talk about a meeting among those agitatin' for vigilance. They say Sanders is in on it, a man named Paris Pfouts, and a bunch of storekeepers over there. Word is they're meetin' this evening after the trial adjourns."

"Well, it's too late to intervene. I best stay here, I can't leave Bannack. Ives is on his own. Let's just think positive and hope this trial will appease everyone who needs placating. All we can do is wish for the best."

Cyrus rubbed his rag on the same spot on the heavy, wooden bar, over and over. "Henry, I think you should leave now. Get out of here. It's not safe for you any longer. I've got a bad feeling."

Henry just shrugged and walked out the door. He didn't feel well. His lungs had started to act up. Henry went home and slept until Martha woke him and insisted that he have some hot soup she had cooked for him.

Much later in the evening, Cyrus came pounding on their door to announce to Henry that after a near hung-jury, the miners had voted, making it a majority decision to hang George Ives by the neck until dead, and that just before they executed him, he had named Aleck Carter as the actual murderer. Carter had run off. Hilderman had been banished, and Franck would go completely free for his testimony during the trial.

"I also heard that vigilantes have organized to, as they say, 'Save the time and trouble with these bogus trials and summarily hang every man suspected of wrong-doing, recently and in the past, until dead.' The story, Henry, is that over a thousand men have been sworn in and that they aim to sweep the country clean of crime."

Henry had no reply for his friend but to say, "Well, Cyrus, you had better think about yourself and how you may be caught up in this. I plan to remain here and bank on people's sentiments; not everyone thinks I'm a leader of thieves, highwaymen. I can't do much else."

Celebrating Christmas proved difficult. Henry watched the quiet demeanor of his friend Francis Thompson and wondered why he would not believe in him and his innocence, but by the time the holiday ended, Henry had become nearly too sick to care. Martha fussed over him, and he made her promise that if the worst possible outcome occurred, she would forward letters to his family in Maine and to Electa in Iowa. He also gave her the other key to the safe deposit box in Salt Lake. She promised but broke down, crying, "Oh! Henry, I am so sorry for my earlier distrust in you. I'm most likely the reason Electa left you, making things even more difficult for you. Please forgive me?"

Henry smiled and gathered her into his arms for a big affectionate squeeze. He grinned and said, "Martha you have been a good friend to me, and I hope we will enjoy this friendship for a long time after we get through this rough patch."

Henry went to meet with his steadfast friend, George Chrisman and a lawyer, giving George the power-of-attorney to collect the debt from the recent sale of his mining claims. Just in case. After the transaction had been completed, George asked him, "Henry, does this mean you are leaving?"

Henry smiled, sad, "No. No, George, I plan to stay right here and face whatever fate holds for me. I've had a good life. Well, perhaps not good, but fine enough. I've done wrong, and maybe it's time I paid for those mistakes. I don't know. There really is no place for me to go. I'm staying here."

By January 1 the Vigilance Committee was fully organized with their leader, James Williams dividing the men up into companies led by lieutenants and captains. Everything, especially their planned action, was to be kept completely secret. On January 4, two companies rode out to the Rattlesnake Ranch to arrest Red Yeager for questioning. When reporting this to Henry, Cyrus protested, "I have no idea why they would go after Red first. They only wanted information about his part in a murder. They've gone after Red only because he has spent so much time with those men who are the suspects."

Henry did not like this news at all. The Vigilance Committee had decided to go after the wrong man for all the wrong reasons, and, he knew Red to be a weak person, one who would sell his mother to the Natives to survive.

Red had also bartended and cooked at many places with the toughs. God only knew what he would say. Henry felt ill as his sick lungs convulsed, and he was forced to take to his bed again.

The Vigilantes found their quarry at the Rattlesnake Ranch along with George Brown, who could only be considered guilty for his warning to Aleck Carter "to get out of town because Ives just fingered you as the actual murderer of Nicholas Tiebolt." They arrested the men, secured them as prisoners, and took them as far as Demsey's Ranch the next day, the last stage stop before the trail became infested and dangerous with robbers. They didn't want to chance being ambushed and losing their prey.

They had all taken refuge in the ranch house from the bitterly cold, thirty-degrees-below-zero and waited two days for conditions to warm. After realizing that the weather wouldn't be warming soon, they thought they had better get on with it. They decided to work on Red Yeager, first. They put the noose around his neck after he refused to talk and hoisted him up, leaving him hanging until he began suffocating, and then they let him down.

After five of these partial hangings, Red folded, quickly naming Frank Parish, Cyrus Skinner, Buck Stinson, Ned Ray, Dutch John Wagner, Jose, the Mexican, Clubfoot George Lane, Hayes Lyons, Jack Gallagher, Boone Helm, Steve Marshland, George Shear, Aleck Carter, John Cooper, Robert Zachary, and Bill Graves, along with Bill Bunton, who he claimed was second in command to their leader, Henry Plummer. He had named every man who had ever been under suspicion for anything. James Williams wrote down each name carefully, not questioning a single one.

The next day, they hanged Red Yeager and George Brown without a fuss.

Then, the Vigilantes traveled on into Bannack to finish their business and met with others waiting for them at a miner's cabin with only a portion of them able to crowd into the tiny space. The men who were present discussed Red's list and made a plan. They knew that Stinson and Ray were in town as well as Plummer. James Williams sent several men out to remove these men's horses from the stable and another bunch to go make ready the place of execution, a partially built structure not far from Yankee Flats. It had become very late so they decided to make their move the next evening.

The next night, Henry, feeling a little better, took to the couch in the main room of the cabin. He and Martha sat quietly for most of the evening, alone, because James had decided to work late at the store. Henry felt distressed and worried because his friend Francis Thompson had been so quietly remote and seemed to be bothered about something during supper. Martha attempted to reassure Henry, "I'm sure it's just this horrible, deadly cold weather we're having. You know how it makes you feel, Henry."

"No," Henry responded, rubbing at his scar. "He's different, almost like he feels some sort of guilt. He looks at me, but won't look me in the eye, like he's guarding some secret. It seems as if he wants to tell me something. I almost felt, when he left tonight, that he couldn't wait to leave. You know? And, where would he be going on such a miserably cold night? And when I asked him what was up, he became all defensive and nervous."

Suddenly insistent, loud knocking could be heard at the door. Martha answered only to have a man rush past her and confront Henry on the couch. "I'm arresting you, Henry Plummer as leader of the gang of robbers, the Innocents, who have been holding up stage runs, wagon trains, and men for the last eight months. You're coming with me."

Martha attempted to intercede. "He's terribly sick, you fool. Can't you see that? Please don't take him now; let him heal up first." She helped Henry with his coat, still pleading with the man to let it go until Henry felt better. The man quickly tied Henry's hands behind his back and she began wailing, wringing her hands, screaming, "Oh, no, not that. Don't do that! What has he done? Where are you taking him? He's a good man, for God's sake."

When Martha threw on her shawl and attempted to follow them out the door, Nathaniel Langford came in trying to comfort her while holding her back and keeping her inside. She fought him, screaming the entire time, "Nate, what are you doing? What is happening? Let me go! What is wrong with you? Henry is your friend, a good friend who trusts you."

Langford spoke quietly, "But, Martha, you don't understand. Henry is guilty of leading a gang of robbers, the highwaymen who have been tormenting and endangering people on the trails. We can't trust him any longer. Justice must be done."

The last thing Henry heard Martha say was, "Justice?! You call this justice? What will happen to him?"

Henry could smell the stench of death. It, along with the ice-cold air stung his nose. He could taste it, like he had so many times before that acrid, iron tang of adrenaline. It was trapped in the circle of seventy-some men and their horses, ambushed in the 30-below-zero-air, like him. They had come and taken him out of his sickbed where he had been attempting to sleep off the latest assault on his weak lungs by this God-forsaken land and its unforgiving arctic weather. Henry coughed a body-wrenching hack, spitting out blood, once again. He almost hoped his own body would rob him of life before they could.

They had bound his hands behind his back, and he walked the circle of men using his last and only available weapon, persuasion. He had talked himself out of so many other dire situations in the past. He stopped before each old friend he saw and tried to reason with him. They only shook their heads back and forth, regretful.

"No, Henry," they spoke out, "not this time. You're on the list. Red fingered you, said you were in with them."

Henry shook his head in denial, claiming, as loud as his poor lungs would allow him, "No! You listened to him? You know what kind of a man he is!"

"Was!" corrected a man as he spit out his juiced-up tobacco. "He's gone now. He confessed and named every man in the gang before we hanged him."

Henry shook his head and searched the enclosure of men for a sane, reasonable person. "There's no gang! Where's Thompson? He knows I'm innocent. Sanders? Where's Sanders?"

The man laughed, choking on the brown spittle left in his mouth. "Hey, boy. Don't yuh know, Sanders and Lott, they's the ones that swore us all in. You's sunk. We's all vigilantes now."

Sanders stepped out from the ring of men who were horseless. "It's useless, Henry. You're to be hanged. Don't beg for your life. It's been decided. Can't be helped. I feel as bad about it as you, but I wouldn't save you if I could."

Henry stood silent for a moment. He hoped this was just another one of his wretched dreams he had been experiencing. He was innocent. He attempted to defend himself once more. "I'm not a thief, never have been. The only men I have killed were about to kill me, and the rest, I was just keeping the law as sheriff or marshal."

The men all around him just shook their heads, and Henry could smell it again, the smell of murder. The men and their horses were restless, anxious to return to their homes, to warm beds and stables. The horses tossed their heads in the freezing cold, snorting out snot and what seemed to Henry, contempt. Their long eyelashes icicled as did the men's moustaches and beards. Many of the men had wrapped scarves around their necks and mouths making them difficult to recognize. Henry mostly identified them by their muffled voices.

Henry asked to spend the last few minutes of his life writing a note to his wife and then one to his family back in Maine, still not believing this was happening to him. He was so grateful that his dear mother had died years ago so she would not have to bear the heartbreak of his untimely, horrible end.

His fingers had almost frozen stiff by the time he finished. He worried about frostbite and then thought, no, no need to worry about such a thing and laughed a bitter laugh. He handed his missives to Sanders. "See that Martha gets these; she knows where to send them."

They had hanged Stinson and then Ray while he wrote his notes. As they walked him to the makeshift, gallows, Henry thought, at least they weren't using the ones he had built. He wondered why. Oh, yes, he thought, they most likely were afraid the infamous, man-killing leader of the gang might get away as they dragged him to the edge of town, and then his alleged followers would be alerted.

They put the noose around his neck and someone said, "May God save your soul." Henry thought of Jesus' last words on the cross and let the ancient prayer pass through his frozen lips, "Dear God, forgive them, for they know not what they do." And, then, he begged for forgiveness for himself. He heard the words, "Men, do your duty," and then, darkness.

Henry woke up to find himself on a soft, woodsy scented bed of pine needles. He looked up at the sky and saw that the sun shone down brightly and that a few wispy, almost transparent clouds floated across the sun's rays, dimming them slightly. He heard a vast array of bird song, and could smell the fresh, warm scent of flowers. He slowly got to his feet and began walking, thinking, he'd found his dream, again, finally.

He walked feeling peacefully expectant until he entered a clearing where the sun shone clean and bright and verdant plants blossomed everywhere. There were creatures running about, unafraid, accepting his presence. He looked across the meadow and could see people coming his way. He looked more closely and could see that it was, indeed, his two sisters, his mother, and Pauline and little Henry, now a young boy, walking toward him. Then, he saw his Grandfather Moses trailing behind. He began to run, ecstatic, realizing he was no longer a lost soul and was home at last. He had people who loved him and he ran to them.

www.ingramcontent.com/pod-product-compliance
Lightning Source LLC
LaVergne TN
LVHW042250070526
838201LV00089B/96